Stop the

Following the international success of *The Fish Rots from the Head: Developing Effective Directors*, this sequel from Bob Garratt explains the public's distrust of the people who govern us – the directors, owners, regulators and politicians – and how this can be changed.

Currently, Corporate Governance is too narrow and fragmented. The growing gap between the angry public and the urban elite, made manifest by Brexit and Trump, is due to a lack of appreciation by both parties of the roles and values of well-governed organizations in bonding a society at both national and international levels.

This book pulls no punches and directly challenges directors and politicians to reframe their thinking about "governance" to address the public's distrust of them. This is the ROT that needs to be STOPPED.

This book is truly radical in going back to basics and then designing a new national action learning system between the four main players overseen by continuous public scrutiny. It is designed to counter the official reports of organizational failure that end too frequently with the weasel words "but the main problem was a failure of corporate governance". Currently this is code for "so no-one can do much about it". This book shows what can be done.

Bob Garratt is a company director, consultant, and academic working on corporate governance; board and director evaluation and performance, organizational learning and change, and strategic thinking issues. He is based in London and consults on five of the six continents.

"Bob Garratt is once again at the forefront of challenging conventional thinking on corporate governance as he fearlessly explores areas that others fear to tread. In his relentless pursuit of excellence in governance, Professor Garratt thankfully takes us beyond yet another dissertation on rules and standards to remind us of the underlying thesis of good governance around values and trust, and seeks to build on the twin issues of competence and professionalism. What I find compelling is his challenge to regulators and policy-makers to demonstrate genuine commitment and leadership in encouraging thoughtful legislation and enforcement that restores the productive, but responsible, capacity of business enterprise."

Philip Armstrong, Director of Governance, Gavi Alliance and Board Vice Chair, International Corporate Governance Network

"An incredibly valuable work. It needs to be studied by the leaders in business and government to begin the processes of correction. As expected by readers of Bob Garratt's seminal work *The Fish Rots from the Head*, the author has not disappointed. *Stop the Rot* will be a handbook for all those involved in corporate entities that are seeking certainty of direction to improve the standing of business leaders in the community."

Denise Fleming, Managing Director, Foresight's Global Coaching, Australia

"This new book from Bob Garratt is clearly needed as a guide to the post-Brexit Trump world. It is visionary in making bold suggestions, and it is ambitious in raising new questions. The book pinpoints the 'demolishing of professionalism' as the critical cultural change that accounts for so much that we regret in today's corporate world."

Robert A.G. Monks, author of *Corporate Governance* and *Corpocracy*

"Bob Garratt adds to his library of classic works on Governance with this volume which builds on the earlier excellent analysis on what is wrong with our boardrooms by dealing with the ongoing frustration over a lack of implementation of previously agreed changes in corporate governance, which in turn has undermined trust. Bob, here, prescribes more fundamental change based on learning which puts humanity, values and ethics to the fore whilst encouraging entrepreneurial direction. Anybody who is unsatisfied with the current state of governance and lack of trust should read and apply the lessons!"

Canon Professor Clive Morton, Middlesex University, UK

Stop the Rot

Reframing Governance for
Directors and Politicians

Bob Garratt

Routledge
Taylor & Francis Group

LONDON AND NEW YORK

First published 2017
by Routledge
2 Park Square, Milton Park, Abingdon, Oxon OX14 4RN

and by Routledge
711 Third Avenue, New York, NY 10017

Routledge is an imprint of the Taylor & Francis Group, an informa business

British Library Cataloguing-in-Publication Data
A catalogue record for this book is available from the British Library.

Library of Congress Cataloging-in-Publication Data
A catalog record for this book has been requested.

ISBN: 978-1-78353-804-1 (hbk)
ISBN: 978-1-78353-766-2 (pbk)
ISBN: 978-1-78353-768-6 (ebk)

Printed and bound by CPI Group (UK) Ltd, Croydon, CR0 4YY

To two feisty nonagenarians:

Queenie Garratt 1923–2016
Jean Bishop   1920–2014

Who lived life to the full and who passed their strong
human values on to their next three generations

Contents

Acknowledgements ix

Preface xiii

Introduction 1

Section I:
Setting the future context for effective governance 25

   1 The value of "values" 27

   2 Towards human values-based governance 67

Section II:
The five future governance roles 115

   3 The directors' role in stopping the rot 117

   4 Owners and their responsibilities 163

   5 Regulators 231

   6 Does government know what "governance" means? .. 267

Notes 297

About the author 309

Index 311

List of figures

Figure 1: The five major players in national leadership........23

Figure 2: The five-level hierarchy of personal values..........43

Figure 3: Learning organization: basic model..................132

Figure 4: Learning organization: complex model............133

Figure 5: Learning board: basic model.........................135

Figure 6: Learning board: full model...........................158

Figure 7: The proposed learning system......................291

Acknowledgements

I have had great support in writing this book. Although it was not written to explain Brexit, Trump or the turbulence in the European Union, its fortuitous timing shows more prescience than is due. I have been pondering the public's and politicians' lack of appreciation of the value of effective corporate governance to their societies over the last decade. In this period, I have spoken in some 30 countries about my practical approach to the future of corporate governance and never had a negative response even from those I was criticizing heavily. Yet, even when they saw themselves as part of a current malfunctioning system and knew that there must be a better way forward, they had little compulsion to take action. Until now. With the exception of the "good guys" mentioned in the book, I exclude the US from these comments as they do not yet seem to recognize that there is even a national problem. Yet.

The idea for the book started when I had two years on part-time secondment to KPMG London. The partners had seen that the "governance area" needed a complete rethink and decided to risk asking me to take time to do just that. So thanks to Paul R. Taylor and David Defroand for taking that risk; and to John Griffiths-Jones, then Chairman, for challenging me to make a difference in what was seen as such an esoteric area. It proved quite a task even inside the practice.

I have interviewed hundreds of people during and since this period, but few wished to be identified by name as they are now very sensitive to being labelled as part of "the distanced elite". I respect their wishes, and thank them for their confidential honesty to me. So without direct attributions this book cannot be seen as a rigorous scientific investigation in search of a law but rather an interpretive one in search of clarifying meaning in the jumbled and confusing world of "governance" words and slogans. This book is my attempt to draw a more comprehensive and provocative map of the area.

However, I can acknowledge some key individuals who have encouraged me over the last two decades to pursue strongly the understanding of the human values and learning processes underpinning effective corporate governance. I thank Charles Handy for his long-standing support since he first helped me switch from architectural education to management education in the late 1960s. The much-missed Sir Adrian Cadbury has been a supportive and constructive critic since 1980, as has Bob Monks in the US, and Mark Goyder and Pat Cleverly of Tomorrow's Company since the 1990s. Sir Michael Bett and David Pearce encouraged me along this track since our first meeting in 1984 on the GEC plc Senior Managers Development Programme.

In the last five years I have had critical support from Professor Janice Caplan at Scala Associates, Professor Gill Atkins at the University of Sheffield, Chris Pierce of Global Governance Services, Professor Georges Selim of Cass Business School, David Prestwich at Mazars, Gillian Karran-Cumberlege and her husband Mark at Fidelio Partners, and Richard Service of the City Values Forum. Internationally, my colleagues in South Africa, Dr Daniel Malan and Lynn McGregor at the University of Stellenbosch, Judge Thina Siwendu, Mervyn King at the International Integrated Reporting Council, Fred Phaswana and Maria Ramos from our time at Transnet, Richard Foster at Old Mutual, Ansie Ramalho and Angel Oosthuizen at the Institute of Directors in Southern Africa, Ram Ramakrishnan in Singapore, Peter Barrett in Hong Kong, Dr Chen Derong in Beijing, Dr Denise Fleming of Foresight, and Logan Chetty, in Australia, Professor Coral Ingley and Ron Hamilton in New Zealand, Peter Gorer in Boston and

Gunnar Walstam of Metellus Switzerland have all been in continuing dialogue and of long-term help in exploring the issues critically.

For the detailed criticism of the more technical chapters I must thank John Plender of the *Financial Times*, Merryn Somerset Webb of *Money Week*, Herve Geny of the London Stock Exchange, Jerry Rhodes and Sue Thame of Effective Intelligence, and Geoff Llewellyn and Ed Straw on the government issues.

On the production of the book I must thank Rhian Williams who followed up from a casual conference conversation to introduce me to Greenleaf Publishing and so to Rebecca Marsh who has been a great supporter through a busy editorial and production process. My worst textual and factual excesses have been picked up by Doug Medland and Dean Bargh, for which many thanks. But the verbiage is still all mine.

Thanks again to Margareta Hult-Gardmo for the use of Villa Gabrielle in Tourrettes-sur-Loup, Côte d'Azur for the quiet to complete the bulk of the writing. But my main thanks are as ever to Sally Garratt who has the wisdom to support me silently when needed, to keep away when I am grumbling over completing the details, and to deliver excellent meals at just the right time. Such empathy is appreciated greatly.

Bob Garratt
London

Preface

I write this book in embarrassed frustration at my inability to answer some simple governance questions asked much too frequently of me by angry and disillusioned members of the public around the world. These include:

- "Why are so many of our business and political leaders incompetent today?"

- "Why don't they seem to know what they are doing?"

- "Have they no professional training and no moral compass?"

- "The evidence of their incompetence is all around us yet why is nothing done about it?"

- "Why don't *you* do something about it? After all, you are supposed to be a professor of corporate governance so you must know the answer?"

- "What will you do about restoring trust in our leaders and the quality of governance of our organizations?"

And that was long before Brexit, Donald Trump or the growing public criticisms of our over-reliance on "experts" and economists.

Part of my frustration is that there is such good news to be told to answer these questions. Yet it is seldom reported. Even when it is, it tends to be fragmented and mumbled in deliberately excluding technical jargon so the public cannot understand that there *is* an evolving new system of governance. Yet for many years I have been helping colleagues set up systems for developing competence for directors and other governors in many countries, especially the UK and southern Africa. We have already created the necessary framework and processes to help answer the public's questions. Ironically, these laws and systems are supported, at least vocally, by national politicians as ways of creating wealth, stabilizing society and reducing corruption. Yet such fine words are rarely supported by political enforcement to underpin the very laws that these politicians have passed. This is a global problem. Why?

At least the UK and South Africa have ensured that the need for director competence is built into their civil and criminal laws. These laws are beacons of hope in a darkening world of political gloom, corporate corruption and the growing use of brute power in so many countries. They are a shining light, as Shakespeare has Portia say in *The Merchant of Venice*, "So shines a good deed in a naughty world." Many politicians have fought hard to get such laws passed, yet oddly they rarely seem to care about their implementation or any systematic learning from them. They rarely feel that such follow-through is their responsibility. So they dump it on their civil servants who have other motivations and rewards. Why?

I have the great privilege of having worked in over 40 countries and spoken with those at both the top and bottom of these societies. I have worked in democracies, with the Communist Party of China, with very different Islamic organizations in the Gulf and South East Asia and, especially in Asia and Africa, experienced the negative effects of kleptocracies, autocracies and plain dictatorships on societies who, despite everything, are still painfully keen to develop themselves around an agreed core of basic human values and effective governance.

It was in talking with so many directors and politicians about effective governance at both national and corporate levels, and contrasting this with the growing choruses of discontent from the majority of their populations, that I began to realize the blindingly obvious – that there are remarkable similarities of education, mind-sets, values and behaviours to be found in the vast majority of directors and politicians. These are the people to whom we give the power of directing and creating values for the organizations that are the bedrock of our society. Surely they must have much to be proud about and to pass on to the wider world? But five years ago, when I started questioning the major players more rigorously about their roles, values and behaviours, I was met with blank stares. Most did not think that there was much seriously wrong. It was as if I was suddenly seen as the Mad Hatter in *Alice in Wonderland* and had asked "Why is a raven like a writing desk?" There was no answer. Nor was it thought suitable to attempt to give one. I was obviously nuts to even ask. Things were how they were, how they should be, and although intellectually change was inevitable it was impossible for them to agree to it.

Yet for me there had to be answers, at least to why there was a growing gap between the current frozen inaction and indifference of politicians and directors, with their over-reliance on very specialized, narrow-visioned professionals, and their increasingly disconnected voters. I was told repeatedly by directors that "politics has no part in business" and "businesses must never compromise themselves with politics". Yet simple observation suggested that the reverse was true, especially in the US, the EU and UK. All sides tried to keep a public face of studied indifference to the other, while short-term deals were frequently done behind the scenes. This signalled a conscious unwillingness to be seen to learn to change the competences and values needed for their future governing roles. I knew that there was much that they could learn from the changes evolving at the boundaries of their current overly narrow world. But to do so they would need to break out of their single-discipline worlds and become comfortable in learning to integrate new disciplines and to use the resulting uncertainty to everyone's advantage.

I have not had a "career". Or, as a PhD student said of me, "In your case, *career* is a verb rather than a noun." A turning point for me was a major row with a group managing director in 1974 when he insisted that it was dangerous for folk to learn at their work and I was determined to prove him wrong. This led me to questioning the roles of boards, directors and senior executives. I have experience that combines architectural design and education, social psychology, management, directing, international development and HR. For over 30 years I have careered around the world being asked to help solve complex organizational problems which have failed to respond to single-disciplinary answers. I have a love for English literature and history, especially the explosion of technology, culture, business and social progress that created the Victorian age. I learned that design education imbues you with the need to integrate all disciplines, especially science, arts and finance, to create sustainable, humane solutions. In my work I have transferred this approach to directing: in itself an integrative process and clearly differentiated from management, which is an essentially convergent, reductive thinking process. Directing is an architectural process. Directors and politicians need to integrate organizational structure, economics, social need, ecology, and technology into a workable corporate whole. Effective directors understand and use this process.

In global politics, great arguments rage about the rise and fall of the power ratios in society between the "super-rich elites", "financial elites", "the hollowed-out middle", the "declining working class" and the effects of "inequality". This is the polity in which both politicians and directors need now debate and design their future. Few do. When I suggest such a widened directoral role and education as a way to resolve many of our societal problems, directors and politicians often squirm uncomfortably in public. But in private they admit that they have no useful answers for building the necessary bridges of trust to an increasingly disillusioned public. Some admit that they are now so desperate that even my odd ideas might be worth a try. They recognize that somehow "values" have become a big issue, but they have few concepts or terminology to grapple with this. They are uncomfortable that they can neither give a simple account of the values that drive them personally, nor of the validity of those they espouse for their version of "professionalism" in their organizations. Many directors and politicians acknowledge privately that they are personally directionless and amoral, including one new prime minister. Then it struck me hard: they are "governance-naked", untrained, untested and so most fearful of humiliation by public exposure. They have little or no training, assessment and development in governance. They have few comrades in adversity.

Consider: both directors and politicians can get into their jobs without qualifications for their directoral tasks. Both can be elected to office without experience, professional expertise or tested values. On achieving office they feel that the public would destroy them if they knew this, so they cannot admit it and quickly learn defensive and obfuscating behaviours. They must appear omniscient in public as the media expect them to know everything immediately upon taking office and hound them if they are seen to be weak in any area even while learning on the job. They assume that they are not allowed to be seen to learn from their mistakes. So they bluster and often fall back quickly to the seeming protection of "groupthink" messages generated either by their board or by party "policy" to hide their embarrassment. Yet without such an admission of their initial weaknesses and their need for sustained learning and competence-building, there is no personal development for them. They are mere cyphers. They remain at that personally disabling level of constant fear of conscious learning – frozen in the headlights of continuous media coverage. The public is rightly critical of, and frustrated by, their non-competence yet it seems unable to accept that all our direction-givers need time to gain competence. The reciprocal is that they then need be assessed regularly on it. We are currently stuck with an illogical, crazy circular dilemma that leaves all parties frustrated. And this is how the rot starts.

This book delves into such nonsense and suggests ways in which directors and politicians can openly admit their need to learn to gain competence for the benefit of all. It then goes beyond the two currently accepted parties of "governance" – politicians and directors – and introduces the need for two more parties to be added and assessed – owners and regulators – before we shall develop an effective national corporate governance system. Owners and regulators are currently submerged parties of the governance system. They must be brought into the public view using the values of accountability, probity and openness and integrated into our national definition of "governance". We then need commitment to the necessary compe-tence-building for all four parties to create a whole system.

In this book I advocate a wider national governance development system where all four parties can learn openly and continuously for the benefit of the public, whether billionaires, millionaires, the mid-dle classes, the working classes or those suffering inequality. Even this is not sufficient. A national governance system must be under the *continuous* oversight of the public. Their trust in the governance of their organizations is the final test of the system. In the end, they are the ones who will *Stop the Rot*.

Bob Garratt
London
February 2017
www.garrattlearningservices.com

Note

This book is a series of six interlinked essays designed to broaden and deepen the future scope and dynamics of the field of corporate gov-ernance. To ensure the integrity of each essay, there is some necessary overlap which I have tried to keep to a minimum.

Introduction

Reframing the national context of governance and leadership towards competence and values

This book is a provocation. It is designed to encourage deep reconsideration of the international development of "corporate governance". This started so well 25 years ago with the publication of the seminal *Cadbury Report on the Financial Aspects of Corporate Governance*.[1] It is now in a torpor, directionless, and needs reframing following the implosion of trust between the governed and the governors across the world. We need to rethink its meaning at national and international levels and then develop the competences needed to deliver it. These competences need developing not only in directors and politicians but also in owners and regulators.

The loss of public trust is seen daily in the soured relationships between electorates and politicians, between shareholders and directors, between boards and executives, between employees and corporations – whether public companies, private companies, state-owned enterprises, trades unions, charities and even cooperatives. But how do you convince a cynical public that effective governance is possible?

This book is a challenge to directors, owners, regulators and legislators to demonstrate that we can fight such cynicism – and win.

Four parties – directors, owners, regulators and legislators – are failing in their duty to balance two crucial roles simultaneously – thoughtful direction-giving and the prudent control of their organizations. The need is to better balance their "designing-their-future" role with their "keeping-control-of-the-present" role. They frequently recognize that they have a "governance" problem but rarely see any hope of resolving it. It matters not whether you follow left- or right-wing politics, whether you are in the private or public sectors or whether you are in the "developed" or "developing" worlds: you can see the old tectonic plates of governance fragmenting and shifting suddenly to force the reshaping of the previously dominant Western mind-sets that have existed for 70 years.

I drafted the above paragraph a year before we were instantly to recognize these issues in connection with the words "Brexit" and "Trump". It was in an increasingly cynical world where I felt publicly challenged to defend the usefulness of "corporate governance". So I set off on a series of self-funded international travels, interviews and debates not anticipating the current febrile climate and the angry public demands in which my thoughts would be published. Nor had I realized just how much existing party politics, economics and business were being rejected internationally by the public as growing negative social forces. What has surprised me since is the size of the global demand for "more human values" in our organizations combined with less self-serving governance from our leaders culminating in a renewed plea for a duty of care among all four players in their field of governance. Currently these pleas are often expressed inarticulately by the public who lack the mind-sets and language to state their demands precisely. They now need to understand governance as much as the named players.

I hope that this book allows clearer expression by all sides and, by clarifying much of the jargon and values in use, leads to a deeper understanding and determination to resolve the mess that we have got ourselves into through a mixture of mainly unthinking greed, intellectual sloth and apathy.

Four major shifts reframing governance

Four major themes run through this book to try to explain the polarizing shifts and the positive solutions derived from them:

First is **the need to re-create *trust* in the leaders of our organizations** by their first showing signs of both contrition at their increasingly out-of-touch governance values, and then a willingness to reform themselves by learning to demonstrate publicly their competence in governing. This is where the Global Duty of Care is most obviously missing.

Second is **the need to *rebuild human values* into our organizations** – private, public and not-for-profit – following a crazy and dangerous era of financial and governance misrule based on anarchically free markets, anything-goes greed and little concern for developing competence in the governing role. This is shown most dramatically by the previous glib acceptance of such terms as "irrational exuberance", "light-touch regulation", and by treating markets and organizations as rational, impersonal machines. This has allowed politicians and directors alike to avoid responsibility for the consequences. It has long been assumed in business that known inputs must have known outcomes without human values disrupting this process. But, as Alan Greenspan, previously Governor of the US Federal Reserve, explained long after the start of the Western financial crisis of 2008, "our models did not work".[2] He conceded that the human values, especially fear and greed, were not part of his self-balancing model; and will now have to be considered.

Little concerted action has been taken, especially in the field of economics, macro or micro, to develop better behaviourally based models. It is now beginning but is nowhere near to being the default position. This lack of human values in organizations has left directors, managers, technicians, workers, customers and stakeholders feeling powerless in their organizations and forever trapped in psychic prisons of some political fiend's making. This leads directly to disillusion, despair and growing public anger at the obvious rot around them.

Third is the need for *assessable competence* and **professionalism** in our leadership and governance roles. We need to feel that those who govern us know what they are doing, and can be dismissed if they do not perform. The public now feel increasingly betrayed by their governors whom they had naïvely assumed must be trained to competence and assessed regularly as such. It is an open secret that they are not. However, the public is beginning to realize that they have a duty to rectify this as no-one else will.

Fourth is **the need to create a system of national** *public oversight* and continuous learning so that the four main governance players – directors, owners, regulators and legislators – can never make the same mistakes again. The problem is that the four main players rarely learn even within their own disciplines let alone between them. And they rarely share their learning with the wider public unless forced to by a scandal or tragedy.

What is governance?

"Governance" has been a founding concept in Western culture for over 3,000 years. The word has had dual and linked meanings throughout – giving direction into the future and simultaneously ensuring the prudent current control of an organization. It derives from the Ancient Greek *kubernetes* which describes the steersman of a ship. Over the millennia the direction-giving meaning has been dominant; but there is a parallel derivation that is now seen as of increasing importance in the modern world – *cybernetics* – the science of control systems and comparisons between the human-made and natural worlds. The word "governance" developed from the Latin *gubernetes* via the Old French *gouvenance* and Middle English *gouvernance,* as used by Chaucer, and into the modern English *governance.* It is now much abused.

The "director's dilemma"

The combined direction-giving and prudent control roles of governance are acknowledged widely as "the director's dilemma".[3] This ever-present dilemma is irresolvable at any given time, which is why we need boards of directors to meet regularly to rebalance it, especially in times of increasing uncertainty. This crucial directoral role is reflected strongly in English and Commonwealth company law as the basis of the "general duties of directors". Sadly, there is no such equivalent yet for politicians, owners or regulators, despite the public's demand for it.

So a key theme of this book is that politicians have much to take from what directors have already learned about effectiveness in their governance system, if they have the courage to take it. I realize that this statement will be treated with a mixture of cynicism, downright hilarity and open disdain by many directors, politicians, and much of the general public. We live in a cynical world, where politicians and business folk are frequently accused of being the two main parties guilty of the biggest destruction of social and financial wealth, Western economic stagnation, increasing global instability since the Great Crash of 1929, and the consequent breakdown in trust. Yet owners and regulators played their part in the destruction. How can they all help each other to help us?

This book shows how they can make amends to their citizens, not by self-flagellation but by applying themselves rigorously to learning and adopting the professionalism and disciplines of corporate governance that have developed over the past three decades. There is much good to be found here, especially when those two existing players – owners and regulators – are added to the mix. We need to create a national action-learning system between these four main players and the public. This calls for a governance re-education programme as so little is known of what has already been achieved, even by many current directors, less so by politicians, owners and regulators and hardly at all by the increasingly critical public. This book is my attempt to rectify this sad state of affairs.

Politicians are usually depicted in the media as ego-centric, self-seeking, unworldly and ultimately powerless when facing those confusing global trends experienced daily by the public and reinforced through exposure to real-time, electronic news. Similarly, directors of companies, government departments and now even charities are often depicted in the media as clueless, passive and sometimes with at least a hint of venal intent against their host community when seeking to create a monopoly and then price-gouge the public of its sparse savings. It is unsurprising that so few organizations are now automatically viewed with affection by the public.

Some directors are considered to be much worse than others, especially since the 2008 crash which was led by financial services. Indeed, bankers still attract much public hatred, as noted by Cardinal Nichols of Westminster Cathedral in his many addresses to the City of London.[4] He stresses especially their lack of contrition for their greedy, self-seeking and often unlawful actions. I have spoken with many in financial services, especially in Europe, the US, the EU and China, who still seriously believe that 2008 was just a large hiccup, but nothing that could not be resolved by even more exuberant trading on the 24-hour, seven-days-a-week money machine. They, investment or retail bankers, still see no reason to apologize and seem inoculated against any feelings of responsibility or morality for their wealth-destroying actions. Their continuing close links to many of our political leaders negatively affects the credibility of both. This lack of concern for their effect on others is part of the definition of psychosis and is a global issue.

The growing failure of "sophisticated states"

Politicians are in the firing line as examples of the failure of national leadership as they are most easily exposed to the media and the public. Democracy may well be the "least worst of the political systems"[5] but it is struggling currently as a system of governance and so, worryingly, losing credibility with the public in many countries. The most concise analysis of what is affecting our increasingly sclerotic democratic nations comes from Jan Techau, Director of Carnegie Europe. He argues that we are seeing systematic *"sophisticated state failure"* – "a cancer that is eating away at the western societies and undermining the liberal world order they have upheld".[6] People are cynical about those who hold democratic power but are ignorant of, or have not experienced, the worse alternatives. This erosion, he says, is hidden and deceptive because for most people most of the time most things still work in the Western democracies. "Systems sort of work yet nationally and regionally nothing much seems to get done". This seems especially true of the EU and US. This spreads discontent and leads to a search by the public and politicians for those simplistic "silver bullet" governance answers that often allow the rise of extreme policies of the right and left.

The five non-communicating new classes in society

I argue that our currently democratic societies are fragmenting rapidly into five distinct and non-communicating classes: the billionaires, the millionaires, the hollowed-out middle classes, the hollowed-out working class and the "unequals". The billionaires and millionaires live in increasingly isolated bubbles mixing only with similar folk. Their gated communities, private jets and limousines with security guards consciously exclude others, but also the ability to learn from others. The hollowed-out Western middle classes have sold out to rampant exuberant capitalism and in so doing have lost the self-respect found in their previous professionalism. In the US, if you are earning annually between $37k and $75k you are trapped with little hope of escaping to the previously offered better life. Some 80% of these folk have net assets of less than $1,000 and therefore no safety buffer against the slings and arrows of life. And these people are meant to comprise "the middle class". The social contract with the politicians for "betterment" is broken for such folk. The politicians have not shown the visionary leadership and competence needed to rebalance and integrate such a society that is, paradoxically, increasingly bitter and divided, yet notionally vaguely affluent. The politicians have taken a niggardly, piecemeal set of expedient minor actions to what is the stabilizing group in any society. They have tried temporarily to rebalance some of the disappearing "working class" and focused little on the "unequals" to whom I shall return in Chapter 1.

Techau argues, for example, that the entry of China into the world economy caused a massive initial surge in the global raw material price cycle. The consequent boom has allowed Western politicians to ride on the back of this boom, despite the Western economic crash of 2008. However, they did not offer long-sighted national leadership but rather played short-sighted party political games with the wealth generated, while being complacent about the growing contradictory national pressures of "entitlement" and "inequality" in their populations. Hence the current political failure and lack of structural reform (infrastructural and constitutional) in, for example, the UK, US, France or Italy during the good years, often despite having working parliamentary majorities. But all such cycles come to an end, and 2008 is the benchmark from which we must reframe "governance" around that Global Duty of Care. Since 2006 this has been legally explicit in the UK's Companies Act, but few seem to have noticed.

As voters become more disheartened by their political leaders, they become more fickle and often seek easier, more comforting answers, however irrational those might seem. Hence the rise of Donald Trump in the US and many new political parties in Europe, the ascent of which strongly demonstrates that many electors have a deep fear of their changing world and so prefer to follow the maxim "always hold on tight to nurse for fear of getting something worse".[7] Meanwhile, "normal" politicians react by trying to hug the middle ground and avoid committing to controversial decisions. Jean-Claude Juncker, President of the European Commission, was unusually explicit in saying "politicians know exactly what they need to do, but they do not know how to get elected again".[8] The result is the increasing paralysis of sophisticated states. "Political elites are disposed to protect the status quo so opportunities for painless change are missed".[9] Techau argues that the only lasting way out of sophisticated state failure is for responsible politicians to worry less about their re-election and more about risking their political careers to get important things moving for the longer-term benefit of their nations – as Margaret Thatcher did in the 1980s in the UK and Gerhard Schröder did in Germany with the labour market reforms in the mid-2000s. Notice that both countries now perform above the EU economic average. But who now will risk their political career for this end? Few it seems.

Which is why the public must lead their "leaders" towards effective governance. The typical current political response is to agree that "something must be done", make a great public noise about it, then leave it to experts and technical committees to sort out the broad details, pass legislation, generate lots of media coverage, bask in the resulting publicity and then forget about enforcement and hope that the public will also forget before the next election. Job done. This is no longer acceptable. In truth, it is "job hardly started" because the real learning from legislated action comes from the feedback after implementation. The problem is that an aversion to open learning leaves the ground fertile for bureaucratic, simplistic, compliance-fixated minds to fill the vacuum by creating more regulation and codes that cripple the purpose of the original. Up until his death in 2015 I occasionally worked, and regularly talked and corresponded, with Sir Adrian Cadbury, the doyen of modern corporate governance. In his last letter to me he wished me good luck with this book and asked me specifically "to ensure that you focus on the entrepreneurial, risk-taking, aspects of good governance and not the Codes and compliance aspects that are now crippling it".[10] I shall return to this warning in Chapter 5 on the regulators.

Can effective corporate governance really help politicians?

Towards publicly agreed general duties of politicians

Despite the cynical mind-sets mentioned, I feel that the time is now ripe for much of what has been learned about effective corporate governance to be applied to help uncertain politicians and their becalmed publics. The objectives of both directors and politicians are similar: to work within their constitution to ensure the success of their enterprise.

The general duties of governance

The legal foundation stones of effective corporate governance were codified finally after some 200 years and are clearly spelled out in Section 171 of the UK's Companies Act 2006 under "General Duties of Directors".[11] There is no political equivalent. There needs to be.

The Companies Act lists seven general duties of directors:

- To act within their powers (their constitution)
- To promote the success of their company
- To exercise independent judgement
- To exercise reasonable care, skill and diligence
- To avoid conflicts of interest
- Not to accept benefits from third parties
- To declare interests in proposed transactions

This needs careful study and understanding by both the public and the politicians. What would they agree on as an equivalent set of "Seven Duties for a Politician"? For example, can a politician ever have "independence of thought", or use "care, skill and diligence" in their decision-making? Could they ever be open to increased public assessment and still stay within an adversarial, two-party system? Who would be their regulators and assessors? And what powers would the assessors need? In the final chapter I suggest ways in which we can move towards the basis of a national governance compact to resolve these questions.

Much of this book explores the parallel cases of our national direction-givers – directors, owners, regulators and legislators – and their needs for significant organizational and personal development. These needs affect all of our organizations, well beyond listed companies, and show that the seven duties are both necessary and sufficient to create solid foundations for effective governance in private business, the public sector, state-owned enterprises, charities and government. If these sound good to you, then read on. There is already much that is transferable.

The need to add two more players to create a national learning system

In this book I argue for governance to be accepted as a national system, then for two more full and publicly accountable players to be added: owners and regulators. Both of these are frequently cursed by existing directors and politicians as being *the* major causes of their current problems. Indeed, all four blame one other for most problems, which is why I am interested in an integrated systems approach based on action learning. All four have important duties of care as dynamic parts of any national governance balancing mechanism. They are not just annoying bit-part players. Having formed these necessary elements of a national system of continuous governance, learning and development, all four must then be held accountable by a fifth player: public oversight. Sadly, at the moment, all five elements are disconnected, often warring, and rarely capable of learning even within their own sector let alone between sectors.

How can we define the values and competences of our national leaders?

As soon as I mention even the possibility of our leaders publicly accepting the responsibility of general duties with assessable and learnable competences, I get furious objections from all four parties. The most passionate revolve around their belief that "our values are very different from each other and from the general public's so this can never work". Yet I doubt the truth of this statement. My experience internationally is that people's personal values and aspirations are remarkably similar, at least in private. However, we are all extraordinarily bad at making them explicit, naming them, agreeing which are good and bad, and then behaving appropriately in public. We find this even harder in our organizational life. This is why we create corporate governance laws and codes to give a societal benchmark beneath which we should not drop.

Human values set the governance context

Before we get into the more technical aspects of the governance competences of directors and their transferability to politicians, owners and regulators, I want to face the "values" question head-on. "Values" is a word used profligately and currently usually without definition. It is a weasel word that can mean anything and nothing. As my colleague at Stellenbosch Business School, Daniel Malan, has written, it is very easy to muddle "value" as a tangible, financial concept and "values" as a set of personal beliefs and behaviours.[12] Once these values are resolved, public oversight of governance competence becomes much easier to assess and develop.

"Personal values" and their frequent conflict with organizational values set the context for much of the argument of this book. We all have different personal histories and objectives, but the cement that should hold the four governance parties and our wider society together are the explicit and implicit set of personal and organizational "values" espoused or assumed as acceptable as "good" or "bad" by our society. Without such boundaries to acceptable human behaviours we would have community, corporate and national chaos. Happily, we do not have chaos yet. But we do have a rolling series of messes caused by our fragmented non-system of governance. Even national governance codes are proving insufficient to cope with the current levels of distrust. For example, in the UK the main corporate governance regulator, the Financial Reporting Council, is encouraging us to consider more rigorously, and then live by, our "values" and "culture" but without specifying what either word means.

What are "values"?

I deal with this fundamental question in detail in Chapter 1. In this Introduction I shall simply try to clarify the term. The word "values" derives from the Latin root *vale*, *val* or *valu* and emerges in the Old French *value*. By the 13th century it is used in Middle English following the cultural impact of Norman (Viking) French on Anglo-Saxon, referring to "valour, strength or worth". All uses of the word have positive meanings and signify that values are "good", signifying "valid" (legally correct), "equivalence", "validity" (truth) and "valiant" (brave).

In our current debate about the foundations on which we should build effective governance in our organizations and society we have assumed the essential *goodness* of "values" without the rigour of specifying them. We have thus reduced them to political and management-speak buzzwords: nouns and adjectives to hide wobbly and weak concepts. It is now so fashionable to use "values" that at least a speaker has a warm feeling about them even if they rarely test the listeners' understanding of the word. Yet it is in the act of agreeing what is good and bad in organizations, and in ourselves, that we uncover the strengths and flaws in our society. This is personally and politically uncomfortable as, once made explicit, we then have to validate them, agree their equivalence and priorities and finally show our valour in proposing, defending and living them. "Value" is a very powerful word. We must clarify, simplify and then use it well for all four governance parties to be credible in public.

Whose values will we use in the future?

The simplest and most practical definition I know of a "value" is *a belief in action*.[13] As humans receive some 80% of their information through their eyes, it is through their behaviour that people visually signal their values to others whether face to face or via the media. For a value to be seen as credible by others, the words spoken must correspond with their actions. Actions are what other people initially believe about you. If your words and actions are out of sync, then people will believe your actions and deduce your real meaning and values from these. Words can be weasel, but behaviours are more likely to be honest. Acceptance of, and living, one's personal values has important implications for the emotional temperature of societal, organizational and personal health. This is why I rate the pursuit of human values so highly.

Clarifying the three basic values sets

A theme running through this book concerns how the development of effective governance allows the resolution of the current clashes between three very different sets of values that permeate our daily life:

- "Accepted" business values   (our daily values-in-action)
- Corporate governance values (nationally espoused "good" values)
- Personal values   (our learned personal beliefs)

Currently, all three are often in contradiction in the minds of many politicians, directors, owners, regulators and the public. The resulting confusion widens the public's distrust in our leaders. The too frequent leadership message of "do as I say, not as I do" then shows hypocrisy and contempt for the receiver. Listening to the current over-supply of psychobabble in the messy public debate about the importance of "values" is rarely edifying. I am reminded too frequently of the lines from Matthew Arnold's *Dover Beach*:

> And we are here as on a darkling plain
> Swept with confused alarms of struggle and flight
> Where ignorant armies clash by night.[14]

Yet there is hope. Historically, our commercial legislation is based on three long-tested basic international business values that have promoted honest trading between individuals and companies over the centuries:

- Accountability (to the owners)
- Probity   (honest dealing between the players)
- Transparency   (openness to allow validation and
                 traceability)

These are the basis of our current corporate governance values.

The necessity to establish national governance competence

I want to change focus here to introduce the rarely discussed issue of developing the competence and values of our governors. A frustrated, angry and ignorant public allows the continuation of poor governance. We get the leaders we deserve. And their careers often end in failure, especially at the personal level. The problem is that the public have little common language, or few agreed concepts, by which to monitor and assess their governors and so turn their criticisms into useful action-oriented learning.

Despite their rhetoric and spin, few politicians, or leaders in, for example, finance, business, health, police, sport, local administration or charities, leave their governing role with their heads held high, with a feeling of a job well done, and to the adulation of their diverse stakeholders. Indeed, the opposite seems true in an age dominated by ever-critical, cynical commentators increasingly using the amplification of electronic media. Too many leaders, even in the public and charity sectors, leave by quietly slipping away often with extraordinarily large pay-offs before their incompetence is later revealed. Or there are later major scandals in which the public and the law become involved.

When the critical public do become aware, it is usually too late to denounce the ignorance, incompetence and arrogance of such leaders. UK parliamentary select committees and their US federal equivalents are beginning to have some positive effects but are usually late in their investigatory process. And few, including the public prosecutors, have an inclination to follow the public's desire for retribution through the courts, especially at the personal level. So, despite a failure to deliver their contractual fiduciary duty to ensure the success of their organizations, many modern leaders are seen by the public to be rewarded for failure.

Yet, perversely, the public still clings to the assumption that their leaders *must* know what they are doing, or at the very least have had some basic training to competence. Neither is proven. The quality of national leadership may never have been as heroic or omniscient as history has painted it. Until very recently the public did not have the power of the internet, the capacity for the instant checking of facts, or the instant global dissemination of criticism, to be able to question their governors. Now it has, and this instant access is opening up to scrutiny a whole new set of the observable behaviours, histories and consequent values of our leaders. Despite the shadow side of the rise of "alternative facts", accountability, probity and transparency are becoming harder to avoid. Governance competency is being brought to the fore.

Markets versus professionalism

However, to establish leadership credibility we still have to battle with two deep political trends where previously effective leadership has been eroded consciously by the political classes. The consequences explain much of the current estrangement and destabilization of our societies. This has enabled the politicians to demean frequently the other three direction-giver players while excusing themselves. This erosion is part of the rot.

1. Idolizing the irrational exuberance of the markets

The first noticeable trend has been the conscious attempt to undermine society's innate common sense while simultaneously idolizing the uncontrolled, irrational and dangerous exuberance of the international markets. For example, the community-eroding effects of the freeing of the US capital markets, the UK's "Big Bang" in its financial markets in 1986, and the stuttering, messy start to the seemingly doomed Eurozone, have all had visible, fragmenting and debilitating effects on the wealth of the vast majority of their citizens. In the West no-one seems to be currently doing well apart from the financial traders who spend the majority of their time trading among themselves for their "turn" on short-sighted market "churn". Hmmm . . .

The disorienting knock-on effects on these new priorities and values have skewed the balance of many of society's problem-solving processes to the point that many politicians now believe that protecting the financial community must always be their national priority and, therefore, "good". This is nonsense. I am not arguing that national budgets should not strive to balance, nor that capital expenditure be opaque about its long-term effects on a nation, but rather that the purpose and value sets of any society must transcend pure financial efficiency and short-term monetary gain, especially if this benefits only a handful of increasingly wealthy and stateless individuals. In an emotionally healthy society based on agreed human values, "wealth" is more than just money.

The three capitals

We recognize this increasingly as society begins to accept that there are now three capitals available for investing – financial, physical and societal – and that all are needed to generate "inclusive capitalism".[15] We are slowly beginning to accept also that there is a necessary moral aspect to the creation of wealth. Those who use Adam Smith's *An Inquiry into the Nature and Causes of the Wealth of Nations*[16] to advocate purely free markets forget, or more likely never knew, that nearly half of this seminal book concerns the key importance of "Moral Sentiment" relating to the moral duties consequent on raising wealth and then distributing it across society. Adam Smith was, after all, the world's first Professor of Moral Philosophy, based at the University of Glasgow from 1751. Without a moral consensus, national leadership leads only to control by the powerful – an autocracy, oligarchy or plutocracy.

Even a cursory look at international finance shows that around 75% of each financial day comprises purely trading with other traders, often automatically through their algorithms. Traders love this as they take a "turn" on each trade and so have continuous cash flow and consequent bonuses. But does even a quarter of this daily flow turn into real, "patient" investments in, for example, infrastructural projects, creating new businesses, developing existing organizations, or hedging against future risk, to protect such long-term investment? Here's a suggestion: open stock, bond and foreign exchanges for only one specified day a week. This should help stop continuous automatic 24-hour arbitrage trading by computers, reduce "flash crashes" and encourage traders to live in a much more modest, patient world.

2. Demolishing professionalism

The second erosive political force is the conscious demolition by the politicians of the professions and their ethos of "professionalism". As with the freeing of markets, the longer-term consequences have not been thought through in terms of the negative impact on society. Some of the more rational aspects of the breaking of the cartels in, for example, law, architecture, banking, accountancy, insurance and medicine, have been partially successful, but at the cost of a loss of focus on the needs and priorities of the very clients and consumers whose protection was meant to be improved. I discuss the detailed consequences in Chapter 2.

I doubt if the politicians were fully conscious of the consequence of their political actions. What is worse is that there is still little conscious awareness of, or learning from, this at national level. Financial efficiency does not guarantee human effectiveness, even if it does have a seductively reductionist single bottom line. The historical development of professionalism was abandoned for quick party-political gain but is having serious societal consequences particularly through the "hollowing out" of the middle class and their stabilizing role in society, while also reducing their potential to improve the plight of the "unequals".

But then few people had a clue as to what "professionalism" meant and, now that it has been attacked so consistently, few care. They should. Historically, the professions were formalized in mid-Victorian times through a conscious political trade-off. The professions would be given the status of cartels with the rights to restrict entry, accredit educational levels, set scales of fees, and self-regulate, including not "touting" for work, provided that they would act primarily in their *clients'* interest, not their own. They were valued broadly as a force for good and stability in society. They would administer rigorous codes of conduct to control the misdemeanours of their members thus guaranteeing justice for their clients. This notion of professionals denying immediate self-interest was so powerful an ideal that it was accepted as mutually beneficial by the fast-growing Victorian middle classes. It held good until the 1970s when it was increasingly questioned by the political left as elitist and by the right as anti-free markets. It is much missed.

It was swept away by Margaret Thatcher's "bonfire of the professions": an attack on professionals, quangos and the trades unions in a sea of free markets, and the dismantling of the barriers to entry and fee scales. The consequences of not allowing professionals a relatively secure and non-grasping lifestyle whether they be consultant surgeons, junior doctors or criminal lawyers are beginning to be appreciated for what they were worth.

This is not just about money but about the beneficial ethical stance of professionals – at the very least their independence of thought in making sound judgements on behalf of their clients regardless of who is paying their fees, just as directors are now required to do for their companies under the Companies Act. Few directors recognize this. We need to build rapidly a new version of what it means to be a professional. This book seeks to do so in Chapter 2. Fundamental to this must be those four corporate governance players: directors, owners, regulators and legislators. This is already being demanded through the international development of the broader concepts of "integrated reporting" and "inclusive capitalism". Importantly, politicians must be integrated into any redevelopment of professionalism to ensure a more just governance system.

This book is not designed as a "banker bashing" tome. However, I am convinced that the lack of professionalism mixed with greed and lust led to the financial crisis of 2008. Most bankers never really "got" professionalism, with the noticeable exceptions of a few discreet and still quietly thriving City partnerships. But then banking was never a profession. Even today it is astonishing how few leading bankers have any banking qualifications. The ability to manipulate the short-term dynamics of the markets seems qualification enough. This is gaming not investment, and we all suffer the consequences.

As this book went to press, the premature takeover bid by the US Kraft Corporation for the UK/Dutch Unilever was a classic example of the two schools of investing clashing in terms of their approach to governance. The bid was withdrawn within days as Unilever and the media attacked Kraft for their short-termist "asset-stripping" approach contrasted with the patient, long-term and inclusive investing approach of Unilever. Kraft argued that by cutting costs dramatically they would release shareholder value quickly for reinvestment elsewhere. Unilever said that it has invested steadily in building brands, customers and their staff over decades and that this has ensured a more stable and future-oriented business. As many of their markets are in the developing world, they argued, their focus on building brands would generate a much better long-term return for all their stakeholders. I deal with this issue in more detail in Chapter 3, especially regarding the conflict between "CRG" and "ESG".

The consequences for national political leadership

Under a democratic electoral system we cannot expect our newly elected political leaders to arrive already competent. They are too diverse. Yet our current final measure of their competence is an absolute: will we elect them to office again? Or do we throw the rascals out? What interests me in terms of effective governance is what happens in between? Seemingly not much in terms of any agreed national process for their personal development. Self-motivation, good luck and party political connections seem the norm. The public's rough measures of competence during their term of office are whether they are a good constituency representative fighting for their electors' issues against state bureaucrats and, occasionally, in being such a party line follower that promotion to a ministerial post reflects well locally. Few examples of professionalism are found. Politicians, especially those in government, should now be developed to agreed levels of competence and values through more rigorous assessment. This should be done at the personal level and especially through monitoring the quality and consequences of their legislation rather than the quantity. I argue there is already much in the development of corporate governance effectiveness for them to build on. The book is designed to help this.

The pressures for all directors to ditch the present corporate governance regulatory system

A key demand of this book is that all nationally registered organizations – private, public and not-for-profit – are brought under the existing national laws concerning the general duties of directors, as has been achieved in South Africa. Then a lot of the present bureaucratic, compliance-based nonsense for all of our nationally registered organizations can be dropped. This includes the vast majority of the current corporate governance codes of many countries.

This requires little legislation: for example, in the UK over 200 years of the piecemeal writing of company law was consolidated into the 2006 Companies Act. This 2,000-page tome has at its kernel[17] those simple seven "general duties of directors". I have already suggested that these become a building block for politicians' general duties. I go further here and suggest that we create:

A National Covenant for directors of all registered organizations

I propose that we make these seven fundamental duties *mandatory* for all registered organizations of any type, including governments and not-for-profits, and that the politicians declare a National Corporate Governance Covenant to this effect. We can then drop some 90% of the current corporate governance codes and all their associated compliance costs and hassle, reduce the number of regulations and regulators, and refocus on the directors' primary task of "ensuring the success of the business"; and the politicians' primary task of "ensuring the success of the country" with due regard to their use of our financial, physical and social capital. We then need a dedicated regulator and prosecutor to enjoy sufficient success in enforcing these duties to nudge every director into taking their roles and liabilities seriously. We need to ensure that directors and politicians realize that delivering these seven duties *is* their job. I feel that this is a modest proposal, not a revolutionary concept. But how will we ensure that the current vested interest see it that way?

The four major players in national leadership

One way is to highlight publicly and bring together these vested interests into a national system of mutually beneficial learning. Throughout this book I define these major players in national leadership as four major groups:

- Boards of directors
- Owners
- Regulators
- Legislators

And then the aim is to create a national public oversight mechanism – a fifth player (see Figure 1).

Currently, they are unintegrated both between each sector and even within each sector. There are still many warring tribes in the current non-system of corporate governance so it will take growing and determined public demand to get them aligned and attuned. It is well worth the effort both nationally and internationally. This book ends with a proposal to create a national learning system for any country linking all five elements so that the present ragged, random and disconnected "governance" nonsense is eliminated.

In subsequent chapters I shall look at each sector in turn. I have been astonished at just how ignorant I was in associated fields to

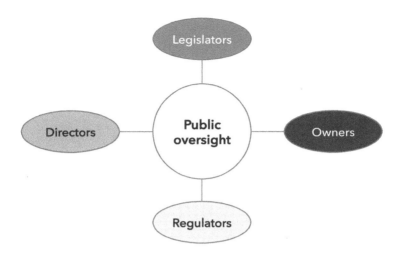

Figure 1: The five major players in national leadership

which I had often glibly referred without testing my understanding of them and the linkages between them. I am still learning and increasingly aware of my ignorant assumptions. I hope that my incomplete and continuing researches will lead to a more informed public debate on this nationally and internationally crucial societal issue.

But I have learned that before I get into a deeper analysis of the needs and issues of each of the four major players there are fundamental issues of values and future trends that permeate the current debates internationally. So I will use the next two chapters to explore the emerging context of effective corporate governance and how a deeper understanding of these trends in values and the external global forces of demographic, political, economic and technological change are forcing our leaders to have to rethink effective corporate governance. It is to these that I now turn.

Section I
Setting the future context for effective governance

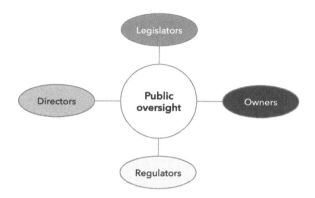

1

The value of "values"

Integrating national, organizational
and personal values to create effective
organizations

Why do our leaders find it so hard to be "soft"?

When regulators begin to advocate building values and culture into corporate governance codes, you know three things are happening, none of which are good. First, the public are so disenchanted with the performance and morals of directors and managers that they are complaining loudly to the politicians. Second, the politicians are putting pressure on the regulators to remove this increasingly uncomfortable burden from themselves. Third, the regulators will try to respond to a political initiative but will always seek to reduce complex issues to such simplicity that they become prescriptive, mechanical and ultimately meaningless. Meanwhile, regulatees then focus their learning on how to beat the system. However, this process allows the politicians a short-term sense of completion while having a long-term cost for the nation.

In this chapter, I explore how the "soft", very human, ideas of values and culture can be used positively in our organizations to allow easier continuous learning and development to deliver the success of the enterprise. Paradoxically, such "soft" concepts can be seen as equally "hard" if understood and used with care, skill and diligence.

The words "values" and "culture" are currently fashionable in both business and politics. Through their use, our leaders demonstrate that they are aware, politically correct, and seen to be siding with the people against, for example, the "evil" bankers, macroeconomists, auditors, commercial lawyers, credit agencies, consultants of all sorts, and anyone else implicated in the Western financial crash of 2008. The continuing casual use of the term "values" is an easy win for the politicians as the public are clearly behind them. But what precisely do they mean by "values" and "culture"? Whose values should be used? Why are the words so confusing and frightening to the business mind? What happens when they are in contradiction, and how do you assess them in practical terms?

Three sets of values

I argue that we are always grappling in our working and private lives with three different and often conflicting sets of values:

- Accepted business values   (what we do at work to get by each day)

- Corporate governance values   (what mainstream society demands of us through codes and legislation)

- Personal values   (what our belief system demands of us)

These conflicts are experienced daily by all yet are rarely made explicit. When personal values conflict with accepted business values, things start to get messy, as values at the organizational level are rarely explicit, let alone codified, but are formed implicitly through accepted work group pressures. When accepted business values are in conflict with corporate governance values, derived from legislation and regulation, matters can become very messy indeed as daily norms are in contradiction with legislated codes. We grapple with these dynamics of all three levels of values 24 hours a day. We often seek to resolve them quickly by glibly using the ambiguous but fashionable phrase "value clashes", but this often means very different things to different people. How can we agree some useful basic meanings?

The basis of "values"

The word "value", the etymology of which I touched on earlier (page 13), has always had, in modern English, a dual, often bipolar, meaning. It carries both an extrinsic, "hard" sense concerning the worth of something tangible, and a "soft" sense, concerning the personal ethics held most closely by a person. This "soft" side has strong tones of "goodness" and "worthiness". Even before Brexit and Trump, the "hard" side in Western societies has tended to signify "greed", "indifference", "cynicism" and "inhumanity" in the public's mind.

This contradiction is expressed well by Oscar Wilde in *Lady Windermere's Fan*. When Cecil Graham asks, "What is a cynic?", Lord Darlington replies, "A man who knows the price of everything, and the value of nothing", to which Cecil Graham responds, "And a sentimentalist, my dear Darlington, is a man who sees an absurd value in everything and doesn't know the market price of a single thing".[18] In a similar vein is a description commonly ascribed to James Thurber, and particularly directed at accountants, who were "without feelings and without bowels". Sadly, the hard sense is still the default mindset for many business folk, and often that of the public. How does one resolve these contradictions?

The myth of "our business values"

The prioritization of the "hard", tangible view, mixed with a conscious lack of compassion in business, is reflected in the accepted values of many organizations, both private and governmental. Financial values – numerate, passionless and seemingly irrefutable – usually predominate in the majority of organizations. So it is odd that much is made, even mandated, in annual reports of so many organizations of their "set of company values". These are usually sentimental and often derived without significant inputs from the reality of experiences of their customers, owners or staff. Instead, they have been written following a quick session of the top executives and are usually untested by them. Their publication leads frequently to the inevitable rude jeering from staff, customers and the public. The consequent demeaning abuse of "our values" creates an antagonistic and subversive subculture which often takes years of expensive damage limitation to rectify.

It is a curiosity of current corporate and political life that there is a deep belief that the values espoused by leaders must be both correct and instantly acceptable to all. Even more curious is the belief by the governors that the governed will immediately adopt the prescribed behaviours without question. This is a nonsense, and an expensive one at that. Such a blinkered approach by directors and executives shows ignorance of history, anthropology or even social science where "value" and the concept of "value sets" as a social principle has been used since 1918 but rarely understood by business.[19]

Lawful organizational values

Context

In the Introduction, I mentioned that there is now a growing acceptance internationally that our organizations, private, public and not-for-profit, have to demonstrate three clear *organizational* values to be trusted by the public:

- Accountability
- Probity
- Transparency

These are the values of an inclusive society and need, therefore, to be incorporated as the basis of company law and public reporting systems. Adherence to these three organizational values allows corporations to be seen as publicly credible, which helps to ensure their success. For many centuries, our commerce has been based on these values through their legal enforcement. They are underwritten in the ancient laws of property and contract (the basis of all free trade) and, when combined with easy access to independent courts of law, form the basis of a healthy society. Without these three fundamental values, an organization is not credible to its clients and customers, and, without credibility, the organization cannot exist in the long term.

Corporate governance regulators are now beginning to insist that, in the future, directors will have to take the monitoring and assessing of business's "values" and "culture" into their regular annual reporting process by giving examples of their use and metrics. The problem is that almost all business leaders, directors and executives find the concepts of "culture" and "values" alien. They are not seen as "normal" business words. Their relevance to the daily business round is barely recognized. Any time given to these concepts is usually considered wasted. So "values" tend to be dismissed without much thought about how they might help leaders develop the future of their business. I argue that they are one of the four key contextual reframings needed for a healthy future. How can they be helped?

Values-in-practice

This book transfers those three organizational values into three levels of values-in-practice. It defines their characteristics, notes their potential for specific conflicts, and then reflects on how development of each organizational value improves a business's future.

Accepted business values

The public's doubts and questions about what really goes on day to day in organizations are as old as time itself. The public often assumes that all "conspiracies against the laity" are true.[20] Frequently, doubts abound about whether publicly espoused organizational values bear any link to reality. For example, people question the accuracy of Volkswagen's pollution metrics for their cars, the safety of Samsung's mobile phone batteries, working conditions inside many clothing factories, the employment of slave labour, the real levels of customer service delivered, or whether HBOS's business recovery service was nothing of the sort. Even more frequently, people doubt the word of politicians. Can they ever be trusted in their duty to protect and develop "the public interest" when their rewards come from short-term party political and personal gains? And can the public ever agree on how an honest person should behave, and so agree a set of values by which we can all live in our communities?

Whose "accepted values"?

Most people accept that just muddling through the contradictions of the working week is prize enough. Thought is rarely given to what the daily values-in-use are, or why they have developed. You meet them from the first day in your new job. You arrive, bright-eyed and keen to demonstrate your skills only to be told with a hint of scorn "Oh! We don't bother to do that around here" and are often shown acceptable but lesser-quality behaviour. The conflicts start here. Do you then compromise immediately for an easier life? Or do you fight for qualitative improvement? Which way will get you more easily accepted by your work group? Which will give you professional satisfaction? Are these in contradiction? And when you go home at the end of the day, which will show that you have been true to your personal values?

The two sides of accepted business values

My colleague Coralie Palmer insists that I stop calling them accepted business values and refer to them only as "disjointed business values". I know what she means. As the old phrase goes, "the tone starts at the top". So, if the directors and senior executives spend little time monitoring and worrying about the values operating within their organization, it is hardly surprising that they run to rot. I argue that there are two sides to accepted business values – a "good" and a "shadow" side. Most people start by striving for good but, over time and under group pressure, slip into easy options that are not so good and sometimes downright bad. A minority of the bad guys consciously set out to game the system and create disruptive "shadow side" behaviours against both their organization's corporate values, and the customers', for their own advantage, as we have seen in the recent Libor, foreign exchange, and "flash crash" examples. These end up as disjointed values when compared with what the wider organization and mainstream society demand. However, even when bad, they are still accepted values.

It often more comfortable to float on top of the sea of organizational contradictions, to moan about them with your colleagues along the lines of "ain't it awful but there is nothing we can do about it", and to actively seek to avoid responsibility by doing nothing. But in the end it is soul-destroying for an individual to live like this. It is so seductively easy to be sucked into the negative mind-set of the accepted business value of "this is what we do when no-one is looking". You may even be rewarded for it by a complicit boss. But are these business values in contradiction with your personal values?

Accepted business values are usually a way of just getting by with minimum personal challenge or moral doubt. But they still leave many individuals with the nagging thought that they are not doing the right things. I am only partially reassured that in private most directors and politicians with whom I have spoken have admitted to such worries. However, many senior people admit often to not having the personal courage to challenge the business's values publicly. They are then hostage to "being found out", which constricts their behaviours and makes them feel even worse.

Amorality and the "shadow side" of accepted business values

The ideal is expressed by the phrase "integrity is in doing the right things when no-one is looking".[21] But group pressure and overriding company "tone from the top" easily erode this. Matters are made worse when strong subcultures are created that consciously flout the mainstream norms, including the legal rules. This has been only too obvious in international financial services over the last decade. From the "Libor Louts" to many other less publicized subgroups, near-impermeable subcultures have been created through tough induction rituals, extravagant rewards and fierce punishments for non-conformance to the group norms, despite the fact that they consciously operate outside acceptable behaviours. Their rules and values are often hidden from, or consciously overlooked by, the organization in pursuit of the short-term advantage, as Nick Leeson and Barings Bank showed. And so the rot begins.

Disruptive accepted business values prioritize amorality and the "shadow side" of business. We see conscious PPI mis-selling, rate-setting manipulation, and keeping existing customers unaware of better rates being offered to attract new customers. Customer loyalty is given a low priority in business and personal rewards. So the public must continue to ask: how does this square with accountability, probity and transparency?

The erosion of positive accepted business values

Historically the values of an organization start from the personal values of the founder. A charismatic and driven leader defines the original organizational value set. If successful, this generates a rosy glow in investors, customers and suppliers from which a brand image and reputation are developed. But these values can easily erode over time as the founder ages or moves on. These founding values are often then forgotten and usually a fixation with "the bottom line" takes over. There is rarely a conscious organizational process for retaining, assessing and developing over time the "corporate memory" to protect the company's perceived reputation. It is left to erode. Instead, sadly, many organizations develop a form of "organizational amnesia",[22] which means that they learn and value nothing from their successful past. This is a hugely wasteful process.

They are then forced to reinvent and promulgate values based on their present, often short-term, conditions generated by the transient personal values of those currently in power. Many of these are "careerist" directors and managers without the founders' drive, ambition, imagination and sheer risk-taking courage. They are driven often by a mixture of expediency and amorality, so their attempts at defining and enforcing the new values frequently fail because so few staff accept them, This is odd, because creating, developing and monitoring the organization's values and culture is a key duty of the board's leadership role – as the regulators are now telling us. As few boards or senior executives are inducted into this "soft" part of their role, few directors place any worth on it.

We are seeing examples on both sides of the Atlantic with the muddled political approach to rethinking and implementing the "new" corporate values of the banks.[23] But, without rigorous monitoring, "living the values" can rapidly become just "gaming the new rules". Such gaming is usually based on slightly modified negative accepted business values: doing what everyone feels that they can get away with to generate short-term profits as easily as possible, rather than aspiring to those human values that chime with our societal and personal values. "Values" in the moral sense rarely come into gaming. This is why I worry about what is happening in Silicon Valley as the much-hailed "disruptive economies" have moved so rapidly from being seen as saviours of the people to displaying the worst forms of rampant, monopolistic capitalism, disregarding the customers and disabling the shareholders.

Corporate governance values

Corporate governance values are the state's push-back against negative accepted business values – its attempt to ensure that we do the right things all of the time. They are the public manifestation of the primary and secondary legislation, and the regulatory control mechanisms, that seek to ensure that our organizations and their governors stay within those broad values of accountability, probity and transparency. They reflect the mainstream political agreement of what is right and wrong, good and bad, in our organizational values and consequent behaviours.

But in most countries these apply currently only to listed companies – a tiny minority of the registered companies in any country. This is why I argue for all *registered* companies, government-owned enterprises, agencies and not-for-profits to be brought under those basic organizational values of accountability, honest dealing and transparency through national agreement on the basic corporate governance values, if we are to have healthy, publicly accountable organizations. Otherwise, it is so easy to slip into corrupt ways. The UN definition of corruption is the simple and powerful phrase "the misuse of public or private position for direct or indirect personal gain".[24] Sadly, corruption and fraud are rampant across the world, even if some Westerners believe they are only to be found in Africa, Asia, the Gulf and South America. They are not. The unfair employment of family and friends, the non-declaration of interest in transactions, the inflating and then awarding of contracts without due process and the casual bribing by gifts large or small: all are ubiquitous.

All fall foul of those three basic values of corporate governance. They are neither *accountable*, use *probity*, nor are *transparent*.

However, progress has been made in the West on some of these issues. The US Foreign Corrupt Practices Act 1977[25] and the UK's Bribery Act 2010[26] have helped modify some behaviours. The US Act applies only to attempts to bribe foreign officials so is more restricted than the UK's. But enforcement has been mixed and, if Donald Trump repeals it as he said he would before the US 2016 election, we may see it slump. So a lot of the growth in this area has been through the development of corporate governance codes and rules rather than primary legislation. South Africa, through the four King Commission Reports,[27] and the UK via the Financial Reporting Council's code developments,[28] are necessary, important but not sufficiently good examples for the establishment of universal business values.

The King Commissions have done much to shake up the contexts for future effective corporate governance by bringing environmental, social and integrated (ESG) reporting issues into the debate, often ahead of pure financial reporting. The UK has tended to focus more on good practice: but only within the FTSE 350 companies, and so has left over 95% of UK organizations to fend for themselves. These organizations often address this by adopting the inappropriate FRC codes as scripture, with very mixed results. It has hardly tackled the deep issue of ownership and its consequent duties, nor of wider public accountability to stakeholders. It constituted a useful start in 1992, but 25 years on, as the FRC/FTSE code has become more pre-scriptive, the whole corporate governance process is slipping towards being "gamed" and demeaned by the players. How long a chairman can remain on a board and what remuneration is paid is a matter for the shareholders and the board, not the regulator and politicians. If the basic law had tougher enforcement, the public might not be so enraged.

This is challenging stuff for directors but even more so for politicians. They always have an ambiguous, if not downright bipolar, position in relation to business. Business and its taxes generate the majority of wealth available for distribution by politicians in a country. So, whether they are of the right or the left, it is dangerous for politicians to interfere too much in wealth generation without risking destroying it and so losing their distributive power. Yet the public is demanding more probity and citizen orientation because of their recent wealth destruction since 2008. How can politicians square this circle?

Ironically, the obvious answer is through laws that the politicians themselves have already passed – but not bothered to enforce properly. The codification and redrafting of some 200 years of case law into the 2,000-page UK Companies Act 2006[29] is a massive national achievement. Yet who knows or cares about it now? It is as if we live in a parallel political world where what is "good" and "right" has been agreed nationally, passed into law and then given to such weak government departments, civil servants and regulators that it was all a façade. Good has been consciously suppressed to deal with short-term political manoeuvring. It is analagous to Gnosticism being suppressed as a heresy by the early Catholic Church in a bid to destroy competing alternatives.

Yet the values of accountability, probity and openness *are* the basis for our current wealth generation within and without our country. Indeed the 54 members of the Commonwealth are increasingly appreciative of, and dependent on, that blend of contract and property law, easy access to courts, swift judgements, and the English language, to underpin their own national corporate governance development. These are beyond the EU and its unhelpful legal system and trade provisions and will need serious scrutiny by politicians post-Brexit to keep our corporate governance system ahead of the global game.

The tensions between business values and personal values

I have never met a consciously venal director, senior executive or even banker, despite the media insistence that the world is full of them. I have met some amoral ones and some psychotic ones (seemingly a growing requirement for chief executives).[30] I have not led a sheltered life and have been privileged to work on five of the six continents with a diverse array of nationalities, religious and tribal cultures. I have met many personally confused leaders who feel that their deep personal values are frequently compromised by the work they are asked to do. "Our Business Values" statements are frequently espoused publicly by these leaders, then embossed on company walls and handed out as glossy brochures to persuade both employees and clients of the inherent goodness of their organizations. Most are greeted with deep cynicism as the staff know what really goes on when no-one is looking. Despite all the grand words, such as "care for our customers", "being number one in . . .", "being environmentally aware", "leading on community development" and "valuing our staff and suppliers", the cynics know that when times are tough cost-cutting, price gouging and reduction of quality service are the paramount "values" used to retain profitability.

Indeed, the major intellectual fights within accepted business values are over short-term profitability versus long-term investment, customer exploitation versus customer development, permanent employment contracts versus zero-hours contracts, and human rights versus casual exploitation. It is a very unusual organization indeed that is not fixated primarily by their bottom line and, if pushed, will do some morally doubtful things to keep achieving it. This is where the exercise of personal values becomes an organizational issue. Sadly, the majority of individuals do not feel entitled to do anything about it and so crumple, even though they might then hate themselves for it.

Most individuals "yield" under pressure

Unless staff have strong levels of personal integrity and courage, sadly over 95% of them[31] will yield to higher authority and obey instructions that they know are "wrong", as experiments from Milgram onwards have shown. This is where an understanding of Roger Steare's "MoralDNA" concept is so helpful.[32] Few people are strong in resisting a demanding authority figure, and few are driven by a clear and developed set of personal values. So the example of General Sir Michael Jackson refusing an order from a senior US general in the Kosovo Campaign "because he had no wish to start the Third World War"[33] is unusual. When asked why he did it, he explained that his role was "to speak truth unto power" when he knew that they were wrong. This stands out as a rare example of a senior leader sticking by their values despite the most dire of potential personal consequences, and winning for the wider benefit of humanity.

There is another aspect to this issue: organizations in general seem to be accepting, however reluctantly, that accepted business values may not be supreme in all circumstances. Yet our organizations – public and not-for-profit as well as private – seem still to be headed down an amoral accepted business values path. This is a growing issue for not-for-profit organizations. Many have joined these non-private organizations precisely because their personal values did not align with accepted business values. This is noticeable in those who believe in a "public sector ethos" or the lived values of a specific charity. Today their personal values are increasingly confronted by accepted business values even in such organizations.

Yet most directors and senior executives I meet are shamefaced about having been engaged in some form of conspiracy against the public, money laundering or corruption, especially overseas. This is despite the US's Foreign Corrupt Practices Act[34] and the UK's Bribery Act of 2010.[35] Since 2015, however, I have noticed the beginning of a small but positive change in, for example, African customers and clients when facing UK directors bound by the UK's Bribery Act. They are now much more careful as they, the customers, do not wish to be involved personally in UK litigation. Some now strive harder to ensure that their business is "clean". So there is hope that more focus on values as a driver of honest business will begin to make a difference when we face the diversity of national cultures. But notice that the driver here is self-regulation through the fear of being found out rather than the imposition of even more draconian rules.

Personal values and the City of London

Given the public hatred and despair of the ethics of the financial services industry in the City of London, I see now some hopes of constructive action even there. Consider that for over some 900 years the simple maxim of "My word is my bond" has been the basis of a business contract in the City. It is entirely personal, and a matter of honour, if you do not deliver on your word. For centuries it has worked surprisingly well in the City – until the last 30 years following the "Big Bang",[36] when ethics seemed to go out of the window. This was reinforced in the public's mind as the increasing number of scandals in the banking world from sub-prime "Ninja" mortgages onwards shook public confidence. We have observed fines for many of the offending companies but few, if any, criminal prosecutions of individual offenders. The jailing of the HBOS bankers and associates in 2017 is a hopeful sign.

Yet I have found in my work that there are many in the City, whose personal values have been shocked and tested, sometimes to destruction, by what their corporate values demanded. These people are often in turmoil but admit in private they lack the personal courage – or access to anonymous organizational processes – to warn their leaders of wrongdoing. The Walker Report on the future of banking[37] made many structural and procedural changes but did not tackle this fundamental tension. However, it is noticeable that individual financial services folk are beginning to want to live their work in line with their deep personal beliefs. The City Values Forum,[38] now led by Richard Sermon, a previous Sheriff of the Corporation of London, has seen a growing number of individuals willing to make the pledge "My word is my bond" publicly. This is not just a piece of corporate PR but a personal pledge made to colleagues. Such a declaration is now being built into the personal oath made by many of the City Livery companies. Members joining my own, the Worshipful Company of Management Consultants,[39] make this pledge in front of their fellows whose role is to hold them to it. Failure means public disgrace.

To maintain this momentum, the public must demand much better oversight of the development of our corporate governance values, and keep asking why they are not enforced by the politicians. It is what the public want. It is what the politicians of all parties say that they want. So why is it not a popular political cause? It smells strongly of "sophisticated state failure". Everyone is just getting by without hope.

Personal values

During our life each of us creates, consciously or unconsciously, a set of values that define us uniquely. They tell us what is "good" and "bad", "right" and "wrong". They reflect the sum of our experiences and learning created by our family, our education, our religion, our work, our friendships, and our innermost thoughts. At their deepest level they form our bedrock beliefs without which we could not continue to function as a human. They are tested and reinforced daily and hence become so automatic that they often are unconscious to us. Yet they determine what others know of us – our behaviours, our attitudes, our values and ultimately our beliefs. They are the cement of our lives – stabilizing and strong, but dangerous if fragmented. When combined in larger groups they form societal values – which we will investigate later in this chapter under "culture". Personal values tend to have been formed by the time a child has its first full physical body change. Hence the old Jesuit maxim: "Give me a child until he is seven and I will give you the man."

Others initially experience someone's personal values only through a blend of their behaviours and their words. If both are in sync, then a person begins to build more trust, even if we do not agree with all of their words. Behaviours and words need to be consistent in order to be credible. If they are out of sync, then, whatever the inner motivation, that person attracts distrust and we prefer not to work with them.

I observe a five-level hierarchy of personal values in humans. I argue that for any leader to be seen by others as effective they must first be aware of their personal value priorities and then have the flexibility to signal this to others so that they can transmit, understand and respond honestly and appropriately.

These five range hierarchically from instantly observable behaviours (the surface-level messages) to often invisible deeply held beliefs (the bedrock of our world):

- Behaviours
- Opinions

- Attitudes
- Values
- Beliefs

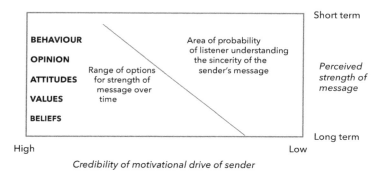

Figure 2: The five-level hierarchy of personal values

A useful definition of "values" is found in Dave Francis's book,[40] in which he describes a value as "a belief in action". He gives practical examples of measuring and developing values. For example, when we first meet a person the impression created is literally superficial – how they look sound, even smell. We interpret our information through their continuing behaviours and words, which we then reinterpret through our experiences, attitudes, values and beliefs. The other party sees none of the internal interpretation process. As we work longer with them, their opinions and then their attitudes become clearer. This amends or reinforces our personal values filters and we seek to find a way of muddling through with them, even if they are "not our kind, really". Only in times of adversity do their personal values become much clearer to us, and ours to them. Do they really believe in "fairness" and "equality"? Do they really enjoy working with "foreigners" (including people from different regions of their own country)? Are they really honest or is honesty a flexible concept for them? Do they really believe in working hard? Do we really like them?

Can values be imposed?

We take our personal values to work every day. They are a uniquely fundamental part of us. There we bump into the accepted business values and the corporate governance values. So I do find it odd that most politicians, directors and senior executives assume that there is only one set of "values" for an organization, and that this is determined by the organization. I argue that there is no easily imposable universal set of values to which all in an organization must subscribe. Monitoring, assessing and developing the mix of personal values that defines an organization at any one point is crucial in creating the "tone at the top" and the consequent culture of an organization. Each organization has different issues and a different history. Governors have a duty to create for their organization a basic values set based on accountability, probity and transparency. Then they must go further to combine these with their legal values of care, skill and diligence, independence of thought, and fighting corruption to ensure fairness and stability in their organizations. Even then, continual "nudging" is often a more effective way of achieving this than any draconian declaration and imposition.

Reconsidering the Seven Deadly Sins

We can go deeper and ask "do humans have common personal values?" While developing this book over the last four years I have raised these issues many times, especially in Europe, Africa, East Asia and the Arabian Gulf. I always expected strong opposition but have found surprisingly little. Indeed, I find that the participants have a great need to discuss not *whether* there are basic personal human values, but rather *what* they are and how we can use them effectively in the organizations that we design and govern. These tend to be private concerns, so there has been little public discussion of them. Yet directors are often keen to air their views. Indeed, a number see this as urgent relief.

So I have taken the risk and gauged my clients' and students' reactions to some historically well-tested value sets. I have been surprised by the very positive responses as regards an ability to categorize, compare and discuss them with others. From the common Abrahamic base of Judaism, Christianity and Islam, many ancient values are seen to hold good, and are reflected in, for example, Buddhism, Hinduism, Sikhism, Confucianism and Taoism. In the Abrahamic religions the Ten Commandments of Moses[41] are still seen by many directors as highly valid personally but difficult to apply, or even mention, in today's hedonistic business climate. Particularly useful in opening up this issue is talking about the personal values as defined in the Seven Deadly Sins by St Paul[42] and especially when compared with the Seven Virtues on a bipolar scale of personal choices:

The Seven Deadly Sins	The Seven Holy Virtues
Three Spiritual Sins	*Three Spiritual Virtues*
Pride	*Fides* (Faith)
Envy	*Spes* (Hope)
Wrath	*Caritas* (Charity)
Four Corporal Sins	*Four Cardinal Virtues*
Sloth	Prudence
Greed	Temperance
Gluttony	Fortitude
Lust	Justice

To help the discussion of how an individual's mix of such personal values can be transferred into acceptable organizational values, I have found that Prudentia's poem of 401 AD, *The Battle of the Soul* provides a useful framework for directoral action:

Humility	cures	Pride
Kindness	cures	Envy
Abstinence	cures	Gluttony
Chastity	cures	Lust
Patience	cures	Wrath
Liberality	cures	Greed
Diligence	cures	Sloth

Board discussion of these generates a lot of comments and often much nervous laughter, especially when I mention that in Dante's *Divine Comedy*[43] the sins are given an order of greatness which are shown from the lowest, Lust, to the highest, Pride.

I have been pleasantly surprised how such a simple list can legitimize and help discussions across many cultures of basic human values, ethics (their relationships with others) and religion (their relationship with their god). These transcend organizational and national borders. But what I notice most on my travels are that the left-hand values defined by St Paul are often referred to disparagingly as "Western" values. When pressed, this is usually modified to "American" values, especially those of Greed and Pride, and are considered in many developing countries as "bad" for humans because they seem to be so contagious. This may seem unfair to many Americans, but it does seem to be a growing world-view, especially post-Trump. The right-hand values are often viewed as more communitarian, better for human development, and characterized as "African", "Asian", "Islamic", "Quaker" and sometimes "English" or "Commonwealth". They are seen as necessary for maintaining the human condition, not at all "soft", because they are aspirational and morally demanding at both the personal and organizational levels. They are a direct challenge to so much of the current becalmed accepted business values.

One of the joys of my working life in so many different cultures is that I can get a good feel of what is valued by individuals and small groups outside of the espoused values of their organization, region or country. For example, I am amused by the still strong links between family life, good food and farmyard humour across China and its diaspora. Some of this has become politicized through the "rights movements" in many countries. The right of life is accepted almost everywhere as paramount. Then the politicians and power groups argue for human rights, labour rights, equality rights, sexual rights, animal rights and now plant rights. Nothing wrong with any of this, and over time they shape the accepted working values of our societies. But note that such "rights" are usually framed in terms of fights about power and its use or abuse and are usually a result of simplistic binary thinking. They rarely include empathy for other different groups.

Organizational reward systems are rarely designed with the desired emotional climate and values in mind. So "hard" rewards are rarely related to any wider psychological and anthropological analysis of people's and organizations' deeper drivers – their culture. They tend to be driven by Envy, Lust, Greed, Gluttony and Pride, which place the personal values of members of any remuneration committee into a very uncomfortable position from the start. However, the long-term sustainability of an organization depends more on the development and continuing historical transmission of these deeper values of diligence, humility, patience, kindness and liberality. These values are way beyond any dry accounting rules.

Organizational assessment tools

Many organizations are faced with having to reverse their reductionist decline to "Western" values, often with few tools to measure their current position or rate their of decline. But assessment tools do now exist and must become part of any director's kitbag. I am particularly interested in the work of my colleague at Cass Business School, Roger Steare, and his book *Ethicability*[44] and his work on "MoralDNA". This is an online personality profile that takes three personal decision-making preferences based on Law, Logic and Love, determines your MoralDNA character – Philosopher, Judge, Angel, Teacher, Enforcer or Guardian – and leads to ten moral values: Wisdom, Fairness, Courage, Self-control, Trust, Hope, Humility, Care, Honesty and Excellence. These are then contrasted with others in the organizational hierarchy. Such tools are being adopted by a number of organizations to give a language and process for helping to resolve the problems of clashing value sets and to rise above the immediate departmental, professional and organizational interests.

A new social contract

Daniel Malan, my colleague at Stellenbosch Business School, South Africa, has dealt well with the issue of ethical values in his paper "A New Social Contract" at the World Economic Forum,[45] where he argues for a global new social contract for organizations based on:

- The dignity of the human person – regardless of race, sex, background or belief

- The importance of a common good that transcends individual interests

- The need for stewardship – a concern not just for ourselves but for posterity

He says: "together these offer a powerful, unifying ideal: valued individuals, committed to one another, and respectful of future generations. Following these values is both a personal and collective challenge."

I can sense the abreaction of some readers at this point. I am used to this. We are reaching issues and disciplines that are rarely considered "proper" for business. We are beginning to enter the "ologies", especially psychology and anthropology, and these are rarely taught at business school – yet. But they will be, especially as the "soft" trends mentioned in Chapter 2 become much "harder", even dominant.

Anthropology, culture and effective board development

Let me explain: *anthropology* concerns the scientific study of the origin, growth and varieties of human beings, and their society's cultural development. It is strange to me that it, together with history, it is not a basic course at business schools but both still seem to be in the "soft" category. You only have to read papers by two stimulating women working in anthropology and relating it to organizations and business – Gillian Tett, US Managing Editor of the *Financial Times* and Kate Fox, Co-director of the Social Issues Research Centre, Oxford University – to realize how apposite it can be as directors and politicians casually blunder into this field abusing and misusing terms like "culture" and "values".

What is "culture"?

When working with a board, I have found a quotation on anthropology by Clifford Geertz[46] immensely powerful for them to study and then work with, even though, initially, they often find the words odd, fluffy and difficult:

> Culture is an historically transmitted pattern of meaning embodied in symbols: a series of inherited conceptions expressed in symbolic forms by means of which men communicate, perpetuate and develop their knowledge about and attitudes towards life . . . Man is an animal suspended in webs of signification he himself has spun. I take culture to be those webs, and the analysis of it to be therefore not an experimental science in search of law, but an interpretive one in search of meaning.

This is very practical, if taken in bite-sized chunks. We create our cultures and then are stuck with them. And, if you don't like the intellectual language, then just go to any business's reception area, look and listen. The way in which you are greeted, the colours and shapes of the space, the general posture and emotions of those employed and whether there is an air of lethargy or of buzz. These will tell you most of what you need to know about the emotional climate of that organization before you even enter it. When these symbols are repeated constantly throughout the organization, they become its unique "webs of signification" by which it is then trapped. Over time, these determine acceptable behaviours, attitudes, values and beliefs, and so inevitably reinforce, often unconsciously, its culture. They tell you what you can, and cannot, do in this organization, who gets rewarded and who punished, who stays and who goes. This is vital knowledge for a board and a top team on which to build a positive culture. It is rarely collected yet it is simple to do.

I argue that the success of future boards and top teams in an increasingly dynamic and uncertain world depends on our national leaders having a more consciously anthropological understanding of their organizational culture, values and beliefs. This is still seen as anathema and academic gobbledegook by many directors, politicians, managers and even some business academics. Yet, if you accept that our commercial life derives from the interactions of the human values of our stakeholders – staff, customers, suppliers, owners and legislators – then this makes a lot of sense.

This assertion will be resisted as irredeemably fluffy by the macho many, but as even Alan Greenspan is studying anthropology to learn from the crash of 2008 it would seem to be a better use of board time than reliance on failed macroeconomics. Directing is a continuous challenge both intellectually and operationally, and the use of anthropological knowledge and skills is beginning to be appreciated by more forward-looking organizations. Yet it still amazes me how many directors and executives see their organizations as impersonal and mechanical entities working on a simple, guaranteed command-and-control system without regard to positive and negative human feedback from their stakeholders. The cybernetic part of "governance" has not reached them yet. Anthropology will help.

Top complaints from employees about their bosses

As an example, a survey by Lou Solomon in the *Harvard Business Review* of June 2015[47] showed just how impersonal many bosses can be. She listed the top complaints in percentage terms:

- Not acknowledging employee achievement: 63%
- Not giving clear directions: 57%
- Not having time to meet employees: 52%
- Refusing to talk to subordinates: 51%
- Taking credit for others' ideas: 47%
- Not offering constructive criticism: 39%
- Not knowing employees' names: 36%
- Refusing to talk to people on the phone or in person: 34%
- Not asking about employees' lives outside work: 28%

It takes little imagination to picture the emotional climate in many such organizations, yet without frequent assessment directors and governors will be ignorant of this.

And the opposite leads to the culture of malicious obedience by staff

Using impersonal change processes like "re-engineering" seems safer to many boards and top teams rather than face-to-face learning with and from their staff. Re-engineering values are seen as "hard", scientific, rational and by excluding most human values are strangely comfortable to many directors and managers. Re-engineering means doing something top-down to others without having to face the human consequences directly, especially the acid test of leadership: whether that leader has any followers. This was not how it was meant to be when the "re-engineering movement" was launched.[48] Its rational values have been eroded slowly through abuse. This leads in many over-managed, under-led, and top-down businesses to the cancerous subculture of "malicious obedience"[49] – "I did it because I was told to (regardless of the fact that I knew it would not work as I had better information than my boss, but I was not asked about the idea or the likely consequences)."

I have worked with so many organizations where both the chairman and chief executive have admitted privately that, even after massively costly re-engineering programmes, "when I pull the levers of power I still have no idea if they are connected". In such organizations, feedback mechanisms are slow or non-existent. Learning is not encouraged. Cybernetics as a key element of governance is unknown. Messages passing upwards are lost or modified to protect the guilty, as we have seen in so many recent UK NHS and Police whistle-blower cases. The rate of organizational learning is not equal to, or greater than, the rate of external environmental change to ensure the continuing success of the organization. Human values have become rejected and demeaned.

Humans love learning

Yet humans love and truly value all forms of learning. The continuing rise of the global middle class is a good indicator that this will continue and grow. They learn "good" and "bad" things, which is where the positive values of effective governance come in. By learning the language and concepts of anthropology, leaders can better clarify and tackle those currently vague "values and culture" issues that the politicians and regulators are forcing on them. In the long term, this means reframing the existing accepted business values to deliver a sustainable, healthy long-term organizational learning culture. But current short-term evasion of such issues is creating a growing number of negative long-term organizational issues for boards and top teams. The board of directors then fails its key strategic board role, in setting the "tone from the top", and in its legislated responsibility for developing and monitoring the long-term success of the business – its legal fiduciary duty.[50] Such negligence becomes a long-term drag on the organization's reputation with customers, staff, owners, suppliers and, ultimately, the regulators and the law. How can the development of a culture of learning help? In times of great uncertainty, many "accidental" (non-professional) directors are now beginning to worry personally about this very issue. Why is it not the same for politicians at the regional and national levels?

People and their values are the key organizational cultural asset

As I have previously written much in this area,[51] I want here to stress that I am not just talking of the technical and legal aspects of corporate governance, but of the "human resource" of which the regulators talk a lot and are making tentative and uncertain steps towards. Hence their early attempts to amend "values" only through HR practices, especially through rules on reward and succession. The more difficult acknowledgement of the importance of "culture" as the key to organizational effectiveness and business success is an unmapped minefield that they still seem keen to enter.

The critical "people assets" make up the third leg of the corporate assets tripod – financial, people and environmental. People are the most flexible capital resources of any organization. People assets may be considered "soft" and "fluffy" but ultimately it is only they who determine the organizational energy, behaviours and day-to-day learning. Only people determine accepted business values, good or bad. Yet they are often considered by "top" people as merely expendable resources. By so doing, the "big potatoes" forget, or are unaware, that these individuals are usually closest to the customer and so determine the public's perception of the brand, regardless of the rhetoric at the top. They are the ones who create, through their learned daily behaviour, the "culture" of the organization. "HR" and "people issues" are often relegated by directors either to the "too difficult to contemplate" or "administration only, and so not our problem" baskets. They are then delegated down to middle executives – people who are aware of the issues but lack the line authority to take action directly from any subsequent learning.

This is worrying. But until the organization, business schools and consultancies accept and teach the primary message that people and their values determine organizational culture and success we shall not improve our effectiveness nor efficiency. Try suggesting to a board of directors or senior executive team that much of their "hard" learning of accountancy, law, risk assessment, operational methodology and marketing is, at best, necessary but not sufficient to give effective direction, and you usually get a very curt response. We are back to the "fluffiness" taunts about new disciplines and thinking. Yet it is these areas where I believe future leaders must go to re-energize and develop their organizations. However, there are international political blockages which complicate competing national cultures.

The corporate governance cultural battle between the US's acceptable business values and the rest of the world

Other "hard", legalistic national cultural values and laws block the development of the learning in organizations across national cultures. In highly hierarchical nations, it is difficult to even open this debate as the working assumption is that only the top people have the right to learn. Large parts of Africa, Asia, South America and Russia, for example, find the notion of allowing people's learning to flow upwards to inform their leaders to be totally counter-cultural. So their organizational and national development is slow or blocked. Like the Bourbon kings, they "learn nothing and forget nothing". Whether this assumption can continue far into the internet age is now being tested. Remember my earlier comments on the unacceptability of "American values" in many parts of the world. They are brought into sharp focus in the current fight between UK and US governance systems.

The cultural clash of US rules and UK principles

The biggest unresolved international values clash relating to leadership and governance is currently being played out between the UK, and most parts of the Commonwealth with its 54 participating countries, and the US. It is a paradox of US culture that, in a nation constantly espousing democratic principles, free will and openness, their legislators do not trust their organizational leaders' values sufficiently to allow them much discretion in their business decisions. Typically, they legislate first at state or federal level, and so rely on a rules-based, risk-avoidance, litigation-driven system of regulation. This is becoming increasingly costly, bureaucratic and has stifled entrepreneurial growth. "Post-truth" or not, this was a constant theme of the Trump 2016 presidential campaign. In Silicon Valley, they seem determined to avoid it, unlawfully or not.

Following the 2008 Western financial crisis, the US legislators have good reason to be concerned about how much more legislation is needed. But their approach is flawed. Their solution has been to develop a "rules-based" system of corporate governance. Any major governance issue then calls for more regulation and so for more boxes to be ticked, which are then argued over and gamed by corporate lawyers. The continuing proliferation of lawyers in the US is astonishing. Everyone seems to want to sue everyone else about everything. Behind it seems to lurk a value of perceived "entitlement" and rights, often blended with greed. The growth of such regulatory laws and rules now risks both generating diminishing returns and adding cost by creating a parallel growth industry in avoiding these rules – as has happened already in corporate taxation. The big problem with a rules-based governance system is that you have to keep adding more rules and laws as human creativity finds ways around the existing ones. In the end, one is left with an expensive and ultimately self-defeating process of *reductio ad absurdum*.

Even the regulators are slowly beginning to realize this and accept that the "people" areas need to be given much greater priority in their prescriptions, as we have seen in the UK's Financial Reporting Council's suggestions. But how do you do that, especially if you have been brought up on values that give primacy to legislation, litigation, accountancy and the belief in organizations as impersonal machines? The regulators and politicians I have spoken with over two decades know deep down that rules-based, compliance-focused and risk-avoiding regulation is an approach guaranteed to fail under the growing weight of its own contradictions and costs. But how do you get out of it? I advocate: trust the people and carry a big stick.

The principles-based approach

Compare the US rules-based approach to governance to the existing "principles-based" approach to corporate governance found in the UK and many Commonwealth countries. Since the seminal and globally acknowledged Cadbury Report on the Financial Aspects of Corporate Governance of 1992,[52] the UK has developed a much more flexible and entrepreneurial approach to governance. This demands that people work within the legislated framework of the law but then trusts them to use their values, judgements and risk-taking competences, linked firmly to personal accountability, to determine the success of their organizations. Directors are still held ultimately accountable to the shareholders, indeed more so than in the US. This principles-based approach frees the directors to explain why they may not be obeying a corporate governance code and gives the owners power to agree or disagree and vote on this decision publicly. It is to be applauded. Here it is not a case of having to first tick all the boxes but then being free to do anything they like if it is not specified by the regulators. In a principles-based system the directors' judgement is always open to question, and there are ways of questioning it. This frees up the greatest resource any organization has: the motivation, commitment and learning of its people.

But the US is playing a high-value card in this game of corporate governance poker by consistently pushing their *political* will through their conscious foreign policy of "extraterritoriality" – to extend US law and taxes by insisting on their use whenever there is the slightest connection to US business. As the current US governance rules are becoming a basket case of how not to govern, as noted by Bob Monks in the Introduction, their rules-based approach is proving a significant blockage to the development of international trade, especially in the developing world. If a nation concedes to such US demands, then its national freedom of judgement and national accountability to an organization's owners goes out of the window. The game has to be played only by the US rules. This cultural clash highlights the contrast between the UK's culture of tolerating, and creatively using, ambiguity, and the US's higher need for certainty and rules. However, even UK politicians and business folk have been weakening their cultural business values by adding many new rules rather than strongly enforcing the basic legislation.

Currently, politicians on both sides of the Atlantic seek a series of easy wins over "greedy capitalists" to pander to their rightly disenchanted public. But they are creating a monster by knee-jerk reactions imposing even more rules and a toxic mix of US-generated anti-banker legislation, blended with that highly corrosive policy of "extra-territoriality". This reinforces doubtful existing acceptable business values, increases the search for the avoidance of sane corporate governance values, and so threatens to destroy our long-term wealth as Western capitalist nations. The European Union is schizophrenic in this area, seemingly actively promoting free markets while behaving to shackle them by more and more rules. The European Commission is not famed for encouraging diversity, fixed as it is on seeking "ever closer union" through increasing standardization of everything from apples to taxation.

Stewardship and stakeholders

It is worth noting that in the two nations seen to be most strongly exploring effective, human values-based leadership and corporate governance, South Africa and the UK, two distinct approaches are emerging: one is *stewardship-based*, which focuses more on the bipolar division of board and owners, the other *stakeholder-based*, which focuses more on creating a wider, more inclusive organizational leadership and learning system. They can be complementary. Much has been said about stewardship over the past decade,[53] so I want to return here to the meaning and use of "values" and their development into long-term "culture".

I argue strongly that neither must ever be the home territory of the regulators or politicians. It is the home territory of directors and managers. It is their role to develop constructive and honest cultures, and positive emotional temperatures, if they are to develop and deliver the continuing success of the company. This requires designing a system of consistent internal organizational processes, rewards and punishments, explicit learning and transferable behaviours. This builds a positive "culture" in their organization. It does not require externally imposed regulation. But that possibility is lurking increasingly and worryingly in the international background as politicians encourage regulators to move into these volatile fields.

In the 2014 Code of Corporate Governance *Development in Corporate Governance and Stewardship* published by the UK's Financial Reporting Council, the new chairman, Sir Win Bischoff, comments:

> The governance of individual companies depends crucially on culture. Unfortunately, we still see examples of governance failings. Boards have responsibility for shaping the culture, both within the board room and across the organization as a whole and that requires constant vigilance. This is not an easy task. Our recent guidance on risk management highlighted the need for boards to think hard about assessing whether the culture practised within the company is in line with what they espouse. Boards should consider what assurance they have around culture. Are performance drivers and values consistent? How can culture be maintained under pressure and through change? Is the culture consistent throughout the business? We will be working to promote best practice in these areas during 2015.[54]

I think that asking such questions and asking individual organizations to respond is helpful – but as far as a regulator should go. These are impossible areas to assess using any current business tools. An attempt by regulators to specify a national measure of an organization's culture will most likely lead to more rules, risk aversion, ineffective compliance and the misapplication of resources, thus speeding organizational underperformance. This has already happened, when the regulators, egged on by the politicians, moved into the area of risk assessment.

We now need to develop transparent (at least to the shareholders) systems of self-assessment by the directors, rapid feedback for the shareholders' scrutiny and have processes for both learning and sanctions if the development of a constructive culture is to be achieved. The regulators should have access to the anonymized cumulative assessment results to see the patterns emerging to refine their rules, but not to a company's individual scores. In the longer term we must include the environmental and societal measures required for effective future governance.

Do such tools and metrics exist? Yes, but they are not currently considered "normal" business tools. The statistics these tools use often work on relativities – non-parametric statistics – and so are less comfortable for those trained on "normal" statistics. I repeat that we have to look to those "soft" and "wimpish" areas like social psychology, board dynamics and anthropology that make more use of non-parametric statistics to make progress here. And when we seek we find. Many "hard" directors' and managers' aversion, indeed fear, of such disciplines is frequently based on ignorance of these areas of mathematics and statistics. If they even dipped a toe in the water, they would quickly see that the concepts of the short-term "emotional climate" of an organization, and the subsequent development and reinforcement of its long-term "culture", are measurable and key benchmarks of organizational health and continuing business success. So boards and senior executives need to track these trends over time. This is invaluable information for directors and managers. Yet they rarely have it. What can be done?

Social psychology, especially the findings in group dynamics from Kurt Lewin onwards[55] and its analytical tools, have proved helpful in understanding the more observable levels of behaviours, opinions and attitudes and the development of cultures, especially in small groups. Anthropology – the study of humans, their origins, institutions, religious beliefs and social relationships – has helped analyse the less visible values and beliefs at a deeper, societal level. Social psychology and anthropology combined explore the anchors of a society's, an organization's, a working group's and an individual's lives. Many such anchors are simply assumed by boards and top teams without testing and so they build their castles on unstable foundations. The public, regulators and politicians know that the gap is there, but do not yet have the language to explain this. Hence the need to integrate the learning from the currently disconnected players – directors, owners, regulators and politicians.

Cultural assessment tools

Most boards discover the weaknesses of their organization's culture
only when there is a crisis, by which time it is often too late to take
avoiding action. But they cannot disclaim liability. There are tools
available to help boards even at both the national and international
level of culture, including some well-tested international cross-cultural mapping tools. At a basic level, there are rigorous and well-
designed emotional climate and organizational capability surveys
which, overlaid with the organization's values data, allow the board
and top team to track the short-term operational emotional climate
and competence changes. These set the benchmarks for the long-
term tracking of changes in the deeper culture of the organization.
Yet these rarely form part of the board's dashboard.[56] Remember
that the board has continuing oversight, leadership development and
responsibility for the learning and culture of the total organization. It
is their duty to create a "learning culture".

The British Army adopts action learning

A good example of how this can work even in an historic organization is that of the British Army. The public and politicians frequently
accuse them of designing their forces to fight the previous war so that
in the next war they face a series of disasters and defeats only to be
rescued at the last moment by the individual and group inventive-
ness of their own troops. Dunkirk and the Battle of Britain come to
mind. Rationally, neither should have been successful. The UK's high
tolerance of a culture of enjoying ambiguity and a strong sense of the
absurd helped greatly. It was their fast rate of learning and continuous motivation by a clear focus on common purpose that pulled them
through. They knew what they were fighting for and demanded great
leadership to get them there. They created strong group values of
support, resilience, austerity and toughness.

The modern UK military, faced with continuing austerity cuts, have
accepted the need to grow an organizational culture of "action learning" to deploy more effectively their increasingly scarce resources.[57]

They have developed rapid feedback systems to let members of each fighting group, however small, know how near or far they are from reaching an objective and, most importantly, what alternatives are available. The critical additional aspect that they have developed, and which most businesses dismiss as too costly of time, are the "wash-up sessions" after *each* activity. Here there is structured criticism of what went right, and wrong. People are encouraged to make their criticism *regardless of rank and without any retribution from above*. This focus on honesty of feedback regardless of rank, plus the guaranteed freedom from retribution by those in authority, has transformed their culture and greatly improved their effectiveness simultaneously with their efficiency. Another good example of cultural transformation is that of BAE Systems under the chairmanship of Dick Olver following the Woolf Enquiry of 2008 into its sales ethics. They have implemented in a very public way all 23 recommendations with good support from the staff, and their progress is published in a section of their annual report.

My worry is that, as regulators try to extend their territory into "culture", they will not have read Geertz or anyone like him and will simply pass on the detailed work of specification and implementation to some soulless bureaucrats to create a culture code. This assumes that specifying clauses and subsets alone will derive the necessary moral values and so businesses can be beaten into compliance. I argue that, as we already have millennia-tested and accepted human values, we do not need another new code, just ways of encouraging the use of the existing metrics more fully and openly. This could be labelled just an additional human rights issue to be added to the compliance list. It is much more, and I shall return to it when discussing the UN Global Compact in Chapter 4.

If the politicians and regulators advocated reinforcement of a national and international climate of the self-application of these well-tested behaviours, values and culture, we would not need increasingly dense compliance codes that conflict with human nature and entrepreneurship. We would then be able to throw out the majority of the corporate governance codes.

International cross-cultural mapping

As trade becomes more global, the importance of our national leaders' understanding of the cross-cultural basis of effective cooperation with international partners becomes critical. Yet few business folk are given more than a day or two's "Introduction to . . . [insert country name here]" type of induction programme for what is often a success-or-failure investment of capital and people. If they are lucky, they may even get a brief programme for their partner or children about the new country. But few get the deep cultural immersion that, say, the Japanese or Dutch invest in such processes. Cross-cultural business effectiveness is usually random at best.

Two helpful but lesser-known approaches

Geert Hofstede's cross-cultural maps[58] and Fons Trompenaars's "cross-cultural dilemmas"[59] have proved effective. Both are essential reading for any director or politician trying to make sense of international cross-cultural working. Both can be criticized academically for the data bases used, but I have found that their utility is not so much in the precision of their findings but in the legitimacy they allow in opening up discussion on such otherwise "undiscussable" cross-cultural issues.

Hofstede takes a relentlessly organizational perspective and focuses on four dimensions that his researches characterize as key dimensions of national cultures:

- Uncertainty avoidance (the need for certainty and national control in the activities of a country, reflected in its organizational behaviours)

- Power distance (the comfort distance that members of that society deem necessary when meeting the power players in that society)

- Individualism/collectivism (the priorities and rewards given to people who either strive to shine individually, or who find more comfort in being members of a defined group)

- Male/female (the values imbued and rewarded in members of a society regardless of their sex)

Trompenaars and Hampden-Turner[60] take a different and equally enlightening approach through their practical use of "Dilemmas" when faced with another nation's value sets. For example, how does your foreign partner's concept of truth fit with their concept of loyalty when faced with a difficult issue regarding a friendship? If there has been a car accident in which the local manager was obviously at fault, will his colleagues deny that it has anything to do with him regardless of the truth? "Alternative truths" are not a new phenomenon. Dilemmas are a very helpful way of understanding and squaring what can be a very tricky circle.

To bring this review of values and culture to a close I have a simple question to ask:

What do Alan Greenspan and Gillian Tett have in common?

In this book I argue that the four major players of corporate governance – the boards, owners, regulators and legislators – do not yet act within an integrated system of learning to improve the governance of their nation. There is little national oversight of each of them, and none see themselves as the key to developing the whole into a national asset to stabilize and grow our society. The final chapter of this book attempts just that.

Here I want to look at the continuing failures of moral purpose and values seen in so many nations following the 2008 Western financial crisis. For example, I looked randomly at two national UK newspapers and found references to corporate governance failure in the media, courts, politicians, boards, the police, health managers, local government, sport and charities. And those are examples from just two days. We are creating a pervasively cancerous culture of distrust of our leaders through the failure of our sophisticated states. The rot is here.

What on earth went so wrong that the joyous social revolution of the swinging sixties gave way to the corrupt noughties, leading to the Western austerity era and the consequent rise of community fragmentation, economic fear, growing authoritarianism, terrorism and distrust?[61] I argue strongly that it was a lack of understanding of the role and moral purpose of organizations in society, combined with a lack of personal courage to say "No" to corrupting pressures, which allowed two insidious attitudes to affect our Western world. First, that it is now considered wrong by many to query any action on moral grounds. So challenges ranging from the support of the Paedophile Exchange to the IRA or ISIS have been made almost impossible as these are evil groups and therefore have been socially non-discussable for decades. Certain words have been banned as societally unacceptable. But as Trevor Phillips, previously Chairman of the UK's Equality and Human Rights Commission, has recently admitted, seeking to ban words and ideas loosely defined by the Commission as "racist" did not extinguish such thoughts and actions from the majority of the population. It just drove them underground where they are proving much more difficult to deal with. We're back to the politicians' silver-bullet, quick-fix attitude. This type of exclusion from debate has eroded the social cement, the explicit values and behaviours, that bonded the values of our organizations, family and personal mental health. We are suffering for it. It is seen in the rise of the "snowflake" generation of students unwilling to debate "difficult" issues and their preference for "safe spaces". The rot really has got a grip.

Second, such international dynamics as the financial "Big Bang" changed our perceptions of what are now acceptable business values and behaviours. Many employers and some employees experienced their organizations as impersonal machines. The erosion of personal values and the prioritizing of "business values" above these human values has encouraged senior staff to see businesses as simply vehicles for personal financial aggrandisement where you take what you can grab and devil take the hindmost. Effective corporate governance went out of the window. Executive remuneration soared despite rewarding the majority for mediocre performance at best. The Seven Deadly Sins were no longer to be avoided but lionized.

Such dubious short-term thinking was backed by the rise of impersonal, financial digital technology so that participants were able to distance themselves from clients and become "players" who could instantly "game" the system without concern for, or even knowing, their effect on others. This is the realm of psychopaths.

What the Masters of the Universe did not value culturally

Yet at least one "Master of the Universe" has learned something from it. I had not realized quite how bad things were until I read *The Map and the Territory*, the memoir of Alan Greenspan, previously the Chairman of the US Federal Bank and so one of the most powerful people in the world – the master of the Masters of the Universe.[62]

Reading the book makes you weep that such economic and social power was wielded in such a narrow and inhumane way. In the book, and especially in subsequent interviews, when asked why such a devastating global financial crash happened, his answer is "our models did not work" [*sic*]. He said that he had 250 PhDs working on them and that the models were tuned to the neoclassical economic concept that markets will always return to equilibrium given time. When they did not self-correct, and with the global financial system crashing around them, no-one really knew what to do because they began to realize that they had not factored in two powers which were then driving and spooking the markets. First was "the nature and speed of market dynamics" [*sic*] and second was "people" and their unpredictable emotions [even *sic*cer]. To me it is mind-boggling that the human and emotional aspects of our global wealth generation had not been considered important enough to be in "The Model".

They did not consider seriously the all-powerful driving emotions of greed and fear in people, especially when fight becomes flight in times of crisis. When this fast-growing instability was then transmitted through instantaneous global communication systems, all of our wealth, social and financial, suffered, and continues to suffer. We are now all poorer but little wiser. Our financial and political leaders have not yet shown the necessary contrition and willingness to learn that they need to gain public forgiveness. So they are currently unable to create the new emotional and cultural climate needed to learn mutually with their society. Consequently, financial and political reputations are rubbished and neoclassical economics, especially macroeconomics, has suffered a continuing nervous breakdown ever since. Behavioural economics is the new hot trend as it slowly being realized by power brokers that human values do matter.

What has this to do with Gillian Tett, US Managing Editor of the *Financial Times*? She is a trained anthropologist, and her regular writings rigorously demonstrate this. She is insightful on organizational and moral purpose. She wrote a devastatingly insightful interview of Alan Greenspan and his book.[63] He was marginally contrite, but did at least admit that he now needed in retirement to study a new discipline, the importance of which has previously eluded him – anthropology! He needed to know much more about people and their values. He has enrolled at college to do so.

Is this a way forward for improving future corporate governance and leadership? Shall we all spend less time on codes and compliance and more on understanding human nature, values and beliefs and their effects on the dynamics of markets and nations? I hope so. But remember that Barack Obama's mother was an anthropologist, and he has some training in the field, so do not expect miracles fast.

In the next chapter, I want to pursue these notions of values and beliefs but now relate them to four international demographic and social trends that I believe will inevitably change the context, nature and development of national leadership and corporate governance permanently. As the failure of neoclassical economics has forced a mind-set change on our governors, I hope that these four forces will do the same.

66

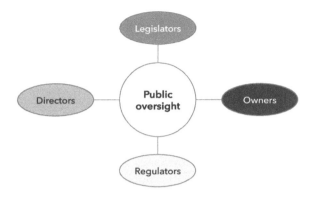

2

Towards human values-based governance

The view beyond executive-led capitalism
towards human values-based governance

When such globally influential figures as Warren Buffett, Christine Lagarde of the IMF, Bob Monks – doyen of US corporate governance and founder of the US's Institutional Shareholder Services – and Mark Carney, Governor of the Bank of England are arguing publicly that our current model of capitalism is seriously flawed, then a change is happening. "Corporate governance" in its current form must respond to this or die. When the doyen of macroeconomists, Alan Greenspan – ex-Chairman of the US Federal Reserve Board – admits that, before and after the 2008 Western financial crash, "we had got it wrong, our models did not work and we did not factor human behaviour into our algorithms",[64] then the public has every reason to be incensed. The consequent loss of their wealth, the continuing political uncertainty and the obvious lack of political and corporate leadership is for all to see. Public estrangement from their leaders is high. Now the cycle appears to be repeating itself without the necessary open learning to escape from it.

Bob Monks's keynote speech, "The End of the Beginning", at the June 2014 International Corporate Governance Network conference at the Mansion House, London, created a chilled silence of affirmation when he adapted the words of the German theologian and concentration camp survivor Martin Niemoller.[65] He said of the declining state of US corporate governance:

> First, the CEOs paid themselves royally, second they took control of the Government. I said nothing because I was not a CEO; I said nothing because I rarely vote. Then they ended pensions, captured Governments, corrupted international institutions and suborned the judiciary. Finally, they came for the owners, me.

The large audience was a sea of international owners, asset and pension fund managers, directors and regulators. There was discomfort but no objections. And this message was from a doyen of the US and UK investment business, a senior Maine Republican and ex-US Cabinet member. The US is increasingly becoming a corporate governance basket case. His criticism reminds me of the psychological concept of the "Dark Matrix" with its unhealthy convergence of three traits – narcissism, Machiavellianism and psychosis. These combine, often at CEO level, to make life hell for themselves and everyone else in the organization. What needs to be done? "CEO hegemony" helps explain the public's distrust of its governors. Overpaid CEOs, and "revolving door" politicians and civil servants are socially unacceptable "rent seekers" and now stand in contrast to the more acceptable risk-taking, entrepreneurial wealth creators.

Public estrangement and the three inclusive capitals

Estrangement between the public and business leaders and politicians is not new. In 1832 in the UK, the passing of the UK's great Reform Act triggered a major shift in political power by declaring universal manhood suffrage – the right for all "men of property" to vote. The gap between the public and the politicians slowly began to close, and the hope generated helped ensure that the continental revolutions of 1848 did not happen in the UK. This social contract grew stronger throughout the two Great Wars. But it has now stalled. How do we resurrect it?

There are two clear complementary issues: the growing public demand for governance change; and the currently unimaginative, puny political responses. The public, and now even the regulators, through their acknowledgement of the importance of "values" and "culture", are pushing for a more rigorous and consistent focus on human values-based governance in organizations. They are moving away from the current financially obsessed focus of the past 40 years.

A hopeful sign is the growing acceptance, nationally and internationally, of the new necessity of accepting three types of interactive and complementary aspects of capitalism – the need for "inclusive capital". This means the integration of three types of capital previously seen as warring rather than complementary:

- People

- Physical

- Financial

Finance capital is an important societal asset as it enables long-term investment projects, ensures adequate cash flows and working capital for growing healthy businesses, generates new employment and allows risks to be hedged. However, the current financially limited focus over-emphasizes those selfish activities that accrete value to only a small cadre of individual traders at the expense of wealth creation for the wider public. This is creating serious risks to the social contract, as the current focus is on "impatient" gambling rather than long-term "patient" investment. Arbitrage, "leverage", marginal trading, high-frequency trading, day trading, unnecessarily complex financial products, and banks speculating with their customers' money, are symptoms of unhealthy, even cancerous, growth in our financial systems. When only fund managers, speculators and bankers benefit from such activities, and justify themselves as being part of a system that is "too big to fail", then we have serious societal trouble.

The growing public push for more transparency and limits to marginal trading activities, however inarticulate, is to be applauded. It will be fought by the combined forces of the die-hard reactionaries for totally free markets on the one hand, and "the business of business is business" brigade, who accept there must not be any social context other than business, on the other. Ultimately, such thinking leads to authoritarian regimes that control their organizations by their personal interpretation of law rather than by the independent judiciary-led rule of law.

The Long March of Everyman[66] continues its inevitable progress through global history. It concerns the seesaws of the balance of powers within a society, particularly between the powerful and the others. I argue that we have reached another tipping point in this power balance. This disruption is caused by four deep, global trends driving change to our currently stalled approaches to leadership and governance. These trends question the nature of "ownership", "governance", "leadership", "regulation" and the value sets that have led us into this current slow rot.

These four global trends outlined below are beginning to have significant impacts on all four key, disconnected, players in governance:

directors, owners, regulators and politicians. In turn, these four players need to develop their policies, strategies and business models to accommodate all four trends. And, beyond this, the demand for increased public oversight will create an all-important fifth player, enabling the basis for a national learning system for effective governance.

Many current corporate governance parties are uncomfortable with these trends because they reflect the growing demand for our organizations to be based on human values. This cuts across much current political, bipolar and reductionist thinking. Boards, investors and politicians are reacting slowly, confusedly, and often dismissively to these four global trends. They are finding it hard to think and behave in ways that will allow these inclusive changes to occur. I argue that, in any healthy direction-giving board or political party, these four trends are becoming the new context for policy formulation and strategic thinking.

The four trends I explore here are currently only partially visible. They are not generally accepted as intellectually connected. And yet they are the tips of four massive icebergs, the size of which we can only imagine. If they can be revealed, their effects will shape the face of national leadership and governance for the foreseeable future. These trends are fuelled by the public's growing awareness of the need to redefine the notion of the "ownership" of our organizations, and the consequent responsibilities of *all* stakeholders within them. The trends are mixed with the public's disgust over the personal-wealth-destroying consequences of many present accepted business values. The demand for continuous public oversight stems from a general feeling of growing "entitlement", indeed public duty, to create a system that allows people openly and frequently to question their business and political leaders. All four trends reinforce the long-established basic corporate governance values of accountability, probity and transparency.

The four human values-based trends changing national leadership and governance

What are these four trending forces? I observe that they are based on fundamental human values, not political or economic ideologies. So, at first sight, they may seem odd, even weird, to many of the current players. They definitely appear "soft and fluffy" when mentioned in the current "hard" business context of "austerity", global belt-tightening, the much-proclaimed "bottom line focus", and failing left/right political nostrums. But my argument goes beyond such dumbed-down simplicity. The first three forces are the consequences of a blend of societal and demographic changes. The fourth, the need to re-establish professionalism, may just seem like an extension of the present. But it is the key to integrating this revolution in governance thinking and action.

The four trends are:

1. **The rise of the concept of inclusive capitalism for sustainability**[67]
   Such thinking can be tracked back to Thomas Hobbes, Adam Smith, Jean-Jacques Rousseau and Karl Polyani. It is again becoming a mainstream concern through the merging of international public discontent with greed-fixated financial capitalism, the negative effects of CEO hegemony following the 2008 Western financial failure, and the more positive attempts at socially integrative trends in developing countries (when not at war). The challenge now for effective corporate governance is to create a system that brings together for optimal societal use the three capitals: financial, physical and social. This demand is linked closely to the *integrated reporting* concept[68] as its delivery mechanism.

2. **The rise of the global middle class**
   This flies against the current Western fashion of focusing on "inequality". Poverty exists globally, as does inequality. Both need long-term processes for eradication. So it may seem perverse to argue that ensuring the rise of the middle classes will help matters. But look at the long-term trends. They do not fit

the doom-mongers' world-view. Using National Audit Office figures, in 1981, 61% of the British population were officially rated as living in "absolute poverty". In 2015, the rate was 20%. Worldwide poverty, disease, hunger and ignorance are in retreat, despite all the media images. The Bill & Melinda Gates Foundation figures show that the global poverty rate has dropped by 70%. The world is doing better than many think. But it can do much better still. And that's where middle-class social, educational and financial aspiration come in.

Through their driving needs for stability blended with growth, and demands for new forms of equitable wealth distribution, combined with their insatiable need for information, their growing confidence and their ability to critically review their leadership and governance, the middle classes are becoming a force for stabilization and growth in many societies. But most of these trends are not happening in the West so do not form part of their political debate. However, even in those "failing sophisticated states" there are signs of an international fight-back by both the "hollowed-out" middle classes, a particular problem in the US, and the still-aspirant working classes. Given the astonishing growth in size and political power of the middle class in developing countries, especially in Africa and Asia, this dynamic has become a significant global force for change. For over 70 years, Western political parties, on both the right and left, have found it fashionable to despise the middle classes – "the bourgeoisie" of Marxist description. But times are changing fast, and the politicians need to reframe their thinking to respond effectively or become even more estranged from their public.

3. **A growing acceptance that people's learning and their moral values are central to developing effective organizations**
   To paraphrase Clifford Geertz[69] in Chapter 1: we humans design, grow, run and are finally trapped by our organizations. People are the only "resource" that can learn flexibly, tolerate high levels of ambiguity and yet still continue to operate – provided that they are supported by human values in their

organization. This growing humane, people-centric, movement is in direct opposition to the greed, piracy and amorality of CEO-dominated behaviour in the notionally regulated "free" markets. Public acceptance of the positive value of *learning* in our society is beginning to influence policy formulation and strategic thinking in private, public and not-for-profit organizations; and is being underpinned significantly by the new communications technologies.

4. **The urgent need to re-establish professionalism**
Currently, this trend is only partially conscious in the public's mind. The demand is there but the concept is not yet explicit. It arises from the feeling that something is fundamentally wrong with the relationship between the "deliverers" – governments, businesses and not-for-profits – and the "receivers": their citizens, clients and customers. But what is wrong? I argue that the professional intermediaries are no longer playing their full and independent roles. Their organizational rhetoric may be "putting the customer first", but the behaviour often seems quite the opposite – how can we extract the maximum amount of cash from these folk without them squealing? Currently, fragmented and uncoordinated political and business initiatives are blended with homeopathic doses of mild pragmatism to hopefully counter public disgust. But existing professional providers, such as corporate governance, accountancy, audit, legal and taxation practices, management consultancy, commercial law and human resources, seem resolutely unchanging and lacking the essence of "professionalism".

Privately, many leaders of the professions admit that they are reaching a tipping point, after which their current narrowly focused client-unfriendly, selfish systems will be unsustainable. The public are seeking a more "professional" approach across society, from their governors, business leaders and the professionals. This is noticeable since the 2008 financial crisis when the public began to realize that so few of their leading bankers were professionally qualified. These current demands for professional changes are not caused by the enlightened self-interest of existing professionals but by national and international public pressures concerning current conflicted and slothful practice. The international avoidance of corporate and personal taxation is a classic example of such public disquiet. Every profession now needs public reassessment of their role in the future governance world. This will force the integration, or abandonment, of previously separate protected business disciplines and challenge the validity of those weasel words "accepted business values" in the professions.

Let us look at these four in more detail.

1. The rise of international inclusive capitalism

Attempts to integrate capitalist financial systems with more effective social and physical natural resource usage have usually failed to impress the corporates, despite growing public enthusiasm. By positioning themselves as "do-gooders" or prophets of apocalyptic doom, "inclusive" advocates often feel happier to distance themselves from the "tainted" mainstream businesses. But in doing so they lose their main channels of communication. One consequence is that the previously fashionable corporate social responsibility (CSR) approach is being quietly phased out in many corporations. It proved too altruistic, naïve and bossy for thoughtful business consumption. The good news is that we are moving to more serious corporate engagement through better delineated "environmental, social and governance" (ESG) debates, which are now frequently appearing on corporate agendas. This is an important step in the movement towards creating a consensus on the future business context of inclusive capitalism. Businesses are no longer the free agents they previously thought themselves to be, as national governments begin to exert new powers. Businesses now exist in changing political force fields over which few have total control. I deal with these new coalitions of powers in more detail in Chapters 3 and 6.

Public anger fed by social media has not abated since 2008, and so, slowly, the global players, including the UK, the United Nations, the European Union, but not yet the US, are beginning to formulate policy and develop strategic thinking to make inclusive capitalism a mainstream issue for national leaders and governments. The most important signal of this change was the "Inclusive Capitalism" conference, organized by the *Financial Times* (29 May 2014) which featured high-powered advocates arguing for a very different form of future capitalism; it has triggered a major rethinking process by corporations, governments, charities and their professional advisors, but so far only glacial actions.

The redoubtable Christine Lagarde, the Managing Director of the International Monetary Fund, warned that, as economies had stabilized to some extent under multinational monetary easing, there would be a counter-attack. She predicted that an integrated approach to capitalism, using an ESG framework, "would face a fierce industry push-back" as the financial services and their advisors tried to re-establish the old status quo.[70] She warned that they were already delaying much-needed reforms, and that this risked destabilizing the world economy yet again. Moreover, she argued that progression in creating a safer, more stable international financial system has been too slow because of conscious and sustained financial, and other, industry attempts to halt the introduction of tougher rules and criminal penalties for individuals. She said that, sadly, the financial sector in particular had not changed fundamentally, and had learned little from the 2008 crisis. She then provided a long list of their continuing shameful activities, including: money laundering; the conscious mis-setting of rates, including Libor, the gold price and foreign exchange mis-fixings; and many forms of insider trading, misapplied "flash trading" and tax avoidance; along with a continuing contempt for their customers, staff and the public, and a total lack of contrition. She confirmed that no banker has yet said "sorry" in any credible way.

She went on to claim that "some prominent firms have been mired in scandals that violate the most basic ethical norms and so damage our social fabric". To add piquancy to this denouncement of many accepted business values, at the same conference Mark Carney, the Governor of the Bank of England, added that "just as any revolution eats its own children, unchecked market fundamentalism can devour the social capital essential for the long-term dynamism of capital itself". He stated that he is determined to ensure that, in the future, banks cannot be seen to be "too big to fail".

This is radical, unexpected and much-needed support from people usually seen as members of "the establishment". They want to re-establish and develop the best aspects of the older *social* contract rather than watch it being eaten cancerously from within by short-term financial greed. They consciously seek a new social contract. This should begin, as I have suggested in Chapter 1, and as many City of London Livery companies have now done, by having their members swear personally before their fellows the old City oath, and motto of the London Stock Exchange: "My word is my bond". There is then working group pressure to be seen to live by it publicly. And there is hope to be found in the new book by Michael Lewis, *The Undoing Project*,[71] which shows how two seemingly diametrically opposed friends learned to debate and cooperate over decades, often by following their gut instincts rather than accepted professional caution. As effective corporate governance starts with an entrepreneurial approach to ensuring a healthy future for their business, this approach is worth studying.

2. The rise and rise of the global middle class and its values

This may seem a strange thing to argue when the majority of fashionable Western politicians, business experts, social science and economic commentariat and literati are bewailing the rising inequalities between the "haves" and the "have nots" in this wicked world. It demonstrates two things. First, these folk do not get out much and observe the reality of demographic trends across most nations. Second, they should not believe everything they see on TV and social media. Having been involved in producing two TV series on future demographic and political trends, I am only too aware that the phrase "poverty makes good TV" is chilling enough even before you consider that many charities now use it as the core of their fundraising activities. This is not to deny that there are appalling levels of poverty in the world and that we are facing the largest mass migrations in recorded history. The UN figure in June 2016 was some 65 million people on the move globally. Against this, it must be noted that the ultra-accommodative monetary policies of many Western central banks has boosted the asset values of the richest 1% globally, an action that still angers a large proportion of the working and middle classes.

But the two positions are not irreconcilable, if you accept that the creation of ever-larger middle classes will begin to act as a counterpoint and balancing mechanism between the powers of super-rich and the super-poor – the two opposing ends of any national income distribution spectrum. Yet the middle classes are still wildly unfashionable in the minds of intellectual metro-Westerners, especially among commentators whose credo of "always hate the rich, always support the poor and always despise the middle classes" seems increasingly challenged by fast-changing socio-economic demography. Globally, the middle classes seek much greater stability and wealth for their societies. They want "democratic" processes underpinned by credible information technology, laws to protect their property and contracts, quality education for their children, and the opportunity to oversee the quality of their national leadership and governance.

In this context, I find the following figures astonishing. In 2014, the IMF calculated that, by 2030, the number of middle-class people in the world will have risen from 500 million to 2 billion. This remarkable figure suggests that over 25% of the world's population will consider themselves middle class by 2030, according to IMF standards. One needs to be careful here as the IMF's definition of "middle income" starts from just US$2 a day, and rises as high as US$23,000 a year (just above the US's official poverty line). Indeed, the Pew Research Center has questioned these figures, but not so much with regard to the middle class as the "unequals".[72]

However, as a result of my travels in Asia and Africa, I can attest that this trend of rising middle classes with their increased discretionary income seems true, with all that this implies for growing economic and social stability in these regions. This will not be a smooth process and there are too many dictators and venal politicians with simple, plausible nostrums to make it a very bumpy road indeed. But it is still a road, and I argue that the sheer volume of the aspiring middle classes will force this change on reluctant, autocratic national and corporate leaders, with beneficial results all round. A form of global Magna Carta of human and economic rights will develop through this same lumpy and disjointed process. My sadness is that neither the EU nor the US is experiencing such changes. Indeed, the reverse seems true.

The IMF also estimated that, in the global economy, the "effective labour force" has already risen from 500 million in 1985 to 2 billion in 2005, and will at least double again by 2030 to 4 billion. This will mean that over half the world's total population will be working and aspiring. "The poor" are increasingly social and economic generators in their own right. Already some 2 billion of the labour force have some form of IT connection, mainly mobile phones, and this number will increase sharply, thus multiplying transparency within and between populations. This is a powerful global force for change which the UN Global Compact[73] encourages strongly. And they are keen to see more human values-based and well-governed inclusive organizations and governments.

This trend is particularly noticeable in China, where I have spent much of my time since 1976. While the country is undergoing another bout of nationalism, and the government is beginning to bring back the cult of Mao to reinforce the power of the Communist Party, they are running into opposition from the fast-growing middle class – the stabilizing factor in an historically chaotic society. You can see the tension in the government's wish to provide "patriotic education" based on the "Chinese patriotic spirit found in morals, language, history, geography, sport and arts", contrasted with the middle classes' wish to have their children educated increasingly at the growing number of international schools inside and outside the country. The Chinese have venerated education for success in their society over the millennia. A 2016 survey by the Shanghai Academy of Social Sciences[74] showed that 57% wanted to send their children overseas for their tertiary education. Even President Xi sent his daughter to Harvard, albeit under an assumed name. Since schooling becomes optional for a Chinese child once they turn 15, and parents must then pay for their education, there will be some tricky squaring of circles needed to compromise the Communist Party's wish for tight control with growing middle-class aspirations.

Anti-business bias

Such optimism sits in contradiction to the Western public's continuing negative perception of "the businessman". This hostility has existed for centuries, whether in ancient China, Ireland, or through Roman Catholicism and their conscious demeaning of Jewish financiers. Such hostility has varied on a scale from mildly acceptable to downright evil. In the last two centuries we can see examples from the villain Mr Merdle in Dickens's *Little Dorritt* or Trollope's Augustus Melmotte in *The Way We Live Now,* via the US's infamous robber barons to Gordon Gecko in *Wall Street,* today's "flash crash nerds", and the Silicon Valley multi-billionaires intent on creating rent-seeking global monopolies while declaring "liberalization through technology". Media images throughout history depict businessmen as unhealthy, greedy, self-aggrandizing, anti-community men. Recently, the brash, vulgar Wall Street bond salesman image has given way to that of the highly unethical "Masters of the Universe" investment bankers. Nowadays, the image has shifted again, on to the unshaven, goggle-eyed, pyjama-clad, burger-munching, home-bound loners who are fixated by their ultra-complex algorithms, and sit at their computer 24 hours a day seeking to get an illegal millisecond advantage on a traded share price. This highly unsavoury image is reinforced by the notion that most still live with their parents, and are unlikely to have a social life, let alone a partner. This is not a role model of a future business leader that any sane person would want. Yet just one such unregulated trader can currently do serious damage to the development of long-term business and societal wealth.

Such people can panic global markets and are without any strong sanctions at present. They refuse to take personal responsibility for the societal effects of their actions; but as their highly doubtful activity becomes exposed we can expect greater demands from a furious public for regulatory and criminal retribution by those whose wealth has been eroded by this over-rewarded, under-taxed, morally worthless and instantly gratified minority. Even that beacon of US capitalism Warren Buffett maintains his consistent belief in *long*-term investment, "slow finance", and in sound but underperforming businesses in need of a kick up the backside.[75]

The continuing shadow side

There is a shadow side to every positive new movement, and the rise of the middle classes is no exception. Whether we are talking of BRIC (Brazil, Russia, India, and China) or MINTSA (Mexico, Indonesia, Nigeria, Turkey and South Africa), there is always a messy intermediate stage that takes decades for each nation to resolve before they establish the hoped-for stable government and corporations. Part of it seems counter-intuitive as their new, cheap workforces are absorbed into the global economy and initially wages remain stable or are forced down. But the wealth released by growth in expanding economies needs somewhere to go, and is then invested, over time, in these growth economies as they give better returns than the sclerotic West. It does not always work like that in the first decades, as the newly wealthy tend to export much of their wealth and invest in properties and companies in the "safe" West. The good news is that, as the decades pass, we see real wage growth in the emerging economies and the start of a recapture by labour of the income share originally lost to capital, followed by increased tax takes and the consequent easing of national government finances and debt burdens. As this happens, I see already the aspirant middle classes demanding better leadership and governance as their default position for supporting their future leaders. They will not pay taxes for nothing.

The new middle class's infectious mixture of youth, enthusiasm for education, wish for growth linked to environmental improvement, love of information, and a growing wish for human rights and social justice (knowing just how unequal their societies have been), will propel them towards more humane governance systems. With their mastery of information technology, they will win, over time.

The stabilizing effects of the new middle classes

Let me give two personal examples that I have watched over decades. The first is from Northern Ireland as it slowly leaves behind the Troubles. When I arrived unexpectedly at Ulster College in 1974 to take the role of Acting Director of Studies at the brand-new Faculty of Management and Community Education [*sic*], I came face to face with inequality. I found a disconnected, overpaid and underperforming set of leaders on all sides, and a disempowered, angry and financially illiterate working class. This was at the height of the terrorist "war". I was astonished to find that there was only a tiny middle class and very little entrepreneurship (the state still provides the majority of Ulster's employment). To my surprise, as a senior academic I was not considered middle class, and was automatically included in the policy-making discussions at Province level with ministers, the police and health officials, and accepted openly into their social circle. I found this quite disconcerting when comparing it to my life on the other side of the Irish Sea. I set to work, encouraging the faculty and students to take part in action-learning-based live projects on the streets, to help both sides of a rapidly splitting community. I found both students and faculty members deeply frustrated with the historic lack of social and economic progress, and almost all of them had grown weary of the war and wished for a more stable and wealthier society.

It has taken a generation for the middle classes to grow and stabilize in Ulster. But rise they have, as the slow rebalancing of employment away from the public sector, the growth of small businesses, state intervention in creating new manufacturing, and the use of information technology to allow businesses to operate in more remote geographic settings have all combined for the good. The Northern Ireland peace process[76] has helped to establish the political future, despite its continuing and obvious faults. The governance of the Assembly has forced previously warring parties to compromise politically on a surprising number of issues for the benefit and wealth of all. It is still a fragile work in progress, but in its significant progress the growing middle class acts as balancing mechanism of growing influence.

Globally, we see similar processes occurring in Asia and Africa. For example, we see the use of the Black Economic Empowerment law in South Africa. The law has many faults, including the disempowerment and unemployment of many well-qualified young, white and coloured South Africans whose roles are desperately needed in the short and medium terms. South Africa is at that historic stage of over-compensating for past wrongs and it needs stronger political will to bring its negative effects back into balance. But it has seen the rise of an aspirant black African middle class at the top of which are the "Black Diamonds" – younger, reasonably well-educated blacks now legally entitled to join boards and own 40% of companies. Despite initial resentment in the white and coloured communities, they are beginning to prove a stabilizing force in a still turbulent, socially split and deeply impoverished society. There have been early excesses by this new middle class, but I see them creating strong aspirational models for the less fortunate to better themselves, especially through education, over the next generation. Matters are complicated by the arrival of over 5 million immigrants from surrounding countries through South Africa's notoriously porous border. But the trend of developing a middle class is firmly established, and the pressures of a rising meritocracy on the current weak national leaders will diminish their powers of patronage and corruption. The ascendant middle classes initially respond to strong national discriminatory direction-giving, but then they like to be left to get on with their social and financial enterprises, in their own way, regardless of what their political and ethnic persuasion might be.

An example of how many of the West's business leaders follow fashionable cost-reduction nostrums based on accepted business values, but then misinterpret them in the developing world, is found in "offshoring". Its current unexpected consequences have surprised many Western directors and managers, unless they are anthropologists. Think of the international rise and fall of Indian telephone call centres. By focusing only on a short-term, cost-centric approach and using only straight-line projections of growth without taking into account national cultural aspirations, Western company directors have created a medium-term wealth-destroying approach for their companies. In the late 1990s, India had a large aspiring middle class of well-educated, young Anglophone Indians looking for employment. Naturally, they were delighted to join the new call centres because they offered good money and a chance to develop their English-language skills. They did not see this as an inspired long-term career choice. Yet many blinkered, fashion-fixated Western HR and operations managers assumed this approach would be a long-term, cost-cutting silver bullet for their national staff shortage problems. Then reality struck. The young Indians found that they would need to work night shifts (when they could be having fun), study *The Archers* daily to improve their knowledge of British customs, and listen to grumpy Brits moan about issues with their bank accounts, insurance, airline bookings, telephone or energy bills in accents they could barely understand. "Received Pronunciation" is not the default dialect of the United Kingdom.

Unsurprisingly, as India's economy expanded rapidly, the aspiring middle classes sought more appropriate and better-paid work, especially in IT. This had two consequences. On the one hand, India's economic and social wealth is still growing. But the West's call centres are now left with fewer competent, well-educated Anglophone staff. New staff members may be happier to work through the night for similar pay, but their lower competence increases the rate of British dissatisfaction, incomprehension and grumpiness at the other end of the phone. As a result, those British companies' brand images and cost savings are being eroded. Offshore outsourcing is now gaining such a bad reputation that some companies are closing their Indian call centres and rebuilding them in the UK. Call centres are reappearing in the North East, Scotland, Wales and Belfast. This is a good example of short-term accepted business values getting their comeuppance, through a misunderstanding of international cultural norms and human values and a dramatic misreading of demographic changes.

But what about inequality?

I am aware that my message of rising optimism stands in sharp contrast to current Western pessimism and both the media's and British politicians' tendency to enjoy wallowing in their self-generated despair and lack of predictive ability. They do not think long-term. For example, who would have guessed that the baby boomers would grow old? And then stick around longer due to better healthcare? Examining longer-term trends seems beyond politicians and many directors. But even medium-term trends are leapt on by politically over-committed journalists and academics, who take politicians' often unsubstantiated claims and transform them into a "crisis", "chaos" or "meltdown" in the subject of their choice. A good example is the issue of inequality. Figures issued by the UK's Office for National Statistics in January 2017 show that the national income gap has *dropped* to its lowest level since 1986, following a 20-year trend. Average incomes for the 80% of households outside the richest 20% were all higher than before the 2008 crisis, after taking inflation into account. Household incomes of the poorest 20% were 13% higher than 2008, while middle income distribution was 5% higher. So it is not wise to follow metro-fashionable analyses without thoughtful discernment.[77]

It is often expedient for Western politicians to focus on short- and medium-term issues, such as perceived growing inequality, to "prove" that they are up to date and that the world must inevitably go to hell in a handcart. Poverty is abhorrent and inequality is always unbalancing in any society. The over-hyping of Thomas Piketty's *Capital in the Twenty-first Century*[78] is a good example of such mass pessimism. Some of the key figures and charts are now disputed, especially by *The Economist*,[79] always a problem for those crunching "big data". Yet his figures sit in contradiction to the United Nation prediction that, by 2030, half the world's population will be in employment and 25% of it middle class. Piketty's main "solution" to such an intractable problem is another single silver bullet: the advocacy of a global wealth tax. If only life were that simple.

My thoughts were reinforced on hearing of the death in February 2017 of Hans Rosling. To quote from the *Financial Times* obituary, "he became an unlikely icon for the world's statisticians, economists and an emerging array of data journalists by developing an innovative fusion of numbers and visuals that enabled him to present global megatrends in a simple, easy-to-understand way".[80] His continuing message was that, with the possible exception of climate change, nearly all the countries in the world were rapidly ameliorating the lot of their citizens. He tried very hard to stick to the facts. Hence his motto "Too much Word, not enough Excel" – one that many politicians would do well to follow.

To be fair, the Western public's emotional response is clear: they like the idea of reducing inequality, if not the solution. The challenge is there for our national and corporate governance systems to tackle. A clampdown on cross-border tax arbitrage, a minimum national living wage for all of working age, and "eating the rich" have all been suggested as solutions, the latter by anarchist groups. I argue that the growth of an international middle class and the consequent redistribution of wealth will, over a generation, provide a more stable solution than any fiddling with fashionable short-term solutions and lots of street protests. But there will be fewer photo opportunities.

Corruption

The rise of a larger middle class is often associated in the public mind as yet another opportunity for the growth of corruption. This is a major cause of public anger: whether in Africa, Asia, South America, Europe or the US. The fact that there are corrupt connections between politicians and international organizations is not in doubt. To quote Louis Brandeis from 100 years ago, "No methods of regulation ever have been or can be devised to remove the menace inherent in private monopoly and overweening commercial power".[81] We see this through the trials continuing under the US's Corrupt Foreign Practices Act and now the UK's Bribery Act. And we see this within businesses as, for example, the Libor rate-fixing, gold and foreign exchange fixing scandals are played out in the courts. Bob Monks's Mansion House speech[82] highlighted the parallel mini-industry of denial created by spin doctors to counter such public outrage. He estimated that, in the US, some $450 million to $1 billion has been spent annually on lobbying since 2008. These "bad" accepted business values are endemic and must be fought continually, otherwise quiet deals will be done between our governors, politicians and business, both nationally and internationally, and the rot will continue.

Along with Max Boisot and Sally Garratt, I had the mixed privilege of working near the top of the Chinese government in the early 1980s just as the Cultural Revolution had ended and as Deng Xiaoping came to power to deliver the "Four Modernizations". I wondered why they had selected three European "loners" to create their first Chinese business school and MBA programme. The pressure had been on since 1976 to allow the US business schools in. A leading member of the Communist Party explained to me, after a very good dinner, that from some six years of observation they trusted the three of us because we were honest, dedicated to education rather than our bank accounts, and so less threatening. Then he explained that the Chinese were a very ancient people with 5,000 years of recorded history and had learned very painfully to keep their people away from the most feared issue for any national leader: chaos. He went on to explain that they respected the Europeans because they had some 3,500 years of recorded history and, despite their many turbulences, had managed to control their continent. But they treated the US, with only 250 years of history, as a teenager. It may have massive financial and military power, but it has no sense of perspective, history or decency, and no sense of how to stabilize its own continent. "They believe that history only begins with them."

I pointed out that, unlike the Chinese Communist Party and many of the Emperors before them, the Europeans had achieved this through some evolving notions of democracy and governance, despite two major world wars. This democratization was derived from the Ancient Greeks, and has been established in the UK since 1215. Magna Carta started a process of governance power redistribution, by taking some of the king's powers and giving them to the barons, and later the people through Parliament. This allowed the people to have some say over how they were governed, and increased their ability to throw the rascals out if necessary. This perplexed my

Chinese friend. How can such a powerful person as a king willingly share power? I explained that such willingness was relative, and that the kings and later landowners had to resort to pragmatism rather than ideology, as a mixture of natural forces, greed and lack of funding undermined their absolute position. Earlier rulers frequently ran out of resources – people and money – when following their national and international ambitions. And then they had to beg from those who had such resources: initially the aristocracy but increasingly the middle classes, particularly the London Livery companies. Occasionally they would go down the extreme route of over-taxing the poor, but this always led to instability.

He wanted to know more, so I argued that, while there had always been corruption through preference, nepotism and graft, two major historical events could explain some of England's relative stability over 900 years. First, the Great Plagues had devastated the national workforce to such an extent that the few peasants remaining were powerful enough not just to demand a major rise in wages but also the end to serfdom (slavery). Without them, the English economy was beached. This created a much more querulous and politically volatile peasantry. Then, in the late 17th century, much of the wealth of the aristocracy (still lending to the overspending kings) was wiped out through their greed, made manifest in the scandal of the South Sea Bubble. This was a classic Ponzi scheme, based on moonshine, and restricted, by careful design, only to members of the aristocracy and the super-rich. The Scottish aristocracy had lost most of its wealth through greed and ignorance in the Darien scheme in the 1690s, which helped force the merger with England. From 1720 onwards, the South Sea Bubble proved once more that investors were often gullible and greedy, and the projects became less and less specific and the promised returns more and more inflated. This is still reflected in many Silicon Valley punts.

The consequences for England was dramatic and unplanned. The sudden loss of wealth by many aristocrats opened a gap through which a strong, rich middle class arose, a class who believed in international free trade, industrial growth, technological advancement, mild conservatism and strong moral values. As the British Empire grew, the middle classes became increasingly wealthy and powerful, despite still being despised by the aristocracy as "trade". I pointed out to my new friend that, as the middle classes grow, in countries such as, Nigeria, China, Brazil and India, we should likely see similar trends and values occurring over the next decades. He remained convinced that China was different and that, because true Communism came only from being Chinese, their Communist Party must last forever. I pointed out the growing public disgust at the corruption of local, regional and even national officials. We agreed to differ and remain friends. But he is now very watchful of the rise of the middle classes.

3. The rise of the human side of enterprise as a counterbalance

Finance fixation

Remember the Clifford Geertz quote on culture in Chapter 1 (page 49)?[83] Here I want to concentrate on that last sentence: ". . . the analysis of [culture is] to be therefore not an experimental science in search of law, but an interpretative one in search of meaning". How do you derive meaning in these "fluffy" areas when you have been brought up as executives and directors fixed on the rugged, manly truths of accountancy, operational research and intellectually wobbly risk management? You will already have had to cope with the fluffier areas of strategic planning and marketing which you still do not appreciate but know that they must be important because you pay so much for them. Now unbusiness-like regulators, pressure groups, academics and legislators are talking of adding integrated accounting, ESG and inclusive capitalism to your overcrowded world. What on earth is going on? Quite a lot. And some of it does have a surprisingly "hard" edge.

Rethinking human metrics

The "human areas" of organizational development, learning, culture and values are susceptible to new types of business metrics far beyond the daily grind of the often-derided HR department. But can they be built into *board* dashboards to improve corporate governance? Can they be developed from balanced scorecards? Yes. We are used to HR statistics regularly feeding the executives cost-related data on, for example, wage spends, turnover rates, sickness rates, labour law compliance and potential litigation costs. But we now need HR to provide the board with new metrics: trends in, for example, organizational capability, emotional and learning climates, long-term value sets, culture development, and customer, staff and suppliers' perceptions of the organization. Some of the latter can be seen by extrapolating rates of turnover, but boards will need a lot more *qualitative* metrics than that. I have used such metrics for years, building originally on the simple metrics designed by Litwin and Stringer,[84] and then developing them into a board and top-team learning system that allows each work unit in turn to see its scores and trends in relation to all the others. The ultimate goal is to have these on an organization's intranet so that the executives can manage the immediate results in real time while the board watches, for example, the emerging quarterly trends in:[85]

- Organizational adaptiveness

- Work quality

- Clarity of personal responsibility

- Financial rewards

- Personal rewards

- Organizational clarity

- Personal performance

- Group performance

- Learning climate

- Leadership

- Customer orientation

- Competitor orientation

It is a revelation to many boards that they, not the executives, are legally responsible for "ensuring the success of their business", and that they are therefore the keepers of their organizations' values and culture. The executives must do the daily developmental work, but, ultimately, maintaining, developing and sustaining the healthy "tone at the top" is the duty of the board. Is this feasible?

The fundamental organizational resource is the quality of its people's learning

I return to the notion that the fundamental resource of any organization is the learning capacity of its people. As Reg Revans has reminded us over the generations, an organization can only survive if its rate of learning is equal to, or greater than, the rate of environmental change $(L \geq C)$.[86] I am aware that many "hard" executives argue that machines, electronic and algorithmic, will be capable of "learning", of being "conscious", and of having "feeling" within the decade. I am sceptical. I have yet to see a machine tie its shoelaces while enjoying a mix of Mozart and Joan Armatrading during a walk up Mount Kinabalu.

The better news is that there already exists a huge, and largely untapped, field of human knowledge and attitudes by which action learning allows organizations to *self*-help by releasing the latent energies of their staff. Few organizations are aware of this. Sadly, few HR departments have the skills to develop their organizations' learning. Yet this is a huge, untapped and cost-effective human asset resource to unleash. It is the basis of any organization's social capital. The "hard" school of management still struggles with such an idea, even, paradoxically, in many universities which style themselves as "centres of learning". But an increasingly angry public, disgruntled shareholders and annoyed stakeholders are beginning to realize that such non-financial questions need to be asked more vocally of the board's policies, strategies and future learning systems at annual general meetings.

Entitlement

This brings us on to a deeper change in the public's values – the growing feeling of "entitlement" – of the public's right to oversee and comment on the performance and competence of our government and organizations whether public, private or not-for-profit. Internationally, the public are frustrated because banks, health industries, the police, sports companies, and even the previously sainted Co-operative Society in the UK, can be treated by their directors and executives as private clubs from which the public are excluded, and about which they should not have the impertinence to ask awkward, discerning questions. This cannot last. Our social media information technology alone will no longer let it. And there is a growing awareness among existing members of "the establishment" that things have to change. They are losing their previous entitlement.

We are seeing a huge change in the public's demand for much higher standards of corporate governance effectiveness. The public's previously supine acceptance of the "you follow, we lead" leadership formula by executives is eroding fast. A more integrated, accountable, honest and transparent system of leadership, especially of corporate governance, is now demanded. This will upset the zero-sum games of many current directors and executives. Yet it is only by taking a longer-term view and then trusting their people to share openly their learning that the future game can have a positive outcome.

The current indifference and amorality of many directors and senior executives currently mixes dangerously with the public's lack of ability to understand, assess and compare directors' and senior executives' *competence*. Their growing feeling of entitlement is mixed with an inarticulacy in demanding and understanding effective accountability, probity and transparency. This has led to the current frustrating impasse and allowed the rot to continue. I argue that this logjam is about to be broken, especially as more and more of the public realize that they are the ultimate, beneficial, owners of much wealth

– especially their pension funds and insurances. It is astonishing that they do not. This may be because this is currently not handled professionally on their behalf. Much the same can be said of the public sector organizations with their massive pension funds and despite their strong historical and emotional ownership tradition.

The unstoppable rise of the "stakeholders"

I want to reinforce here the unstoppable rise of the diversity of the other *stakeholders* involved in modern corporations: the increasingly powerful *emotional* "owners" (non-financial), and their growing access to external legal sanctions to constrain the corporation's ability to operate without thought for their interconnected community and environmental contexts. This complex chain of stakeholder connections comprises a mixture of, for example, staff, suppliers, planning and taxation authorities, community groups, the media, and environmental and social pressure groups. While many have no direct legal ownership rights over a company, they have an increasing mix of other control mechanisms – including direct legal sanctions. And they exert new forms of power and influence, both directly and indirectly, through emotional ownership in the community. Their strength comes from a growing aspect of corporate governance: *stakeholder powers and control*. This opens up new dimensions of governance way beyond the well-established accountancy capture. We see new and growing public and international pressure on sectors such as financial services, "ethical pharmaceuticals", oil and gas, mining, farming, shipping, aeronautics, and retail supply chains. In turn, these "emotional owners" are questioning the key support mechanisms of much of today's amoral business: the professions and the very nature of "professionalism".

4. The need to rethink the meaning of "professionalism"

The professions, especially those supportive professions of the international financial services – accountancy, audit, law, management consultancy, and company secretarial – have had a very profitable run for over 30 years since the UK's Big Bang in 1985 and the deregulation of the financial markets in 1986. In the UK, as the Labour Party administration finally became aware of their job creation and taxation potential, they reversed their previously hostile position on finance and the professions and adopted a "light touch" regulatory position. In 1998, they embraced "greed" as a force for societal good [*sic*]. Peter Mandelson, then Business Secretary, said that he was "intensely relaxed about people getting filthy rich as long as they pay their taxes". This reflected Deng Xiaoping's comments on releasing capitalism in China: "It does not matter if the cat is black or white as long as it catches the mice."[87] This has proved economically successful in the medium term for both of them. But this strategy is now bringing on itself its own downfall, following the 2008 Western financial crash, and there are similar signs of a bubble economy in China. Politically, greed is a very difficult value to control.

The lack of moral business values was evidenced by the sudden drop in the UK's global business trust and credibility ratings, as tracked annually by Transparency International.[88] Britain dropped from the fourth most admired country for conducting honest business worldwide to the fourteenth under Tony Blair, although it has since crept back to tenth in 2015 under David Cameron. And we are just above middling position on the Bribe Payers Index, despite all the political rhetoric. This drop was not because other countries became more honest but because British politicians and their civil servants increasingly turned a blind eye to rule-bending and bribery. What was most worrying for me was that the allied professionals went along with it so easily, if not in public. They rarely warned their clients to stop. Their much-vaunted codes of professional practice and ethics committees were seldom seriously activated. Their loss of fees was their main concern. So the public became increasingly disenchanted with the notion of "professionalism", and now we all suffer. No-one expects politicians to be completely honest because they are known to duck and dive for personal advantage all the time. That is the sad nature of party politics. But the professions are meant to be disinterested and need to keep the *clients'* best interests at heart. They are not expected to do their client's bidding regardless of the law and ethical considerations. Their perceived altruism was why the professions were given their monopolies in Victorian times.

But, in modern times, their focus has been less as a client's dispassionate conscience and more as a willing executive, delivering increasing financial returns through minimum compliance to the growing number of regulatory requirements. In my experience few modern professions have been concerned publicly with the development of stakeholder effectiveness and human values in business. Even fewer have been warning their clients of the consequent growing public anger nor the need to rebalance financial measures with appropriate metrics for those two other sources of capital: social and natural.

Mervyn King, in his highly readable "Integrate: Doing Business in the 21st Century", says that

> Integration is the new way of thinking about running a company today. Businesses ... have the same issues to contend with: greater expectations of their stakeholders, rising consumer power in the digital age, environmental constraints, economic uncertainty in the aftermath of the global financial crisis, and social uncertainty on rising income inequality.[89]

I know of only one large international accountant/consultant who is taking this trend further and has even invested in a human rights division. Well done Mazars: a beacon for the future?

What are the future roles of the professions in supporting more effective leadership and governance?

I mentioned in the Introduction that the professions came into being through a conscious national deal with Victorian society: the professions would be allowed to define educational and practical competence, restrict entry, ensure discipline, and set the fees for their profession, if they were seen clearly to put the interests of their clients first while demonstrating their independence of judgement. This latter point is now highly criticized publicly. It is always a problem for any professional not to fall into the Stockholm syndrome[90] where you become so close to your captors (clients) that you end up empathizing with them and fighting on their side, regardless of what the external, rational world expects of you. It is easy for any professional consultant to develop this syndrome, especially if they have had a long-term relationship with a client. As an extreme example, KPMG and its forebears had a contract to audit the Bank of England which lasted 100 years. Was this wise for either party? Following the 2008 heart attack of the Western financial system, there are moves, especially from the European Union, to, among other things, rotate auditors every ten years. Clients need sound dispassionate advice, stimulation and *challenge*. They do not seem to get that very often.

But the questions for the current professions go much deeper. How can they balance their perceived primary purpose of delivering a defined operational solution for a client while maintaining their professional independence of judgement? Are they now too aligned with clients' interests, especially financial services clients, to have lost any semblance of independence? Have they lost their old "conscience of the client" role? If so, should they continue to be treated as a profession by society, or seen as just a very expensive outsourcing contractor? What real value do they add? As an extreme example, the ratings agencies in the US were a crucial part of the evolving sub-prime mortgage scandal. If they had not given good ratings to the bundles of "securitized" mortgages pushed onto the markets and certified as investment grade AAA, the markets would not have been able to trade them so easily. This has led to general disgust and public approbation of the agencies and the whole financial system. However, in a cynical manoeuvre, a recent US court judgement has allowed such agencies to continue "because legally the markets must have ratings"![91] Christine Lagarde and Mark Carney eat your heart out.

Six professions that need reframing

Here I want to take a more detailed look at those professions associated with the Western financial crisis of 2008 leading to the continuing loss of public's wealth. I look at six of the professions now under public criticism relating to finance-fixated governance:

a. **The accountants** Their public credibility has not been enhanced by their performance during and since the 2008 crisis. Internal and external accountants will continue with their present work but with greater uncertainties hanging over them about their future roles and employment. The simultaneous changes in technology ethics and professionalism will deeply affect their future roles, incomes and costs. Their basic information-providing and assurance-checking services are creakily holding up. Modern information technology systems now allow not only the collection of much larger quantities of data but they also allow more sophisticated systems of analysis – and in real time. So real-time accounting is feasible. Whether one is already "in the cloud" or not (currently still risky as there is significant uncertainty as to who owns the data/IPR if the cloud service provider goes bust), there is no doubt that big-data-crunching processes will allow real-time reporting systems, giving greater accuracy and relevance than ever imagined by accountants and their clients even a decade ago. Potentially this is great news for effective governance, as the owners and other stakeholders will be able to demand and get more accountability, probity and transparency.

This means that boards and managers can be held accountable sooner, as one can trace transactions more accurately and quickly; and any internal audit function will be able to better inform the board of directors directly via board dashboards of any worrying financial or other trends without reference to the editorial powers of the executives. Board dashboards will be more accurate, up to date and relevant than before. If the new data on trends in organizational capability, values and culture are integrated into annual reports (it is good to see organizations phasing out the use of the expensive non-sense of quarterly reporting), along with their reporting on the optimal use of financial, social and natural capital, the board's role will be more focused on assessing future uncertainties, while also improving prudent control as demanded by law. This will allow them to better handle their duty of independent judgement. And it will reframe what we think of currently as "accounting".

b. **The auditors** are under even more public criticism than the accountants. The public cries of "How could they have cleared Enron, RBS, HBOS, AIG, The Co-operative, FIFA (or whoever)?" are now so common that they must be taken seriously to restore public confidence in the credibility of national and international financial reporting systems. The major criticisms have been over the general quality of audits, especially for complex organizations and especially those operating across national borders. Again the old, stereotyped auditing process is undergoing serious public questioning. This is often characterized simply as the external senior audit partner having quiet chats with the board chairman, the chairman of the audit committee, the CEO and the finance director, to ascertain any broad financial and contextual changes from last year, then having a more detailed session with the chairman of the audit committee of the board to cross-check any significant details to watch for before launching shoals of relatively junior accountants and trainees to trawl records looking for probity and anomalies. These are fed back to the client, usually the CEO rather than the board, through a series of meetings and a negotiating process that determine what are likely to be the "facts" that need to be transmitted to the shareholders, the public and the regulators. Then the chairman, not the executives, can sign off the accounts as "true and accurate" for presentation at the annual general meeting; and the auditors are reappointed for a further year.

Shareholders should employ the auditors

Few shareholders continue to believe in the efficacy of such a process. Matters are made worse by the simple fact that the auditors are not paid by the owners, or the shareholders (who need a level of independence to protect their interests), but are usually paid by the company itself! There is no absolute guarantee of "independence" when the professional role of auditors is under attack. If you have been auditing a company for, say, 20 years, a level of Stockholm syndrome is likely to be present, however unconsciously. In 2014, the European Commission published rules to rotate auditors of larger listed companies every ten years. These rules are being opposed by many companies and auditors. It seems to me that auditors are in danger of drifting into rearranging the deckchairs on the *Titanic* while the iceberg of combined regulatory reform and big data crunching gets ever nearer. I suggest that a good start is to agree that auditors should be paid by, and report to, the shareholders directly.

An interesting alternative approach is being proposed by Professor Mike Mainelli which drops this old business model.[92] Instead, it is more in touch with the growing ethos of future audit. It firmly places all the responsibility for the stewardship of "the figures" with the board and then the executives. The chats with the chairman, audit committee, CEO and financial director are more structured and rigorous and, crucially, are based firmly on the company's espoused *business model*. The subsequent independent critical analysis is carried out by the external audit team. The auditors must still give advice on good reporting practice but the previous in-depth saturation of the company by junior audit team members is dropped in favour of much deeper analyses of carefully selected issues (hot spots) generated by the critical examination of the business model. The old in-depth junior trawling tasks are selected more as random spot inspections to sample the accuracy of the total system.

The new audit output is then not the "true and accurate" statement signed by the chairman, but an independent statement by the auditors to the shareholders of the likely issues coming from the existing business model; and the *probabilities* of benefits and risks occurring from its pursuit. This model seems to have a lot going for it. Importantly, it allows in the new business model the integration of the social and natural capital accounts alongside the financials. In some ways, companies like Shell have been publishing a version of this for many years through their *People, Planet and Profits*, as have Novo Nordisk. Other organizations should copy them as the legislators and regulators become more demanding of audit and (alarmingly) are beginning to design and "manage" the future financial reporting systems themselves. That way box-ticking lies.

Internal audit

Internal auditors are often treated as the Cinderella profession, despised and neglected by powerful executives yet full of unused relevant information and useful ideas. Unlike external auditors, they know where the bodies are likely to be buried. My thinking has always been that they are too often wrongly positioned in a business and need a direct reporting line to the board through the audit committee chairman as recommended by their professional body, the Institute of Internal Auditors. This idea is hated by most chief executives as it removes their editorial powers over the information the board receives. It is the internal audit team's job to "speak truth unto power" – both to the CEO and the board. It is this independent stance that can mark them out as professionals in the best sense. Yet few are truly independent. Many get their pay-and-rations via the CEO and so are implicated deeply in the organizational micro-politics of information flows and blockages. This is why I have juggled and experimented with clients the idea of having the internal audit team as part of an expanded chairman's office. This design comprises the chairman, the chairman of the audit committee, the company secretary, and the head of internal audit. It worked remarkably well. But it led to howls of protest from the executives, so I assume that I am onto something.

c. **The corporate lawyers.** I find it hard to comment here without getting angry. I know it is an old joke that, when asked what the financial results will be, accountants always ask "what do you want them to be?" In aiming to develop effective corporate governance, my experience with organizational lawyers is similar, but sometimes worse. The lawyers, corporate counsel and external contractors rarely take the stance that their job is to explain to the client the spirit of the law as well as the letter; instead, they seem to feel that they are paid to bend their interpretation of the law as far as possible for their client's needs without the client ending up in court or jail. Such comments might be seen as calumny by some, but it is my experience. I have seen so many lawyers at work in boardrooms not explaining and defending the importance of the primary law – especially the seven "general duties of directors" – to their boards. They tend not to stress that "a director is a director, all are equal under the law and have unlimited liability for their actions". Rather, they tend to allow the weasel words "non-executive director", "executive director", "executive chairman" "senior independent director" etc. to be applied as if they were the primary law. They are not. And, to my despair, they have found it expedient to let them slip into the corporate governance regulations. It muddies the water, and over time the words are assumed as correct. They then become the norm and are followed by many directors, a non-comprehending public, and many not-for-profit organizations. This has allowed general semantic confusion to reign in the UK and the many countries that have copied their lead. Matters even more complicated have emerged under the new UK Banking Act of 2015, which has created two more categories of director: accredited and non-accredited. I shall deal with this issue in Chapter 3.

Only once in 30 years have I heard the opposite case stated, when I sat in on an Asian board listed in London. They had already received two warnings from the regulator, the then Financial Services Authority, for corporate governance offences. They were on their third and final warning when I was invited in as a corporate governance advisor to work with the senior partner of a major law firm. He had been specially selected by the top team back in Tokyo as he had been voted "the best corporate lawyer in London" for consecutive years. I made my case about sticking with the primary laws and he not only backed me but told them clearly and abruptly what would happen to their company and them personally if they didn't get their corporate governance house in order. They were shocked by this revelation, as their previous lawyers had not explained this to them in such stark terms. I, on the other hand, was delighted to be able to restore, at least temporarily, my faith in corporate lawyers. After much debate, the board decided to de-list in London, because the UK's evolving corporate governance culture was too counter-cultural for them and their corporate values. They did not want to lose face by being brought before the courts.

d. **The management consultants.** Whereas London has many small, personal and "boutique" management consultancies, providing truly client-centred independent professional services, there is still a tendency among the big players to use a more mechanical business model that relies on standardized analyses and solutions to continue their relentless pursuit of partners' billable hours. This is often backed by long-term and rotating relationships with clients. These can be rewarded greatly in the annual partnership financial distribution. So, over time, Stockholm syndrome can overcome notions of professional independence.

Having seen some of the big consultancies from the inside, I was always amazed that they were not that interested in helping design a distinctly better future for their clients. They offered such services, but these were not central to their business model, nor were they central to the training of their future consultants. Their induction "training" creates the consultant's brand for its next generation. But, in doing so, it often continues the existing rewards, values and long-term culture of the practice. I had been working on a radical design for a future management consultancy offering. Over drinks one evening with two senior partners, I raised this issue again. They said, "Look, Bob, think of us as a garage – you must understand that we are really a jobbing shop. That's how we make our real money. People bring their damaged businesses in, we find the quick, operational problems, knock the panels out, refit any damaged parts, and then we push them back onto the road. We are not really interested in your 'futures' stuff, so we give low priority to investing in our future intellectual capacity, nor have we much motivation to do so." Professionalism, anyone?

Happily, there are at least some medium-sized consultancies that are increasingly concerned by such an old-style approach and have much richer services to offer. A good source for this growing debate is the Worshipful Company of Management Consultants.[93]

e. **The company secretaries.** These are increasingly appreciated as the governance "good guys" of many messy corporations. They also have a legal role as an independent professional. Company secretaries are not members of the board of directors, but are "officers of the board". Much of their role can be seen as purely administrative, as they ensure the due process of creating, recording and filing the necessary corporate papers during the year to stay within their company constitution, the law, and the corporate governance regulations. An important and expanding part of their professional role is explaining "due process" to the board, by checking the current behaviour of the chairman and board, that the general duties of directors are delivered and that corporate governance regulations are adhered to. Their duties include the creation and circulation of properly constructed agendas and minutes and, most importantly of all, playing the role of "the conscience of the board". This not only involves ensuring that the board stays within its articles of association and regulatory remits, but also that the board is pursuing its policies and strategies to ensure the success of the company. A key part of the effective company secretary role is to keep asking discerning questions about the board's objectives, processes and values, and then carefully recording their replies. This reinforces effective board behaviour, and is vital to the board's understanding of their governance role.

f. **Human resources.** I have already suggested that this is still a very messy area, as neither the title nor the roles have been clarified at governance level. The "human metrics" paragraphs above indicate HR directors' desire to break free from their purely administrative and operational focus and contribute to strategic thinking. This is growing, but only very slowly. HRDs have yet to provide the dashboard tools by which boards can value their inputs at the policy and strategy levels. There is still a noticeable lack of HR expertise at board level in most countries. HRDs need to develop further their organizational learning systems, dashboard metric trends, values and culture, and take a more anthropological approach to understanding their organizations. Currently, I am unsure whether they can become truly independent professionals and make a big contribution to governance development. I hope that they can, but there seems little motivation for most boards to do so.

The shadow side of professionalism

Many professionals now use the legal entity of the limited liability partnership (LLPs) as a way of protecting partner wealth without having to create and register a limited liability company which has tax advantages but also demands much greater public disclosure. In its short life, the LLP has been a boon to partnerships. Its creation featured highly in the political argument for "lighter-touch regulation" under the Blair government's 2000 act. It shelters partners' earnings and has the great benefit of not having to disclose its

STOP THE ROT

ultimate beneficiaries. From the public perspective, this is its biggest weakness. It is not easy to find who the final owners of an LLP are, particularly if they are registered offshore, as many are. This legal form may suit legitimate partners but it also attracting the shadow side of global wealth movements. A growing number of non-professional LLPs have been implicated in money laundering, drug dealings, people trafficking, and modern slavery. So the concept and validity of the LLP as a suitable vehicle for professionals is coming under worldwide scrutiny.

Increasingly, professionals cannot afford to be associated even indirectly with criminals who are also using this legal entity to hide their ultimate beneficiaries. I know of a number of partners of truly professional organizations who are considering registering as a limited liability company to avoid being associated with this "shadow" side. They feel that they cannot advocate probity, accountability and transparency to their clients while seeming to be even loosely associated with the opposite in private.

It is a paradox that, in an age when information technology and public oversight is being advocated to make communications more transparent, many corporations are trying to move scrutiny of their wealth and their decision-making away from the public gaze behind closed electronic doors. This is not happening just in the private sector. The number of growing governance and leadership scandals within corporations that many in the UK had previously seen as bastions of moral integrity, like the BBC and the National Health Service, clearly reflect this movement towards secrecy, despite the existence of the Freedom of Information Act. It is particularly ironic that a public corporation will often use the cover of "commercial confidentiality" to hide its actions. This is part of the rot.

Which leads us on to a deeper exploration of the parallel governance fields of anti-corruption, probity and taxation, and the roles of the professionals within them.

Three global trends: anti-corruption; probity and taxation; and transparency

In the US and the UK, the anti-corruption trends are being played out publicly as society questions the current practices of corporates and their professional advisors in the areas of corruption, bribery and taxation. How these will be resolved now by the courts and new legislation will determine much of the new governance value sets for the two next decades.

Anti-corruption

Principle 10 of the UN Global Compact states that "Businesses should work against corruption in all its forms, including extortion and bribery." The UN's definition of bribery is "the abuse of private or public office for personal or political gain". I mentioned earlier that the UK position in Transparency International's long-tested Corruption Perception Index has slipped by a number of places in recent years. Post-Brexit the UK must strive hard to rebuild its dominant position as a champion for its organizations and their values and so rebuild its slightly tarnished national brand. This is a key to the UK coping with the four international trends which I have described above.

It is enlightening and reassuring to note what happens on one of the very few occasions when an organization is successfully shamed in public, shows its contrition and rectifies matters. Following the Woolf Report in 2008,[94] BAE took serious steps to stamp out corruption in its UK and its overseas activities. It changed its internal processes and its external reporting so that investors and the public can see and, most importantly, track its progress in improving these governance aspects. The improvement at board level is noticeable, as is the rebalancing of powers between the board and the now less dominant executive team. The annual report has since become a model of how to report on, measure and develop effective corporate governance.

Hopefully, such improvements will be applied to, for example, Rolls-Royce and GSK and their selling issues in China. GSK's 2010 Corporate Social Responsibility Report[95] makes for puzzling reading. It says that its CSR Committee "had reviewed and strengthened our approach to preventing, detecting and addressing bribery". It also says that "GSK makes payments to healthcare professionals . . . and has clear standards about how much we pay". It says that all payments in China are above board but does admit that it runs different programmes in different countries. In 2014, the arrest of GSK's Mark Reilly in China forced the company to release a statement declaring that "Certain senior executives of GSK China who know our systems well, appear to have acted outside of our processes and controls".[96] In my eyes, this means that their central ethical values need to be more explicit and transparent in order for them to be enforced and thus credible for members of the public, national or international.

The UK's 2010 Bribery Act strives to improve organizational probity and directoral professionalism. It applies to *all* registered UK companies operating anywhere in the world, and to any foreign business operating in the UK. It applies to *all* employees, agents and contractors, and leaves the business open to prosecution if bribes can be shown to have been paid. Distortion of "the honest flow of business" can be created by cash payments, expenses-paid trips, receiving or asking for a bribe, failing to prevent bribery, or bribing a foreign public official. Cash does not have to change hands as, under the act, the prospect of offering an inducement is regarded as an illegal act. The penalties include personal fines and imprisonment for up to ten years and, for corporations, unlimited fines and the possibility that the organization could debarred from tendering for public contracts. Initially, directors, executives and professionals were flustered by the act, questioning whether one could still entertain corporately, give gifts, take clients to dinner or to sports events. The answer seems to be that you can, provided the individual cost is well below £100 per head. But the ultimate goal of the act is much grander: to change the ethical and professional nature of the way UK business is conducted in the future.

The low limit on gifts is important. It is a classic example of "nudging" behaviour – a method to change behaviours rapidly and to influence opinions (initially), then, over time, attitudes, and finally beliefs. Firms are encouraged to create and publish their own bribery policy based on a careful assessment of how they do business in each country, then to build these aspects into their existing and new *employment* contracts, while communicating the new rules across the business, and having the policy endorsed by the directors and top teams.

The political and societal wish is to make probity a self-regulating process in any organization. It is not meant to be a rules-based system because then participants will game it. The real test will come when the first cases go before the courts. These interpretations will then form the basis of our new case law. Sadly, few cases have appeared yet and there seems little political will to enforce the act quickly. Indeed, in the 2012 Guidance Notes issued by the Bribery Act Working Group (on which GSK and BAE both sit), the talk is only of box-ticking "adequate procedures", so do not hold your breath. Probity in the governance of our organizations still has a long way to go. Yet in Asia and Africa, where I spend so much of my time, I am both reassured and mildly bemused that UK companies are usually seen as "straight" in their business dealings. What can the rest be like? However, I was reassured in February 2015, at a Fidelio Partners Breakfast Workshop on African Business Development, at which people on all sides agreed that the UK's Bribery Act had made a difference to the attitudes and behaviours in which their national business was now conducted. It was noticeable just how much their *clients* felt that they had to respect the Act and how they did not want to appear before the much-admired UK courts. All felt that their business dealings had moved towards a higher level of probity.

US legislation recognized this problem earlier with the passing of its tougher Corrupt Foreign Practices Act, which makes it a criminal offence to bribe a foreign official. Indeed, some business folk have not just been fined but jailed by the new act.

It still takes values-driven, strong-minded and courageous individuals to do the right things when no-one is watching. There are still only few who would risk using the upward-reporting "whistle-blower" systems to allow the truth to flow. It takes very strong professional directors and executives to praise, protect and promote the bringers of such messages. Such whistle-blowers are more likely to be dismissed and harried, especially when executive bonuses depend on being deaf to such information. Sadly, in most organizations, there are no formal processes that allow the truth to be spoken to the powerful, so most employees still "yield". It is only in a publicly high-risk industry like the airline industry, with its Airline Safety Reporting System, in which whistle-blowers can file reports safely and anonymously, and with the knowledge that rapid remedial actions will be circulated and then enforced. To have such a system within financial services is years away. To have it in the NHS is still a dream.

Tax and probity

I have included taxation as a probity and professional governance issue here as it tells us much about corporate attitudes, values, culture and future reporting. Decisions on where and when to pay tax set the "tone at the top", which then permeates the company's ethics. It is a paradox that, in a "borderless trading world", companies still seek to hide behind the borders of the weakest taxation regimes. This is usually justified by the phrase "we pay exactly what the law demands" and "our duty to the shareholders is to maximize their returns in the short term". How will this rationalization continue to work in an age of inclusive capitalism and integrated reporting?

There is great public anger about the perceived underpayment, or non-payment, of taxes by companies operating across international borders, especially those involving the reporting of sales and intellectual property generation. This public anger will not go away. At its base is the question of whether tax should be incurred in the country in which a sale is made rather than in the one the corporation chooses to book the transaction. This question particularly applies to businesses that choose to register their headquarters in a country because of its low corporate tax rates.

This is a serious and growing issue. Starbucks was boycotted in 2015 because of its pathetically low tax payments on its UK turnover of £8.1 million.[97] Amazon, Microsoft, Google, Apple, Johnson & Johnson, and now Uber are similarly vilified and risk losing their reputations as "good", "customer-friendly" companies. There is also a growing public backlash towards the countries in which these companies are located, especially Ireland, Luxembourg, the Netherlands, Singapore, Bermuda and the Cayman Islands. The probity issues seem twofold. First, should this tax avoidance be encouraged by the professionals and, should companies be allowed to get away with it? By consciously using the rules to reduce or avoid tax, these companies are depriving the country in which they trade of tax income, in a time of recession. Is this just?

A prime example of such a problem is Vodafone. The British company has been criticized internationally for years for paying below the average tax rate of countries in which it operates. For example, what seems extraordinary is that, in its UK figures for 2014, Vodafone has a tax *credit* of £14.8 billion.[98] As far as I can see, this is because the company has "recognized" the future tax benefit of £17.4 billion of losses in Luxembourg, equivalent to losses of some £70 billion booked there. This is doubly odd, and stretches the bounds of corporate credibility as Vodafone sells no phone contracts in Luxembourg; and the losses claimed equate to twice that country's GDP. But the public is told that it should not worry itself as these are not "real" losses but EU agreed reliefs from Luxembourg's predatory tax system, based on the write-down of recent acquisitions that include Germany's Mannesmann 2000. Confused? I am.

How has this been allowed to happen? The UK government had set up a Treasury/Business "Monetary Assets" Working Group", and included in the membership were Vodafone's tax director, and ex-HMRC director, John Connors. Eyebrows were raised and this time not those of the Governor of the Bank of England. It is time that the intelligently naïve public asked many more questions of such deals, and questioned whether participants in such political working groups and committees are conflicted to a point that they should not be allowed to vote or even participate? Do such working group members have a *primary d*uty to that group? If not, why not? Effective governance is at stake.

Vodafone says that, "for a significant number of years", it will be able to channel its UK and other profits into Luxembourg and so pay no corporation tax in the UK. What are the ethics of such actions? By avoiding paying tax in the countries in which they are trading, Vodafone is not allowing those countries to benefit from their otherwise substantial taxation payments, payments that help to pay for social services including health, welfare, transport and future infrastructure. Vodafone are therefore decreasing the potential wealth and financial stability of that country. The US Joint Committee on Taxation estimates that, in 2015, some $96 billion of revenue was lost over a decade by a range of companies using such techniques in a similar way. They are concerned that, if the US Congress gives in and creates a tax holiday for the repatriation of the vast sums held by US corporates overseas as proposed by President Trump, it may well then create the expectation of even more tax holidays in the future.

Which brings us on to the second probity issue with "tax limitation" schemes. There has always been a tension between paying government-determined taxes and the rights of individuals and corporations to arrange their affairs so as to pay as little tax as possible. But in a long-term recession, the question is not what is a reasonable balance here, but why, when the public still have to pay their personal taxes, are the corporates getting away with tax limitation, and why are they also allowed to create those vast offshore cash piles? Such activity seems massively inequitable, but there seems little political will, nationally or internationally, to tackle this. This is an affront to inclusive capitalism. A *Financial Times* survey conducted in May 2014 estimates that in the US alone some $500 billion [*sic*] is held in offshore cash by just 14 technology and pharmaceutical companies. On average, they paid just a 10% tax rate in 2013. During the past eight years, their overall tax rates *fell* as their lightly taxed foreign profits grew at nearly three times the rate of their foreign sales.[99] No wonder the public cries foul! Long-term international resolutions need to be agreed on the source and rate of taxation across national boundaries. Tax arbitrage is now firmly in the public's firing line. In the meantime, the long-term brand and probity reputation of these companies will be increasingly eroded. Their power to hold such vast sums of cash offshore potentially unsettles not just markets but entire countries. What was the definition of "plutocracy" again? And isn't plutocracy the very opposite of democracy?

Transparency

Which brings us to that third major organizational professional value: transparency. Most organizations could help themselves just by starting to be less opaque in their information flows to their owners, let alone to the public. Directors, and especially executives, are not bound by a sworn code of secrecy to keep as much as possible from the owners, yet this appears to be their accepted business value, particularly in the US. The notion of being forced to be secretive to protect "commercial secrets", including intellectual property, is debatable in an age rife with internet hacking and cyber-attacks. Such defences are often a convenient cover for directors who cannot provide answers to intelligently naïve questions from the increasingly frustrated shareholders and for Ministers and civil servants keen to avoid the Freedom of Information Act.

In an internet-enabled world of instant digital data, corporate leadership and governance is presented with a paradox: on the one hand, having so many forms of social communication available means that organizations face the daily threat of being overwhelmed, both from within and from without, by public requests and views (not all of them intelligently naïve and some plain barmy). On the other hand, organizations are frequently accused of withholding too much information.

At least for publicly listed companies, professional rules on communicating with the owners are clear and reasonably well policed. The fundamental objective is to ensure the equality, the "symmetry", of information between shareholders. So warnings to the market, uploading of trading or financial information, and the declaration of results – at strictly prescribed times and in a prescribed sequence – are the law. Or at least this was true until the "flash boys" created unfair asymmetry of information and rigged the technology of the markets. The financial authorities and politicians are panicked and are now seeking to get to grips with this change.

An oath of professionalism for the professions

I shall conclude this chapter on the four broad trends affecting future organizational governance by making a modest, values-based suggestion that directors, executives, civil servants and their professional advisors take an oath to build on the fundamental organizational and human values of accountability, probity and transparency to renew public trust and credibility. I advocate a professional oath that covers:

- The sovereignty of the client
- Independence of thought
- Necessary care, skill and diligence
- Regularly assessed professional competence
- Personal courage
- Humility
- Temperance
- Oversight
- Wisdom

We could even call them the Nine Virtues of Effective Governance.

Section II
The five future governance roles

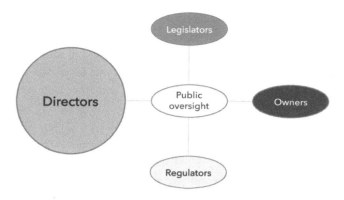

3

The directors' role in stopping the rot

The argument for effective corporate
governance values as the basis for national
leadership and governance

The current Western fashion for denigrating directors of all types is emotionally understandable following the financial crisis of 2008. However, it demeans the many directors who are still determined to develop their people and organizations, but often without sufficient ideas, models or vocabulary to deal with the deep governance issues that beset our society. This chapter is a personal attempt to ease this unhealthy situation. It forms a fifth of my proposed design for a national corporate governance learning system.

People are comfortable if they feel well led. This allows them to get on with their lives while retaining the security of having the democratic right to eject the rascals if the quality of their governance fails. In the UK, we have two millennia of models of effective national leaders from Boudicca, Alfred, Elizabeth I, Cromwell, Nelson, Wellington, Churchill, Elizabeth II, to Margaret Thatcher. All have passed the key test of any leader: that the majority, with the often grudging acceptance of the minority, are willing to follow them to achieve a greater cause. Each had very different personalities and, at a time of national emergency, had a passionate belief in what was right for their country. None of these leaders was universally popular, and not all of them were loved. But all were effective in their own way.

The problem with many of our current leaders of national institutions such as Parliament, international business, local government, the National Health Service, the BBC, the universities, schools, the police, the trades unions, media, sport and our charities (and this is only a partial list) is that they appear disappointingly purposeless and colourless personalities. Opinion polls show frequently that the public no longer see our leaders as effective. Their deficiencies are magnified by real-time criticism, disseminated over the internet and the wider media, and so any credibility is continually eroded. This process is nationally debilitating because the public have not yet learned to ask discerning questions of their leaders' competence. The public needs agreement on what is effective political and organizational governance and leadership, especially between the legislative, directoral and the executive functions. Paradoxically, despite the criticisms, we have already invested in and built the legal infrastructure, so I argue that we can benefit much by accepting what has been learned about effective corporate governance already, and then using that as the default position from which to disseminate widely a system for the necessary direction-giving to cope with our turbulent future. And I do stress the importance of creating a system of continuous *learning* to achieve this aim.

I am not advocating the creation and development of a cadre of national super-leaders of the "dominator" stereotype.[100] Despite Donald Trump, the "leader as action hero" single stereotype is of limited use in stakeholder-based, inclusive organizations. Alternatively, I advocate that the conscious national development of the concept of a *range* of effective leaders is accepted by the public as a key to their sustainable health and wealth. This depends on the development of learnable, agreed, assessable competences, linked to a set of values and behaviours for leaders of any organization: public, private or not-for-profit. As the UK and South Africa currently have the world's most developed systems of effective corporate governance, we should use these countries as the benchmark from which we can then develop our future organizations internationally. This builds on my suggestion in Chapter 2 that we treat the practice of effective direction-giving as a *profession*, that we regularly assess practitioners' competence, and have sanctions for professional malpractice.

The current muddle over the title of "director"

But first we need to clarify the much-abused term "director". I have mentioned that the use of the title "director" is unlawful in most Commonwealth countries, unless you have personally registered your title at Companies House or the national equivalent. Yet the title is constantly overused, usually unlawfully. The term is distributed like confetti in good times, when there is a need to retain senior staff, and in bad times when remuneration cannot be increased so other forms of compensation are deemed necessary. This demeans the title, exposes those folk not registered to the legal risk of unlimited personal liability, and it causes great confusion in the public's mind as to who is a "director" and whether the title has any validity. In that growing basket case of corporate governance known as the USA, the term "director" is doubly confusing because it is used to describe both members of the board of directors and to the position directly below a vice president.

Matters are made worse internationally by the consciously lax use of the term "director" in organizations. Existing boards and HR departments often offer the job title "director" to employees as if it were a compensation prize, especially if larger financial rewards are not on offer. This is particularly true within financial institutions. If the exposure of a director's personal wealth to unlimited liability is not made clear when a non-registered director title is offered, then this exposes a business's key employee to high and unnecessary risks. They become what I call "accidental directors". This is equally true if people are offered such job titles as "Director of . . .". Strong case law also exists which shows that people "holding themselves out to be" or "purporting to be" a director, will be treated by the courts as if they were. Such people are then accredited with the same responsibilities and liabilities as a lawfully registered director, but without access to any insurance cover. Few people in this position seem to know that they are exposed to unlimited personal liability. They only start to care when indicted, by which time it is already too late to cover themselves.

Internationally, regulators have allowed this sloppy use of the "director" title to become the norm. In the UK and most of the 54 Commonwealth countries, you are either a registered "director" or you are not, from the legal viewpoint. However, the regulators have let the terms "executive director" and "non-executive director" become the norm in many countries. Yet, legally speaking, neither term exists. This was administratively convenient at the time of the Cadbury Report and has just been copied by other regulators without care. What is worse is that the financial services' lack of understanding of, and contempt for, this basic legal point means that they, together with the financial regulators and politicians, have not only continued this bad practice but now compounded their folly by creating yet another class of directors – approved and non-approved – without squaring this with the Companies Act 2006.

The foolishness of "the senior management regime" in the UK

In a desperate and rushed effort by politicians and bureaucrats to save the reputation of banking and the wider financial services of the City of London, the regulators, together with the Financial Conduct Authority, the Bank of England and the Prudent Regulation Authority, have created the fearsome "senior management regime". This is a triumph of arrogance over, and dismissal of, the hard-won general duties of directors. Directors should carefully note the title. All three words are incorrect. It is not a "senior management" position as the drafters have not appreciated the basic legal differentiation between directors and managers, and instead have attempted to tar all with the same brush. Their intention is worthy – to ensure that all "senior managers" accept personal responsibility for their actions and any risks taken, a laudable aim in that it brings the actions of the top executives under legal scrutiny. It is very odd that they were not before. They now have a *statutory* duty to take reasonable steps to prevent regulatory breaches in their specified area of responsibility.

Early experience shows that this has caused fragmentation of board and senior management's *collective* responsibility, as each individual now seeks to ensure that they cannot be held personally responsible. This is against the essence of the General Duties of the Companies Act 2006. These values of domination by the regulator are reflected in the "regime" title. It suggests little discretionary ability under the UK's long-established value of principles-based governance. This is not cooperative language. If anything, it suggests that the politicians are seeking revenge on the banking sector in two ways: first, by encouraging the regulators to abandon the basis of the Companies Act; second, by being so strict in their desire to impose some form of qualification on banking directors that they are now screening out suitably diverse people for directorships who could guarantee the "independence of thought" and ensure the "care, skill and diligence" demanded of banking directors under the Companies Act. Their panic is consciously reducing the gene pool from which effective future banking directors can come. This is a classic short-term fix that will create unhealthy long-term problems. They have created four different categories of directors on banking boards none of which are in the Companies Act: "non-executive directors", "executive directors", "approved directors" and "non-approved directors". These strange combinations are guaranteed to create confusion and division around what is meant to be a "unitary" board. As Henry IV says, "uneasy lies the head that wears the crown".[101] This is not conducive to effective governance.

The confusing words used to describe directors

In an attempt to demonstrate how confusing such titles can be, I have drawn up a list of the more common current "director" titles in general circulation:

- Registered or statutory director (the default position)
- "Accidental" director (the most common category – they are unaware that they are legally acting as directors and have not registered, nor are they aware of their exposure)
- Non-executive directors (a nonsense title as they may be part-time but have the same statutory duties as all directors)
- Executive directors (another nonsense title: most executive directors don't realize that they need two different employment contracts, one as a director and one as an executive employee)
- Shadow directors (who influence events from behind the scenes; they, too, rarely realize that they have the same duties and liabilities as a registered director but usually without liability insurance)
- "Representative" directors (who are unlawful; see below)
- The chairman of the board of directors (which is correct; but note that they are not the chairmen of their companies but only of the board)

- The managing director (but not the chief executive officer, unless they are also registered as a director of the company)

And that is before we get into the fashionable US title nonsense.
So let us go back to the basics of corporate governance.

What is corporate governance?
The "director's dilemma"

As I have already written much in this area,[102] I have chosen to explore here only the key issues relating to the present rot.

Based on those basic governance values of accountability, probity and transparency, "corporate governance" seeks to solve a fundamental problem for anyone charged with giving direction to an organization: how can we drive our organization forward, while keeping it under prudent control – otherwise known as the "director's dilemma"? Directors are legally responsible for both, simultaneously. The "drive forward" aspect of the dilemma is to "ensure the success of the company", according to company law, while also ensuring that the company and its executives are "under prudent oversight of their actions". This is the complex, continuous and difficult intellectual challenge for every board. Yet most boards focus only on the prudent control aspects as they tend to be populated by executives who will know a lot more about this. "The future" is seen as too difficult. It is full of uncertainty and risk which, being executives, they are still keen to avoid.

In the UK, the Commonwealth and the European Union, I advocate that the director's dilemma should be applicable to all nationally registered organizations – including state-owned enterprises, trades unions, partnerships, local governments and not-for-profit organizations. In stopping the rot, we are all seeking to invest heavily in creating and regulating effective corporate governance, so why restrict it only to the directors of listed companies? Surely our nations would derive increased social and financial wealth from such a comprehensive approach? The competent delivery of effective corporate governance demands the continuing resolution of the director's dilemma.

The competence of our national organizations' leaders and governors should be regularly tested against this.

Defining direction-giving

The modern, global corporate governance movement derives from the intellect and energies of the Quaker and human-values-driven Sir Adrian Cadbury, who died in 2015. The publication of his *The Financial Aspects of Corporate Governance*,[103] commissioned by the then International Stock Exchange, London, and the Institute of Chartered Accountants of England and Wales, shocked most directors and politicians. They suddenly realized that directing was a proper job, a crucial role and not just a (honorary?) title. Unfortunately, the backing by such heavy financial services groupings has created two myths. The first is that the report only applies to listed companies and their financial business values. Paradoxically, the second myth is that the report is complete in itself and not a work in progress. It is seen by many politicians internationally as a fixed template for all organizations. Many have subsequently tried to apply it regardless of whether or not it fits. The report was a belated response to Lord Halifax's comment that "the trouble with British companies is that they mark their own examination papers".[104] It undoubtedly raised the profile of "corporate governance" internationally and introduced it to many. But now, despite its "comply or explain" ethos, it is becoming mired in ever more regulatory processes that add little. For over 20 years I worked with and was in correspondence with Sir Adrian. Just before he died, and in relation to this book, he insisted that I must do all I can to get the focus of corporate governance back to the primacy of ensuring the success of the business. He was increasingly concerned about the growing fixation with the primacy of compliance.

Feedback for the board

The second derivation of *kubernetes* (the origin of the word "governance") (see page 4) – "cybernetics" – is highly topical today and yet unknown by many directors, politicians and the public. Its meaning comes from sense of *kubernetes* relating to the feedback control and learning systems of a direction-giving mechanism. It seems that this second meaning has skipped a couple of millennia, but it resurfaced after World War II in the work of Norbert Weiner,[105] Reg Revans,[106] Stafford Beer[107] and W.R. Ashby[108] as the "systems thinking", "feedback loops", "requisite variety (diversity)" and "action learning" concepts that emerged to drive our organizational development thinking forward. Boards are becoming more comfortable using these sustainable learning systems, especially in the "age of uncertainty". Politicians, directors, regulators and owners: please take note.

Directing not managing

To go deeper into the current corporate governance debate we need to review a very common public misperception. Most people assume that the words "managing" and "directing" are synonymous. They are not. They are abused continually by the media, managers, politicians, owners, regulators and by directors themselves. This does not make such abuse right. Legally, registered directors are jointly and personally liable for the total performance of their organization, not managers, nor politicians. "Directors" are personally bound by a tough set of laws, usually the Companies Act or ordinances of their country. Their personal wealth can be at risk if they take unlawful actions in not ensuring the success of their organizations. Managers are much less constrained. Directors', not managers', general duties are specified under Sections 171 and 172 of the UK's 2006 Companies Act and are followed in many of the Commonwealth countries. I feel that these duties are so fundamental in the induction and development of any leader of any organization that they are worth reinforcing here:

- To act within their powers (the company's constitution)
- To ensure the success of their company
- To exercise independent judgement
- To exercise reasonable care, skill and diligence
- To avoid conflicts of interest
- Not to accept benefits from third parties
- To declare interests in proposed transactions

Moreover, I argue that these basic directoral duties are so important for the nation that all registered directors should be regularly assessed on them. These duties are, after all, the basis of their professional competence.

Managing

The directors' role is to ensure the success of their businesses through their strategic thinking and consequent decisions on coping with uncertainty. This relates to their changing and complex external world and their consequent broad deployment of the company's scarce resources to achieve their legally defined purpose. It is a critical *oversight* role, a helicopter view by the board of the future and their role in creating it.

This is quite different from the executive's important but separate daily "managing" role. The word "management" entered the English language in the late Tudor times, and most agree that it derived from the rather macho Italian word *manegiarre*, which relates to the handling of a wild horse and subduing it to one's will. "Manager" is later also related to the 17th-century French word *maneger*, which relates to the domestic organization of a kitchen and household. Both of these "male" and "female" characteristics still apply to the modern English term "management". This has been forgotten in many accepted business values, which often over-emphasize the macho aspects and so run themselves into difficulty on the "caring" aspects.

Modern management concerns the overall control of the day-to-day *operational* roles of the organization. Managers may control up to 95% of the daily time and resources of their organization, but that does not mean that they are directing it. Curiously, unlike directors, managers have very few laws to define their role, apart from civil obligations and criminal issues like the breaking of health and safety legislation, employment, environmental protection, bribery or anti-slavery laws. Managers do not create policy or strategy, but they should generate key information and ideas for the directors to work in and then work with them on the implementation of that strategy. But it is the directors who are liable for that strategy. In the final part of this chapter I give some examples of what can go well and what can go wrong. More detailed examples are found in *The Fish Rots from the Head*.[109]

What corporate governance is not

UK corporate governance drifted slowly into a cul-de-sac after the initial wild enthusiastic, awareness-raising and attitude-changing launch by Sir Adrian Cadbury and his committee. The direction-giving and leadership focus aspects of corporate governance have since been diluted. It has, like risk management, been captured by a mixture of operational managers and risk-averse bureaucrats. I am talking here more of the new corporate governance "experts" within organizations than the regulators. It is in these "experts'" career interests to avoid the very essence of corporate governance: i.e. exercising their *personal* judgement and taking thoughtful risks to ensure their organization's continuing success. Those currently involved in corporate governance, or its growing support industry, have rarely had the necessary training or experience to *take* thoughtful risks. They are not chosen for their imagination, ingenuity or tolerance of ambiguity. Neither are they assessed regularly on their competences.

Instead, they work to reduce the complex governance concept to a box-ticking exercise, and they thoughtlessly assume that a ticked box must indicate compliance and therefore good governance. This is *reductio ad absurdum* nonsense. This is a rules-based approach from the board that allows the executives to do anything they want without using moral judgement. Remember that Enron ticked all the boxes, was 100% compliant, and became a noted criminal failure because the directors and executives did not fulfil their roles honestly. Prudent control and compliance is only one aspect of effective corporate governance. But, until the legislators and regulators enforce the primary legislation of the seven general duties of directors as a national development policy, it will remain compliance-bound.

Sadly, current corporate governance thinking tends to be moving sideways, rather than forward, like a crab, scuttling to create more rules to evade risk and avoid the future. This is the antithesis of inclusive capitalism. Until regulators refocus their aim, and start reinforcing the intellectual and human behavioural demands of the director's dilemma, the rot continues. The public will remain angry, querulous and frustrated. And rightly so.

Director induction: the crucial legal aspects missed and their human values consequences

The casual and unconscious acceptance of "unlimited liability"

Most directors that I have met, and almost all managers, dismiss my focus on directors' legal duties as overdone, on both a personal level and in their stewardship role of their legal entity. "Nobody really takes them seriously because if they did we'd all end up in court" is a typical response. In so many countries, the induction of a new member to the board is only a chat with the chairman, a long and often baffling session with the company secretary on roles, responsibilities and legal liabilities, and then the handing-over of a vast pile of papers – including the memorandum and articles of association, and selected sections of the Companies Act or equivalent. It is not expected that the new director reads these documents carefully, and is tested on them, nor is there any expectation that they are meant to live by their instructions. This is seen as an unrealistic demand.

If the new directors are lucky, they will get a quick tour of the organization. After which, it is assumed by both parties that they are automatically "inducted" and, therefore, miraculously "competent". Yet the law expects omniscience unless there is a very good reason to show otherwise. Such induction is nonsense and very dangerous nonsense at that. It has negative effects on the long-term social and financial health of a nation. It is in no way a personal benchmarking and development process. Board competence metrics are rarely specified, benchmarked or monitored. Yet this is what so many new "directors" are offered as the prelude to their acceptance of their duty of "care, skill and competence". Moreover, at the induction stage, directors will have little notion of what these mean in practice. Yet it is usually at this stage that they sign their registration forms as a director and so put their personal, and often their family's, wealth on the line by accepting unlimited liability. I go into the messy history behind this in Chapter 4. No wonder most directors feel that they are exposed – they are. HR directors and company secretaries need to be much more aware of this key aspect of director induction and be more careful in their directoral induction processes.

The differences between "managing directors" and "chief executives"

Confusion is caused by the lax use of these two job titles. They are not interchangeable. The only difference between a "managing director" and a "chief executive" is that a managing director is automatically a member of a board because they must be registered nationally as a director. A chief executive is not a registered director. If he or she is registered, then his/her legal title is managing director. The frequent misuse of the term "chief executive" is the result of a continuing British fashion to import US words, regardless of whether or not they fit with the UK and Commonwealth legal systems. These terms are dangerously confusing to owners, directors and the public. Sadly, through a mixture of ignorance, arrogance and fashion, the term "chief executive" is currently thought of as more sexy than "managing director". But, given the mess that many American CEOs have made of their listed businesses, this is a dangerous path to follow.

I mentioned that I feel that the US is becoming a corporate governance basket case. This is not only because of CEO hegemony but also because of the distorting and confusing power battles between the federal government and state legislatures over the power of development and control of corporate governance. This is best avoided by other nations if they can escape the vampire squid of US extraterritorial foreign policy. This does mean that all foreigners have to be prepared to fight that wretched American political policy. It is worth the battle. It will take many decades for it to be rectified because of the current constitutional stalemate in the US.

The politicians' troubles with corporate governance

The arrogance of politicians and civil servants, together with the ignorance of the corporate governance laws and codes they themselves have passed, are at the heart of much of the public's, and many directors', misunderstandings about the value of effective corporate governance. Many politicians cannot even quote two of the seven general duties of directors from their company or ordinance acts. Test this by asking them. Their lack of such basic knowledge is deeply worrying. Yet most politicians talk publicly, posture, and ultimately legislate, on these issues of national importance – sadly only on the orders of the party whips.

However, rising public anger and continuing daily media examples of corporate governance failures mean that pressure is rising on boards, owners, regulators and the politicians. The main public demand is that directors, owners, regulators and politicians are assessed regularly on their governance competence. But, currently, it seems highly unlikely that any of these four players will willingly submit themselves for such an assessment. This is why the public must demand it. Such political tests are usually restricted to elections every four years or so. We have yet to convince the public that they need to become the fifth active player in a wider national corporate governance action-learning system.

Corporate governance as a learning system

Learning as the human values-based culture

In some of the world's leading economies, including the UK, South Africa, Canada, Australia, but excluding the US, we are seeing the evolution of an agreed set of human values, processes and regulations for leadership and national development: usually under the banner of "ethical leadership".[110] An article in the *Financial Times* by Klaus Schwab of the World Economic Forum, written on the 11 January 2017 shows this concern well.[111]

Why, if we already have such good, and codified, national leadership and corporate governance knowledge and practice, do we treat it as virtually confidential? Why is the public excluded? This is partly because the term "corporate governance" is not understood by the public and sounds intimidating to them. Politicians will therefore use it to claim that they are doing something big, important and topical for the public. But the words scare off all but the very bravest of intelligently naïve enquirers. The phrase is not accepted as a key aspect of developing our national social and wealth-creating culture.

Such public enquiry is resented by those power brokers currently running corporate governance. They find it restricts their freedom of organizational actions. However, following the Western financial crash of 2008 and the continuing wealth-destroying effects of quantitative easing on the general population, such enquiry must be encouraged from the public. South Africa is a nation that accepts that such discipline must apply to all of their organizations. Their understanding of the universal nature of the director's dilemma is thought to be crucial for their national development and the detailed questioning needed is made explicit in their King 4 Report of 2016.[112]

The learning board in a learning organization

Having written so much on this issue over 30 years, especially in *The Fish Rots from the Head* and *Thin on Top*, I shall sketch out here only the rationale and outline of the "learning organization", with the "learning board" as its central processor.

Reg Revans[113] showed that, for any organism to continue to exist, its rate of learning must be equal to, or greater than, the rate of change in its external environment – $L \geq C$ (see Figure 3).

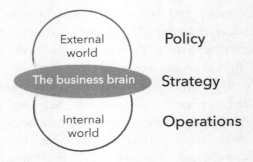

- Accepts that good and bad learning occurs continuously at all levels of the organization
- Focuses on systems for capturing learning fast
- Values people and their learning
- Forgiveness culture, provided one learns

Figure 3: Learning organisation: basic model

Learning is based on the acquisition of information, its interpretation, and then the action to test and refine it consciously to ensure an organism's sustainability. This is as true for a single cell as for an individual or an organization. "Learning", which is derived from Anglo-Saxon and was used by St Cuthbert, has always had an intensely personal meaning quite different from "teaching".

The learning organization

The learning organization (see Figure 4) takes the concept of $L \geq C$ as its basic organizational design. Most of its managers and staff will spend over 90% of their time in the internal, managed "operational" world, trying to deliver plans and projects through their prudent control systems to generate the necessary levels of performance from the system. This is daily "work" for most folk. Our operational world is full of risks. These risks manifest themselves as deviations from plans and they disrupt the smooth running of the organization. Then most organizational energies are put into getting back on track, often in panic mode. "Hurry-up-and-wait" is the disrupted reality of most people's working lives.

Figure 4: Learning organization: complex model

Simultaneously, the wider external environment continues to change in random and uncertain ways – political, economic, social, technological – and trade patterns are rarely predictable. Few directors pay any systematic attention to these uncertainties. This is often because they are life-long managers and find it difficult to rise to the broader intellectual challenges of a new director's role in handling uncertainty. So they stick to the known comfort of managing. They are more used to, and get immediate satisfaction from, "solving" immediate organizational problems than taking time out to consider longer-term external changes and trends, many of which will have no short-term, tangible results. But this then leaves a huge hole in board responsibilities if no-one is paying attention to the external changes and trends caused by disruptions to the environment. The board's key role is to ensure the integration of the operational and directing cycles. This is why we have to have a board of directors. In Figure 4 this integration process is shown as a figure-of-eight or a "continuous double loop of learning" – a lemniscate curve.

The learning board

The board's key role is at the intersection of those two loops of learning – the thoughtful bringing-together of the operational and the strategic worlds to address the perennial director's dilemma: how do we ensure the success of the business while keeping it under prudent control?

There are two activities the board must then undertake continually to resolve this dilemma:

1. Ensuring future success
   - Policy formulation and foresight
   - Strategic thinking
2. Ensuring prudent control
   - Supervising management
   - Ensuring accountability

This drawing, like all business consultancy and education figures, is based on a two-dimensional model. The vertical axis focuses on the board's internal and external perspectives; the horizontal axis focuses on its long-term and short-term perspectives. My observations show that the majority of boards concentrate their time on the bottom-left box – supervising management. This is wrong, but hardly surprising. Having been brought up as managers, this is their comfort zone. But they then overdo it, and an overdone strength is usually seen as a weakness by others, especially staff reporting to such a director. "Managing from the boardroom table" is a common complaint from exasperated managers who are trying to do their own job when the directors are also trying to do it for them.

But then the directors would, wouldn't they? My research into the thinking preferences of such directors[114] shows that only 5% of

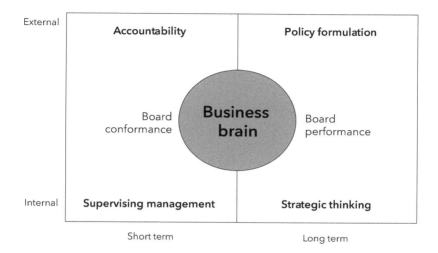

Figure 5: Learning board: basic model

directors prefer structured thinking about the future. They feel that this denies their prime supervisory role of the daily operations. They are much more interested in the micro-politics of the present and are comfortable to spend over 80% of their time there. This helps explain why the necessary, and intellectually stretching, aspects of policy formulation – clarifying and testing purpose, creating vision and values, developing a long-term culture, regularly monitoring the external environment – are avoided. Crisis seems the preferred thinking style of most directors, as opposed to thoughtful policy-making. We are back to the rejection of "soft" aspects here.

This means that the interface between policy-making and strategic thinking – monitoring the external environment – is not often prioritized by the board. It is not handled systematically, and is often relegated to just a one-day "away-day jolly" as a way of legitimizing socializing over good food and drink. Which means that true systematic strategic thinking rarely occurs. Even worse, the "thinking" aspect is often replaced by the erosive managerial concept of strategic planning: a dangerous oxymoron. Planning is a purely managerial role relating to plans, targets and performance measures. These are necessary, but not sufficient for governance. They should not be substituted by the board for the higher-level process of strategic thinking. Remember what I said in Chapter 2 on the four international trends forming future corporate governance? This is a key aspect of developing board professionalism. Figure 5 is developed in detail in Figure 6 on page 160.

I stress the key role of the chairman and the board as the "learning leaders" in any organization and the role of the chairman's office and the managing director in being seen to be the central processor of the learning organization in their drive for professionalism. Here I want to focus on some of the key practical aspects of directoral development.

What should effective corporate governance look like in action?

Directoral competence

You have to have some sympathy for those appointed as directors because so few are offered serious induction, assessment and self-development processes. So three good questions for the public to ask of directors at AGMs are: "How rigorous are your board induction, training, development and annual assessment processes? And how transparent are they to the shareholders and the stakeholders? What evidence is there for this?" The general indifference to assessing directoral competence is, I argue, a major cause of the current rot in our institutions.

Is there any hard evidence for promoting board competence? Yes. In May 2014, Hermes Fund Managers published an analysis of the MSCI World Equity Index[115] for the period December 2008–2013. Hermes is a leading proponent of assessable board competence, and adds environmental, social and governance (ESG) dimensions into its evaluation of company and investment performance. It directly manages investment funds of $43.5 billion and has more than an additional $163 billion under stewardship. It found that well-governed companies outperformed poorly governed ones by 0.3% points *per month*. However, the environmental and social factors are not yet statistically significant in terms of governance. The research saw no outperformance for their investors from the best-governed companies, but the 20% less-well-governed companies underperformed significantly in investment returns. Of special mention in continuing underperformance were such issues as lack of board independence, excessive remuneration and complacency due to poison-pill defences. Underperformance in Asia was 0.6% points a month, but was much lower in the US, where stronger regulation and the constant threat of litigation helped at least with compliance aspects of governance.

It is not that directors are by nature incompetent, stupid or lazy. But they are frequently ignorant of the full legal range of their roles, responsibilities, personal liabilities and the necessary developmental strategic and policy formulation processes to fulfil them. It is nonsense for both directors and the public to allow this unsatisfactory and organizationally debilitating situation to continue. The fish truly does rot from the head.

Learning from three examples of corporate governance failure

Case study: the Co-operative Bank Group

Corporate governance failure is not just confined to banking. A surprise has come from a previously well-trusted and loved national institution: the Co-operative Society. Founded in 1844, "the Co-op" was a "mutual", founded on strictly ethical values, created for and by working-class people. Its constitution states:

> It is to be the most socially responsible company in the UK; our purpose is beyond profit ... some things are plainly unjust and need to be tackled with or without a business case. We've learnt that we need to manage and develop our business in a sustainable manner and will always be transparent and accountable in our pursuit of this. We are guided by the long-established co-operative

values of self-help, self-responsibility, democracy, equality, equity and solidarity.[116]

So all the fashionable words are there and in the right order. What could possibly go wrong with such espoused values? The answer is found in the Co-operative Bank, founded in 1872, its conflict being between its espoused values and its accepted business values, and the supine behaviour of the board. They were "good" people who had agreed that the bank had to become "more business-like". It took over the Britannia Building Society, an area in which it had scant experience. This was queried by Co-op members and by the City of London. But the board persisted. Public and membership criticism increased sharply when it then failed to conduct full due diligence in its proposed takeover of 600 branches of the TSB bank. Then it transpired that the Co-op Bank was on the brink of bankruptcy. Where was the board? How could they go along with such a seemingly random business model? And why did they not feel bound by their espoused corporate governance and ethical values?

The surprise promotion of the inexperienced Reverend Flowers to chairman of the Co-operative Bank, his subsequent relations with his "unruly board's" lack of directoral competence, together with the weak ethical values demonstrated by the regulator in allowing him to take the post in the first place, caused greater public outrage. This outrage was fanned by the media as the business rotted quickly. Its humiliation continued, following the arrest of the Methodist Reverend Flowers on drugs and sex charges. Brought before the Treasury Select Committee, he could not even give the figures for the basic assets of his own bank. The saga continued in March 2014 when the new group chief executive, Euan Sutherland, resigned after spending just a few months in office. He claimed that the group was "ungovernable" and that he could not convince the group board to support his rescue plans because they were unwilling to accept the reality of their situation, and because they refused to accept that "good people like us would do bad things". He felt that he had entered a Kafkaesque nightmare, trapped in a psychic prison. The board was unable to give direction, nor demonstrate prudent control. The director's dilemma was left unaddressed.

Ironically, this all occurred in a business that was publicly perceived to be whiter-than-white. Mutuals like the Co-op are founded and owned by the community, based on strong ethical values, and "led by the needs and interests of their customers". With an example like this, you can understand why the public has generally lost their trust in all business leadership and governance. In May 2014, the Co-operative members finally agreed to implement the previously rejected Myners Plan, and began a structural and cultural rethink of "the Co-op". As ever, the test will be in its implementation. In February 2017 the Co-op Bank was put up for sale but with seemingly little buyer interest in the whole. So, in the public's mind, it is left to the redoubtable John Lewis Partnership to carry the flag for the mutuals and the notion of employee participation and good governance.

The rise of the new disciplines in corporate governance and the fall of the old guard

Restoring such trust and co-operation is not just a case of reinforcing existing business disciplines and attitudes. Directors must also accept that different value sets must become paramount. As Alan Greenspan has discovered,[117] human values, behavioural economics and anthropology are needed to cope with the psychology of human dynamics, the continuing effects of fear and greed, and the need to work with higher levels of continuing uncertainty to achieve their purpose.

Only when nations recognize directing as a distinct profession linked directly to the collective responsibilities of the board, and develop the appropriate training, assessment, ethical and disciplinary codes, shall corporate governance be acknowledged as a self-regulating national asset. The good news is that we are closer to this than many realize. Below, I outline some current trends.

Restoring honesty in business

The worried public assume levels of professionalism and competence in their business leaders which frequently do not exist. This is one reason why management consultancy exists – a corporate service to sort out damaged organizations and to get them back on the road as quickly as possible without major redesign. But rather than keep making the same mistakes we need to accept the deeper value that all business relies on the validated behaviour of "My word is my bond". Without it, no financial credit can be given or taken, nor can organizations be governed. We saw during the era of "self-certified mortgage applications" that automation does not allow human judgement to assess the risk that both parties to a transaction are honest. Look at the mess that this got UK banks into. Honesty was not considered a central value of the contract.

The public are still puzzled and angered by the duration of the Western financial crisis, as they watch their pensions and savings disappear. They ask, "But surely businesses should have been much better at forecasting, tracking, and managing their risks to stop the rot before it caused the crisis?" After all, the larger companies have entire departments devoted to horizon-scanning, business intelligence gathering, risk assessment, forecasting, compliance and marketing. The results of these expert information flows, their cybernetic learning system, are then meant to reach the very top of their organizations, where the board of directors, not the managers and executives, is charged with delivering on those two fundamental horns of the director's dilemma. It seldom does. And the rot starts.

Case study 2: "market-based" NHS health practitioners

As an example of what is happening in the UK, and of the mixture of ignorance and contempt with which corporate governance is treated by politicians and civil servants, I have spoken with groups of primary care medics – general practitioners ("GPs") – who are setting out to help create allied private businesses to serve the changing needs of the UK National Health Service (NHS). They are being given alarmingly large sums of public money to implement this process, seemingly without sufficient governmental oversight, training, assessment of competence levels, a conflict-of-interest reporting system, or external audit. I have grave doubts about the rigour of the implementation of this initiative, and of governmental accountancy, auditing, and the ethical processes for monitoring the emerging "purchaser/provider split" of these new "businesses". I predict that there will be more public enquiries into this sloppily designed and monitored process.

But I have even graver doubts about the quality of corporate governance thinking and design being deployed. Remember that, in the UK, people can simply register as a "director" once they have signed the appropriate forms at Companies House. This does not guarantee that they have any training or experience to be a competent director. Nor does the NHS encourage them to get this experience. I have asked GPs, setting up new businesses, if they would let an untrained doctor operate on their patients in the hope that they might "pick it up as they go along". Every GP I asked replied, "Of course not." So why do ministers and civil servants let medics blunder naïvely into this area of business?

Directoral competence does not seem to be a commodity among such business-bound GPs. Nor does the NHS demand any such guarantee of competence in the directors of new businesses. From most of the GPs I have spoken to, I get embarrassed eye-avoidance, some throat clearing, but little contrition or time commitment towards developing their new profession. The future court cases that are likely to emerge from their likely lack of competence, even fraud in the misallocation of contracts to members with conflicts of interest, coupled with questionable purchasing deals, will be enlightening but very expensive for the nation. Few seem to have heard of, or care about, the Fraud Act. Anyone willing to advocate an NHS Businesses Hippocratic Oath? Effective corporate governance and directoral competence are rarely seen as obligatory in the NHS, until a disaster is made public. By then it is always too late, and, even then, the focus is only on the single organization involved, as we have seen with the Mid Staffordshire hospital disaster.[118] So the rot of disaster, public enquiry and a call for "better corporate governance" is repeated.

Case Study 3: the immoral brilliance of marketing to the US Ninjas

Public trust in the US government was eroded massively during the Ninja ("No incomes, no jobs, no assets") loans scandal, otherwise known as the "Sub-prime loans scandal". A fashionable get-rich-quick financial business model was developed, generated by the US *government's* Freddie Mac and Fannie Mae housing agencies' need to keep selling mortgages as the politicians released ever-increasing amounts of "cheap" credit into the financial system. This encouraged growing indebtedness in the public. The problem was that the market for home loan mortgages was already flooded, so what business model could now be used?

The immoral brilliance of the solution that private finance developed still beggars belief: to consciously sell mortgages to people who could not afford them. Any rational, ethical board would not have allowed this, but in the febrile and corrupted "animal spirits" system of the early noughties in the US there was serious money to be made if you were quick and had no moral conscience. And the government seemed happy to turn a blind eye. It became fashionable, therefore, for financiers to move into this "sub-prime" market, despite the obvious business illogicality. Financial services are a fashion business, so everyone seemed keen to join in. Remember that, in the US, this was mainly government money being punted out via agents to poor folk who were desperate to get on the housing ladder to give their families shelter and possibly some equity. Obviously, they could not repay their mortgages, but the new business model approved by their boards asked, "Who cares?" So they developed plans to expand the lunacy of their risky game. And soon the "sub-prime" disaster started to unfold, eventually triggering the 2008 Western financial crisis.

Matters may not have been so disastrous for Western economies and politicians had the complexity, interactivity and remorseless continuity of the international financial system not been developed to such a level of 24/7 "sophistication". There is always a continuous demand for quick personal rewards by executives and investors, and especially ones with an over-long string of intermediaries each demanding *their* cut. Greed and gluttony were infectious. It seemed obvious to any outside observer that you could not sell on Ninja mortgages without finally breaking this dubious business model. Their boards should have asked "And then what?", but none did, because clever manipulators had developed an answer even to that.

Such irrationality did not worry the cunning financial marketers, who believed that the velocity of credit generated greater short-term profits and bonuses than any thoughtful longer-term investment could. However, the "normal" business model still needed to be corrupted further, in order to answer the reasonable question, "How would you find a willing buyer for such an obviously toxic investment?" This is where the immoral, self-seeking attitude, which came to characterize our international financial markets, came into play. In boardrooms and executive suites around the country, it was argued, with a straight face, that, if you could take these underperforming mortgages and "securitize" them – by chopping them up into smaller, mixed packages, then getting a supposedly unbiased credit rating agency to add a small sliver of highly prized Triple A rating on top (for which they would get a higher and questionable payment) – then these packages could be punted out into the markets for trading and everyone could take their cut. This was entirely reliant on the "pass the toxic parcel" game never stopping. If, like the financial marketers, you are blinkered by only immediate returns, then you can create an Alice-through-the looking-glass world in which everyone must be a winner, everything will be OK always. The customer must never know that the scam was taking place. But, if the music stops, then all hell breaks loose.

And so it came to pass. Inevitably, the music did stop and, following the Lehman Brothers Bank crash in 2008, customers and shareholders around the world discovered a rotting pile of bad debts, mis-selling, and dodgy financial instruments way beyond the consequences of the sub-prime scam. Even today, these deals are so baroquely complex that no-one knows who owes what to whom. As a consequence, we see countries in massive debt, with an addicted financial "system" and a disillusioned public seeing no, even negative, returns on their savings and investments. The financial and political elite permitted a ruthless scam on the punters; and many made themselves super-rich, and the rest of society much poorer. Little wonder that there is still massive public anger towards bankers. And remember that this crass example was only in the *retail* banking sectors, which was meant to be the boring, stable part of the financial system.

In the investment banks, matters were just as bad. The Big Bang took the banks' eyes off of the primacy of service to clients (trading only for them) and onto trading for the bank itself. It did not take long for investment bankers, especially traders reinforced by big bonuses, to subordinate the clients' funds to their own, thereby massively increasing the clients' risk, without necessarily keeping them informed, and building banks' funds for continuous reinvestment. The development of ever-more complex instruments to support such investments seemed to baffle clients and, later, the bankers themselves. We still see them trying desperately to unscramble such mis-selling as credit default swaps especially to smaller businesses who never understood the instrument or the risks involved, and never needed them in the first place. This was a bitter pill to swallow for otherwise sound medium-sized businesses, some of whom were forced into administration by the banks' own actions. This scandal is still being played out in courts, with the jailing of a handful of middle-ranking HBOS bankers, hopefully the start of a much wider process.

This is worlds away from the concept of partnership banking, where the partners sit together, across partners' desks, assessing risks and returns, debating them openly, and then putting their own capital at risk. Sir Brian Pitman's worst fears were realized. When he died in 2010, he was trying to build a new version of a high-street retail bank along the old, successful lines that the public still demanded, trusted, yet could not find. Where do you now find a trusted bank?

In all these cases, the public is right in asking: where was the board? And what had happened to its critical oversight role? It seems that CEO hegemony is rife in banking. This is still a mystery to the public, particularly as the "great and the good" sit on these boards and have not been punished for their laxness. They are charged legally with both the forward development of the enterprise and its prudent control. So why did they not do this? I argue that it is because they did not understand the absolute nature of their general directoral duties, as distinct from demonstrated managerial prowess, nor had they been trained in, or had much experience of, the industry that they were now directing.

"Non-professional" bankers

Matters are made worse in the public's mind by the fact that no contrition has been shown, as Cardinal Nichols, the Catholic Archbishop of Westminster, has frequently pointed out – to the point where he has created the "Blueprint for Better Business".[119] In the UK, bankers are now rated by the public as the least popular work group, below even estate agents and journalists.[120] In 2013, at Cass Business School, a school noted for its large graduate recruitment by the City of London, not a single management graduate wished to go into banking as a career. Previously there had been a scrum to join such Masters of the Universe.

Giving back and the modern Liveries

This gut reaction by the Masters students demonstrated an interesting volte-face. Graduates were more interested in becoming entrepreneurs and manufacturers; which sounds a lot more healthy and human values-based. It allows them to do something much more constructive than being a mere pawn in gaming the financial system. They wanted to participate in creating social, natural and financial capital and, most importantly, to be able "to give something back to society", rather than trade parasitically on the ignorance of others. The rise of the "modern" Livery companies in the Corporation of London is a useful example of professional people wanting to rise above narrow professional interests. One outstanding example is the Worshipful Company of Management Consultants, of whom I am a Past Master. With only 180 members, they have run a pro-bono consulting programme for 14 years for "small and unfashionable charities", and have helped 1,200 of them by working as mentors or consultants giving the equivalent of over £5 million worth of consulting hours for free. The demand continues to grow. It encourages me that their motto is "Change Through Wisdom" – very human and professional values. They are humble enough to realize that in giving back they improve their learning processes and derive wisdom from this.

Directors and their necessary learning processes

My focus on the centrality of learning is because of my belief that, in developing the truly effective corporate governance values of accountability, probity and transparency, building individual and board competences can stop the rot. Ultimately, the development of a broader and more effective *national* learning system of corporate governance oversight will stabilize and then help develop a better civil society. Effective governance is a learnable asset. We need *national* agreement to achieve this. The final chapter of this book (Chapter 6) maps the dimensions for such an initiative and suggests the necessary mind-set changes and practical steps needed to get there. But we have to clear some directoral blockages first.

Despite all the rhetoric about the UK "having the best corporate governance in the world", the truth is that there is no national *system* of corporate governance in the UK. I argue that Sir Adrian Cadbury peaked too early. From his brilliant intellectual and practical analysis of 1992[121] we have built pragmatically, over some 25 years, unintegrated elements that have failed to become a system. We have responded to political whims but there is little integration even between the corporate governance requirements of listed and unlisted companies. There is almost none between directors, owners, regulators and politicians. Sadly, neither is there the national political will to do so. But then many directors put little energy even into their own learning.

Blockages to directoral learning

Why do directors still baulk at the necessity of being *seen* to learn? I believe that there are two major reasons. First, the perceived threat of not being seen to be omniscient – of not knowing everything about everything. In truth no-one can know everything, and the admission of ignorance is the first step to gaining knowledge and wisdom. But, if you do not even know the seven general duties of directors, then you are hardly going to admit your wider lacunae. Second, there is a lack of systems thinking prevalent in our society and in directors. Its integrative nature is not encouraged in most schools or universities. So many directors and politicians are ignorant of the nature and utility of cybernetics, ironically at the time when the manipulation of big data is coming into its own.

So our present leaders fixate during their working lives on the micro-politics of managerial thinking rather than directoral thinking. Directors are not yet trained to think both creatively and systematically, so we consider any consequent learning in these areas irrelevant or even personally threatening. There is still a discernible arts–science split in our societies, with many politicians either arts-inclined or partly seduced by the soft science of "social science", as distinct from psychology or anthropology. C.P. Snow's dire warnings of this continuing "two cultures" educational divide live on in our elite classes.[122] This affects our ability to think critically and dispassionately *across* disciplines. Thus we are condemned to repeat our mistakes because we cannot integrate and rigorously review the facts and likely consequences of our complex organizational data, ideas and actions. Only the modern military seem different in having almost an obsession about learning from their "wash-up sessions" after their *daily* activities. They are focused on continuous learning and training and are a model for business and not-for-profit organizations. They have a vested interest in not being killed. But have you ever seem a training and development budget *increased* to facilitate fast learning?

Divergent thinking and long-termism

A major problem is that, throughout our secondary, tertiary, professional and managerial training, we are taught "convergent thinking". Instant success is defined by focusing on a single "solvable" issue often to the exclusion of any wider contextual consequences. This delivers "single shot" solutions which may have a short-term pay-off for managers. But, when directors are dealing with longer-term and higher-level issues of complexity and uncertainty, they need to develop a more "divergent thinking" approach – focusing first on the wider contextual and messy environments, before refocusing much more sensitively on reaching an integrated, multidisciplinary solution better at adapting to its changing environments. And even then they must be willing to change it rapidly if the uncertain environment changes again. For many executives these are alien processes. If they are made directors without a conversion process, they will fail.

John Maynard Keynes, "inventor" of macroeconomics, recognized these issues back in 1924 in relation to the development of effective economists:

> He must be mathematician, historian, statesman, philosopher – in some degree. He must understand symbols and speak in words. He must contemplate the particular in terms of the general, and touch abstract and concrete in the same flight of thought ... No part of man's nature or his institutions must lie entirely outside his regard. He must be purposeful and disinterested in a simultaneous mood; as aloof and incorruptible as an artist, yet sometimes as near the earth as a politician.[123]

I believe that such a description perfectly fits an effective professional director. Keynes continued with a hope that economists were at their best if they were "humble, competent people on a level with dentists". But then he was always a dreamer.

Decision-making in uncertainty

Directors are not trained to tolerate high levels of external uncertainty and yet must make strategic decisions that generate risks in the business's wider environments. As F. Scott Fitzgerald remarked, "the test of a first class brain is to be able to hold two contradictory thoughts in one's head and still be able to operate".[124] This is the opposite of taught managerial thought. Yet such toleration and use of uncertainty is the essence of *directoral* competence. Directors are called "directors" because they are charged with steering the company into an uncertain future. So the building of professionalism and competence based on *directoral* care, skill and diligence demands a major broadening of a director's comfort zone to be able to process, and react to, changes in the political, environmental, social, technological and world trade environments. This means that the public demands for professionalization through the regular assessment of directors, owners, regulators and legislators must include their ability to cope with high levels of uncertainty.

"Uncertainty" as used here was defined by the US mathematician Frank Knight in 1924 as "real or possible events that reduce the likelihood of reaching [business] goals and increase the probability of losses".[125]

So with my board development work we have worked on developing board members' thinking so that we differentiate between "uncertainty" and "risk" in the following way:

- Risk is where the probabilities of different outcomes are known, but not the outcome itself

- Uncertainty is where the probabilities themselves are unknown

So risks are the province of the executives. Uncertainties are the province of the board. Which is why they need to learn to cope with them.

This may seem an unrealistic demand of directors' intellect, but I argue that, in the UK, as we have already invested in the necessary elements for a national corporate governance system through our laws and codes, we now need the national political will to encourage and train these key main players to rebuild our damaged and organizational competences and reputations.

It is a national scandal that the primary law in this area – the seven general duties of directors – is not enforced more strictly. It is treated as optional by so many. The Act's sponsoring government department, Business Energy and Industrial Strategy, seems to have no great enthusiasm in publicizing the Act's relevance to society or in enforcing the law that it took eight painful years to pass through Parliament. It is still adding to that law without ensuring the effectiveness of what it has already. Separately, the UK has invested in the Corporate Governance Code[126] and now the Stewardship Code,[127] which ventures very slightly into the developing area of ownership duties.

Effective corporate governance and the UK's Financial Reporting Council

These codes are under the separate supervision of the Financial Reporting Council – which is still accountancy-oriented rather than corporate-governance-led, has few strong enforcement powers, is not a committed intellectual powerhouse driving for a better society, and has been acquiescent in the "light touch" political approach which helped increase the current rot. Sadly, it has proved easier for most businesses to yield to the costly, time-wasting codes and compliance rather than to fight for the spirit and implications of the original Cadbury Code. So "compliance" has become the name of the game for the vast majority of corporations, even charities, and the ticking of boxes has become the highest corporate governance aspiration of many boards. This is unacceptable if we are to have sustainable organizations in the future. The primary duty of "ensuring the long-term success of the business" seems to have gone out of the window, as Sir Adrian Cadbury reminded me in his final personal letter.

Corporate governance and the emergence of inclusive capitalism

I am concerned still about boards' over-reliance on the Berle and Means philosophy of free markets: that if shareholders don't like what's going on they can always sell. Berle and Means,[128] and later Ayn Rand,[129] are still held up by many directors and executives as business beacons of free-market "rationality". The "owner", in the form of multiple shareholders, was considered insignificant in such an "agency-based", CEO-dominated system. Indeed, the US system was designed specifically to *exclude* the shareholder-owner, and the directors, from executive control. If the owners chose to disagree with executive strategy and actions, then they were free to sell their shares. That was their only choice. They only had legal residual property rights to the company. They had no right to control it or, particularly in the US, regularly and rigorously to review the actions and performance of the executives, or to comment on their reward system. This is the antithesis of what I propose as an effective national corporate governance learning system based on inclusive capitalism. Yet it exists in many forms in most countries today.

CEO-hegemony capitalism exists in its most egregious form in the state of Nevada, and at its most blatant in Delaware state's Law of Plurality. This law proclaims that a new board member can be selected only from a slate drawn up by the existing board and executives. A shareholder can then vote for the proposition to the board, or abstain, but has no right to vote against it. So much for notions of shareholder democracy. And consider that the majority of large US corporations are registered in the state of Delaware. In the West, it is still too common a business mind-set that "executives rule, OK?" They often have primacy in the total running of a company and so the board of directors, and the shareholders, become annoying irrelevancies to them. I believe that this mind-set, combined with a conscious disregard of the growing power of the "stakeholders", has caused the current rot in corporations, and has led the public to perceive that all directors and executives are incompetent, uncaring and self-serving. This executive domination is as true in the public and not-for-profit sectors as it is in the private sector. It will continue unless there is a major public demand, backed by a political will, to abandon this form of executive–led capitalism and to replace it with something with a much wider, more community-inclusive model. Is there any hope of this happening? Yes.

What needs reframing

It is already starting to happen in a surprising number of countries, although many would not recognize it by this name. Some would call it "stakeholder capitalism"; I prefer "inclusive capitalism". It is capitalism, but with a much wider owner and stakeholder base, and so a more democratic debate occurs both inside and outside the corporation over its impact on natural, social and financial resources.

My work in China, East Asia, Southern and Western Africa, the Gulf, Australia and New Zealand suggests that strong socio-economic trends are already reshaping our concept of the future of capitalism, and that new corporate governance systems are being introduced to reinforce this. It is noticeable also in many of the "emerging economies" that, while they aspire to a form of capitalism, they also seek inclusive characteristics more in line with their cultures than in the West, especially the US. They do not like the Seven Deadly Sins "Western" value set. They tend to aspire to a more inclusive, national or regional mind-set that strives to consider all members of their society, despite the many hierarchical problems of achieving this. This is not purely altruistic, but more a way of signalling that, to reach sustainable growth, the benefits will need be shared more widely. This does not always currently succeed but, in time, it will.

However, I accept that in the early stages of socio-economic development, emergent economies are often characterized by a few powerful plutocratic and authoritarian owners, complete with their own shadow side of kleptocracy and nepotism. These are the nasty stages of development when open learning is difficult. This saps national resources through the effects of inefficiencies, corruption and state-organized crime. But the trends behind the public's desire for a safer and wealthier society still continue even in such societies. This is why it is so important for a country to develop a stabilizing middle class.

Towards a "licence to operate"

Two trends strike me as forcing corporate governance change in such emergent societies. Both have major implications for boards and directors internationally. First is the growing public demand for "recognized national development benefit" from the output of any corporation, private, public or not-for-profit in their country, especially from international businesses. This can be as simple as a country paying relevant taxes to ensure its people of their continuing development. But it can be as complex as ownership and revenue-sharing deals with the national government on a fixed-term contract. Recognized national benefit development is a major issue even in "developed" countries. For example, in order for it to work, a wholly owned subsidiary in any country must, however reluctantly, fully obey the company law of that nation. Many directors still have to learn this. It alone is beginning to break many international corporations' iniquitous "extra-territorial" mind-sets. Increasingly, such companies have to obey local law rather than ride roughshod over it, if they are to remain operating in that country.

This is forcing reconsiderations of *what is a company for?* as Charles Handy asked in his seminal lecture at the Royal Society of Arts in 1990.[130] This question reinforces the concerns of Adam Smith in 1776, who questioned the seemingly unlimited powers of the new joint-stock companies. He was excited by their development but he foresaw later trouble because he realized that, under the new law, such companies had been granted "the four unlimiteds": unlimited life, unlimited size, unlimited licence and so unlimited power. This was valued as a good thing. It greatly enhanced the capitalization and risk-sharing abilities of UK companies and their trading partners. It powered the fast development of the Empire through easier capital access and liquidity.

But in the 21st century, current "unequal" issues, like the payment of tax and obeying local laws, are bringing Smith's old doubts about unlimited powers into sharp focus. Behind it all is the deep and often unasked question: "should corporations automatically have unlimited life?" The old argument has been not to worry as if they were not successful they would die. But now we see some mega-companies with such global power the question needs asking again; and some developing countries are asking it. The concept that corporations should now be granted a limited "licence to operate", and must be subject to regular national public review of their economic *and* social benefit, will become a major aspect of the future corporate governance debates. Many business folk will hate this, especially those in corporations that use their unlimited size to exercise their unlimited licence. The use and abuse of such corporate power, together with the exercise of state legislative power to give or terminate life to corporations within their remit, will become a major international issue. It will not go away. It must be faced.

The concept of "recognized public good" is not new. It has been discussed for many decades. For example, within the West, the idea of integrated "triple-bottom-line reporting"[131] has been quietly gaining ground. The agency theorists have been losing ground to this idea because their assertion that the only important bottom line is financial is just not believed in many countries. If you are not making profits with a positive cash flow, then you are no longer in business. So for a board to focus only on a single bottom line is very unwise. It is necessary but not sufficient. It excludes the social and environmental contexts. There are now so many laws demanding reports on, for example, the environmental impact of a corporation's operations, and the impact on the local community, employees and suppliers, that more companies are seeing the light and changing their annual reporting systems so that both the owners and the wider public can assess their wider corporate performance. As previously mentioned, Royal Dutch Shell and Novo Nordisk have good records, over some 15 years, of clarifying and refining such annual triple-bottom-line reporting.

Stakeholders

The second trend to strike me as forcing corporate governance change in developing societies is the concept of a wider network of "stakeholders" – those involved in a corporation's activities who are not shareholders need regular, external critical reviews of a business and its operations. They include staff, suppliers, local communities and environmental conservators. These are backed increasingly by national legislation. Currently, these laws are not coordinated internationally, but they are starting to emerge, as shown by the UN Global Compact. For example, local communities are having a greater say over the environmental and economic outputs of a company through local and regional planning and employment legislation. Labour and suppliers have a growing body of laws to protect themselves, including human rights, anti-slavery and anti-people-trafficking. While these legislative powers include the owners, they are also giving such stakeholders wider sanctions over a business. These sanctions call for greater cooperation, which is the very nature of inclusive capitalism. This leads to a growing debate about reframing of what "ownership" means, which is the focus of Chapter 4.

In many countries, noticeably those within the European Union, we see a determined political push to raise the rights of such stakeholders to intervene, critically review, and sometimes stop the strategies and actions of national and international corporations through legislated powers. This has stimulated the growth of non-governmental organizations (NGOs), usually as single-issue pressure groups. Goodhearted and well-funded the NGOs may be but, having worked with two global ones and many smaller ones, I am aware that they can rot too, and suffer from the very same governance and power issues as the corporations they fight. "Good" human values are not always employed by them, despite their rhetoric, and infighting with similar agencies over fundraising, power and resources, together with the inevitable local corruption, can make them as much of a governance problem as any other human endeavour.

"CRG" versus "ESG": cultural differences affecting corporate governance

The inclusive corporate governance trend is beginning to gather momentum after 25 years of relative calm. You see it clearly in the current fight within the international corporate governance community itself. When addressing the future of corporate governance, the US mainly uses the abbreviation "CRG": compliance, risk and governance. This fits their "rules-based", cost- and lawyer-heavy antagonistic reporting system. As an example, see the financially and administratively onerous effects of their Sarbanes–Oxley Act of 2004.[132] Yet this is still seen by their federal legislators as sufficiently avant-garde to satisfy their reporting requirements for the foreseeable future. However, the majority of European countries, the 54 Commonwealth countries and many of the other emerging nations, prefer to use the term "ESG" – environmental, societal and governance – to develop more inclusively their corporate reporting relationships with the communities in which they work. They are less concerned with the introverted, operational governance foci of compliance and risk and much more with their corporate purpose in developing the governance of sustainable businesses in a turbulent and uncertain world. The abbreviations tell it all in terms of mindsets for the future.

The battle is now whether CEO-hegemony-led capitalism wins over inclusive "stakeholder"-led capitalism. Will CRG- or ESG-based reporting win in the global fight for corporate governance dominance? It is a political battle that will test whether "extra-territoriality" will reinforce US world leadership or continue its decline. I feel it will be the latter. The Western financial crisis, followed by Brexit and Trump, has shaken the public and forced them to question the leadership, ethics, elitism, effectiveness and efficiency of their organizations. They are now demanding better performance of their organizations and investments and they are unlikely to pipe down. This will ensure that directors take a much wider, broader, deeper and more integrative "helicopter view" of their role than before.

Rebalancing the future content of corporate governance to include uncertainty, strategic thinking and human values

Following the Western financial crisis, there have been discernible moves occurring in Europe and the emerging markets to unseat accountancy as the prime professional discipline driving corporate governance. We will always need some form of quantification to be able to measure business performance. This is not disputed. But, in future, there is no need to assume that the financial figures are the only ones worthy of attention. As with the CRG versus ESG debate, the rise of integrated reporting[133] and "long finance",[134] and proposals for the reframing of audit, we are now witnessing the evolution of a more integrated set of performance measures. These take people, society and the environment into account. With stakeholders being taken seriously by the regulators and politicians, the next two decades will see their ascendance.

This will cause many problems for existing boards and top teams, as their need to understand the "people-oriented fields" – including behavioural economics, group dynamics, rights laws, values, culture and integrated reporting – will not go down well with accountants if their power in the boardroom is eroded. This conceptual shift will mean a complete rethink of the meaning of effective corporate governance. The outcome will become central to our national learning system.

Developing the business model

One practical way of dealing with these changes is to incorporate a more rigorous and constructive assessment of the board's business model into the reporting system for shareholders and stakeholders.

"Business models" are becoming fashionable. However, as management consultancy and business education is a fashion industry, one needs to take care. For example, the UK's revised Corporate Governance Code is demanding that the business model is made explicit in the annual report of a company. However, it does not specify what a "business model" is. This is unsurprising, as curiously little is known about them. Like "corporate governance", it is a phrase that everyone thinks they understand yet, when questioned, there are many conflicting answers.

I will use two definitions that I have found useful, both in my own businesses and with my clients. First, a business model is the board's agreed mind-set (ideas) from which to design their future. It allows them to achieve their espoused purpose by monitoring the many trends and changes in their external environment, while simultaneously monitoring the operational performance of their executives, after having decided where to place their scarce resources to achieve their purpose. It is the translation of their wider strategic thinking into a business strategy and a subsequent business plan. Second, the business model is the central processor and testing framework of the "business brain"'s role in the learning organization (Figure 6). It creates a common language between the board, the executives, the shareholders and the stakeholders for assessing progress. It is important because it reinforces the professionalism of the board.

Figure 6: Learning board: full model

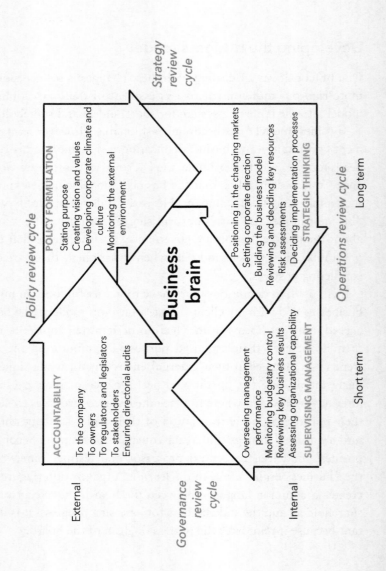

POLICY FORMULATION
Stating purpose
Creating vision and values
Developing corporate climate and culture
Monitoring the external environment

ACCOUNTABILITY
To the company
To owners
To regulators and legislators
To stakeholders
Ensuring directorial audits

STRATEGIC THINKING
Positioning in the changing markets
Setting corporate direction
Building the business model
Reviewing and deciding key resources
Risk assessments
Deciding implementation processes

SUPERVISING MANAGEMENT
Overseeing management performance
Monitoring budgetary control
Reviewing key business results
Assessing organizational capability

Business brain

Policy review cycle

Strategy review cycle

Operations review cycle

Governance review cycle

External

Internal

Short term

Long term

The chairman's role in ensuring inclusive capitalism

An effective business model allows professionalism to be seen to start from the top: the chairman of the board of directors. Remember that the chairman is not the "boss of the firm" but is "the boss of the board". It is the role of an orchestral conductor who may have the final say, provided that the articles of association give him or her a casting vote. Having worked with hundreds of chairmen, and been one myself, there are two innovations I propose to help clarify both the chairman's and the directors' roles in creating effective corporate governance.

The chairman and chief executive's monthly report

My original idea came at a time of crisis in a massive and complex business. The business was in trouble on all governance and financial fronts and the board, which met only every three months instead of once a month, was unable to cope. The enterprise had been misdirected, mismanaged and abused by politicians for a decade. Board morale was at rock bottom. And 75% of the board members were being replaced with a challenging mix of very experienced directors and very inexperienced younger folk as part of a national political initiative. All board members were expected to play an active and immediate role in this turnaround. This was more time-consuming than many had expected, or were paid for. And they were constantly in the media's eye, which they found very uncomfortable. They realized that they all had to be much better informed about their company's complex activities including the failing relations with the owners, stakeholders, managers and staff. But this was proving impossible until they could agree a process by which the business trends, operational performance and customer and stakeholder satisfaction levels were given to them more frequently. They understood that, as a board, they should not try to manage the business, but that they still needed to be better informed to understand the performance trends. Their fear was to be wrong-footed and humiliated in public by the media for not knowing information about the business.

Their new chief executive was a highly intelligent and feisty woman who rapidly realized that a short, weekly briefing of the directors on the relevant happenings during the last few days would help them greatly to understand better the current issues against trend-lines agreed by the board. But the directors were widely spread geographically and not very internet-literate. So she guaranteed them a weekly email news update. She called these her "love letters" to the board. They came out regularly on a Friday afternoon. They were a boon. They helped to bond what had been a fragmented and nervous board, helped the chairman set priorities at board meetings, and they created both a common language and a greater trust between the board and the executives as they more openly discussed trends and any deviations from the business plans.

This increased transparency allowed, within the listing requirements, the sharing of monthly performance trends beyond the board to shareholders and stakeholders. All were reassured. A big worry had been that this would leak immediately to hostile members of the media. But, even with volatile unions, once the trends were seen as positive, nothing leaked in a four-year period.

The building of trust between the chairman, the chief executive and the new "top team" was palpable. The chairman proposed the creation of a "chairman's office", which would comprise him, the company secretary, and his own PA. This was accepted immediately, and it has proved a powerful governance force. It is seen now as "the soul of the firm" and the centre of all organizational learning. Additionally, a "dotted line" reporting system from internal audit to the chairman of the audit committee has greatly improved organizational learning.

This structure has been applied in other organizations. It leads me to recommend that generally we set up similar structures, that we ban quarterly reporting, and focus on the long-term, patient creation of the success of the business to improve corporate governance. We should strongly encourage a minimum six-monthly chairman's commentary on the trends of the business in relation to its business model and strategy with legally appropriate release from Investor Relations. All this helps the move towards directoral professionalism.

The Chartered Director award as a model for the development of modern professionalism

So we return at the end of this chapter to the issue of director professionalism. The public now needs to demand that the selection and performance of all boards is based on competence, transparency, accountability and probity. Which is why I, along with John Harpham, Barbara Lady Judge, Professor Chris Mallin, Colin Melvin, Chris Pierce and Bernard Taylor, helped found in the 1990s the UK's Chartered Director national award – a truly professional development process, which examines knowledge and practice, and continually assesses continuing professional development. Bankers, please note. I argue that legislation should insist that all UK registered directors have passed part 1: the basic knowledge of the director's role, responsibilities and liabilities before they are fully recognized as "directors". Moreover, all directors of corporations – public, private or not-for-profit – must have a development plan to take them through part 2 to the practical, and the oral examination of recorded professional experience in part 3. Most of the existing directors of major organizations will hate this. But it will help hugely with the professionalization of directing – and the restoration of trust in our leaders. Not all corporate directors need be accredited in parts 2 and 3 but the majority of the board should be. They would have to formally report annually to the shareholders why they are not.

However heavily boards of directors are criticized, it must be remembered that there is an opposite and balancing party to the board – the owners. Owners seem to have avoided most of the criticism and legislation that have affected directors, so they are often portrayed in public as the injured parties. This leaves boards as the main focus of public ire. In the next chapter, I hope to show that there are many questions about the roles, behaviours and responsibilities of owners that need investigating much more deeply to rebalance this issue.

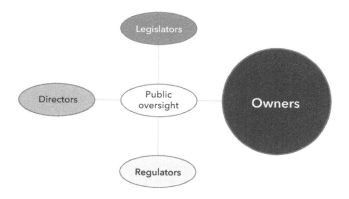

4

Owners and their responsibilities

Why should the values of Lust and Gluttony
defeat Patience and Temperance?

Blending legal and emotional ownership values for effective governance

Ownership is a highly fashionable buzzword, in both business and politics.

Like all buzzwords, it is easily said but not necessarily understood by either the speaker or the listener. As I researched this chapter, I found that we are all coping with a series of contradictory assumptions. For example, shareholders do not own companies, despite much of the present rhetoric. The public does not "own" in any legal property way our state departments or enterprises. So what are we actually talking about? The deeper I talked with the experts, the more confused I became until I realized that so were they. This chapter is my attempt to clarify matters.

"Ownership" is a fundamental element of the human condition. The need for it triggers strong positive and negative reactions based on our learned personal values. On the human values scale, ownership ranges from lust and gluttony to temperance and charity. Given such an emotional range, humans have developed laws and acceptable behaviours to protect themselves against its excesses. In the West these are particularly well developed in relation to the legal aspects of property and contract ownership, but much less developed in relation to its emotional, non-physical aspects. The personal concept of ownership is usually clear to an individual and their personal circumstances but rarely clear when "owning on the behalf of others". The the well-developed legal concepts of "agency", "fiduciary duty", "stewardship" and "duty of care" should be paramount. They rarely are. Why?

What can we do to clarify the current imbalance between the property and emotional ownership aspects of effective corporate governance? The word "own" seems so simple. It arrives in Old English, via the Anglo-Saxons, from the Old German *agen*, meaning "possessed by". This term can still be read ambiguously, which explains some of the current confusion over its legal and emotional usage. Oddly, its usage died out in the 13th century, once the Normans took over, but was renewed in the 1580s when the modern meanings of "the fact of being an owner" and "the legal right of possession" became firmly established in English law. It had to be. It was the period leading up to the granting of Royal Charters for companies, the consequent rapid expansion of international trade, and the very start of modern business ideas and practice. The first "modern" chartered company was the British East India Company founded in 1600.

From the start there was a tension between the legal right of possession and the *emotional* state, of "being" an owner or "feeling" like an owner. This has confused political ideologies, of the left and right persuasions, ever since. It has reinforced class, religious and racial prejudice, leading, over time, to winners and losers, oppression and cultural greed in a long history of zero-sum political games. Semantic confusion over ownership still infects our ideas about organizations and corporate governance, and therefore contributes towards the rot. We need to introduce some sunshine to disinfect its worst characteristics.

Corporate governance and ownership: current contradictions

Having long experience with boards of directors' approach to corporate governance, I had naïvely assumed that I knew enough of the obverse side of the corporate governance coin: ownership. I was wrong, very wrong. The board side of the coin is currently in the public spotlight, is much discussed and criticized, and faced with increasing legislation. Ownership is rarely seen as the reciprocal of directing, and in need of similar accountabilities. Rather, the ownership role is seen as dull, murky and simply assumed as a given by most players on both sides. I disagree. I had guessed that I needed just a little top-up of knowledge. But, as I interviewed so many of the known players on both sides, I found that few had ever really considered the concept of "ownership" deeply. They just played the game as it was. The legal facts often surprised them, sometimes to the point of disbelief; and the emotional aspects were an unexplored mystery.

Players were often at odds over the ethical values needed. Few were able to answer my, hopefully, intelligently naïve questions.

For example, property owners were skilled at working the existing ownership mechanics of the legal/contractual system, but often had little vision or strategic objective other than to always be on the winning side of a zero-sum game. For them, the whole notion of human values-based ownership and governance was always subordinated in favour of the bottom line. On the other hand, those who were strongly influenced by the "emotional ownership" camp seemed to feel that property ownership is always inhuman, unfair and somehow unclean. It shocked me that the idea of seeking an inclusive "ownership" definition was rarely considered by the professionals. It was a warning signal of my problems that followed. So this chapter is more anecdotal and messy than I would like, but ends with some hopeful new structures, approaches and conclusions.

Two types of ownership

Legal ownership

I started with the simple assumption that there are two types of "ownership" that exist simultaneously in the public's mind. First, and most obvious, is legal ownership: the property right over an entity, physical or intellectual – its "title". Once established legally, this property right is protected by the courts. Through legal ownership, contracts for sale or exchange can be made – for many centuries the basis of our commercial law. I have not met anyone who disagrees with this concept, even in Communist countries. The main questions here seem to be: "Who controls that title?" and "How is any conflict resolved amicably?"

Emotional ownership

However, for many people there is a second, deeper, often invisible, emotional need: possession of something they love or respect but have no legal title over. I call this "emotional ownership", to differentiate it from property ownership. It is a surprisingly powerful force. For example, an individual does not legally "own" the BBC, the NHS or "their" football, rugby or cricket team, locality, region or nation; but they can be emotionally bonded to it, sometimes obsessively so. If an external authority tries to change, take it over or create new legal property rights, all hell is then let loose. If the incomer's cultural and ethical values are not the same as the existing emotional owners, then there are major ructions. Public campaigns are created, the internet boils, and the private lives of the "invaders" and their families are made public, and they are harassed. Emotionality reaches a crisis point. Rationality is rarely in abundance. A cyber-mauling is not a pretty sight for either side.

Something deeper is happening. Emotional ownership triggers our deep-felt personal values and beliefs – the anchors of our lives. For me, this helps explain Brexit, and the similar growing feelings in many countries, when a super-rich elite establishes itself outside the value systems of the majority and is seen to profit from it continuously and unfairly. A balanced, fair society is the reasonable expectation of all. The current discontent shows a visceral concern that the majority have been betrayed, regardless of their political affiliations. The leaders' duty of care has been abandoned and the current governance system is incapable of responding.

Ownership and the private sector

Although individuals are ultimately responsible for protecting and developing their social and financial wealth, most people devolve such actions to agents to do this for them, whether to pension and insurance funds, specialist advisors or friends and family. This means that it is in the financial sector that both aspects of ownership are currently most obviously likely to be in contradiction. Handing over the legal title to an agent does not mean that the emotional ownership is transferred as well. The "hard" extrinsic values of finance rarely correspond with human emotions and "soft" intrinsic values.

So you might expect that these issues are long considered and understood by both sides. Wrong. Among the general public, I found a worrying mixture of ignorance over both how their own personal finances work and how public finance operates. This meant two things. First, they had no language or constructive mind-sets to discuss and understand what was happening in the financial and legal fields of ownership. Second, consequentially, they were in blissful ignorance of the sometimes doubtful values, behaviours and reward systems of the professionals to whom they had delegated an assumed duty of care, skill and diligence for managing their wealth. The fact that such "players" are agents – pension fund trustees, fund managers, hedge fund managers, mortgage companies, insurers, etc. – means that they can easily be in conflict with their role of generating maximum returns for their clients while also supporting the different accepted business values of their own corporate culture. Given their current behaviours and reward systems, many do not see their *primary* duty as the professional care of the client.

Nor are they incentivized for this. It is more normal for agents to give their primary duty to their employer, and their consequent focus to their quarterly payments and bonuses, rather than ensuring the long-term health of the individual or enterprise on whose behalf they are investing. The sainted Warren Buffett[135] is one of the few notable exceptions to this rule, although even he can wobble. Given the amount of adverse publicity towards boards of directors, following the crisis of 2008, owners, especially agent-owners, have kept a low profile. What makes matters much worse from the public's viewpoint is that owners and agents have growing rights but few duties. Why do those sound corporate governance values of accountability, probity and transparency not to apply to ownership? They do, but few seem to know or care.

Do owners and agents have duties?

This myth that owners do not have duties is built on three common assumptions found in current corporate governance practice. Each is flawed:

- That boards of directors must always work under the directions of, and on behalf of, the shareholders. This is incorrect.

- That executives must work on behalf of the directors. True in law but rarely in practice.

- That all three parties – shareholders, directors and executives – have the long-term success of the enterprise as their common goal. This is doubtful in current practice.

I challenge all three myths. To complicate matters, in any three-party system it is always possible for one party to play the other two parties against each other for short-term gains. As the current commercial system is based increasingly on short-termism, this needs rethinking if the current property owners and agents are to restore their credibility with the angry and puzzled public. Sadly, few of our national political and financial leaders seem to recognize these issues, care about them, or be willing to take responsibility for changing them to benefit our national well-being and wealth.

This is odd, as our legal definition of ownership, with its consequential rights and duties, is the foundation stone of our commercial law, effective corporate governance, and so our national stability. Why is ownership so little understood or appreciated even by those who earn their living from it? This is a core part of the rot that must be stopped.

What is "ownership" in practice?

My researches show that few involved – with some noted female exceptions such as Merryn Somerset Webb and Gillian Tett of the *Financial Times*, Gillian Karran-Cumberlege of Fidelio Consulting and Jill Atkins of Sheffield University – seem to have much intellectual curiosity about, comprehensive understanding of, or a feel for ownership's significance at either the national legal or emotional levels. "Ownership", in most people's minds, seems a given: unquestioned and immovable. If questioned, there will be many different, contradictory and partial meanings given. Shareholders and agents generally show deep commitment to their traditional role, and proponents tend to fight for their ground even as the external environments change, however irrational this is. I began to realize why my questions generated so much heat and so little light.

The need to "own" something, or a relationship with someone, is deep in the human psyche and in many animals. It is valued positively or negatively depending on the individual's needs and ethics. Ownership involves a mixture of complex personal values, ranging from securing the basic human needs through gaining identity and certainty by acquisition to self-actualizing as described in Maslow's Hierarchy of Human Needs.[136] However, taken to the extreme, the need for identity and certainty can turn to lust and greed, to the detriment of others.

The fight between the legal and emotional meaning of ownership is played out politically and globally in, for example, the continuing global battle between capitalism and Communism, and in the power plays when balancing the roles of the state, religion, families and the individual. In corporate governance, it is currently focused on the increasingly fractious debates between the need for wealth generation and the exploitation, and development, of the physical and social environment: "fracking" and rainforests being current examples.

Ownership and avarice

The greatest international governance dilemma of our time is how to balance continuous wealth creation for a growing world population while optimizing our use of scarce natural, social and financial capital to develop inclusive capitalism. Developing effective national corporate governance competence is central to its resolution. Argument has tended to be dominated by the economic and financial aspects of business over the past 50 years. But, after the 2008 Western financial crisis, the social, ethical values and emotional aspects of ownership, especially the duties of care and cooperation, are becoming more central to public debates.

Yet economic and financial bias is part of our history, with greed and avarice displaying some of the worst human values. In *Owning the Earth: The Transformational History of Land Ownership*,[137] Andro Linklater quotes US Senator Henry Dawes, who, in 1877, condemned the Cherokee Nation's tradition of using land communally by saying that such a concept "contained no selfishness, which is at the bottom of civilization". The use of the ambiguous word "bottom" highlights our current confusion over whether the value of selfishness/ownership is at the root of our current civilization, or is the least acceptable part of it? The values of selfishness, greed, individualism and the thoughtless pursuit of "happiness" can be argued as the bane of our times, and the basis of at least US civilization. Has the addition of the words "and the pursuit of human happiness" to the end of the American Declaration of Independence paradoxically condemned the US to centuries of continuing emotional frustration?

Gordon Gecko[138] is imprinted on many Western minds through the phrase "greed is good". Henry Dawes was reflecting not on greed as we now see it, but on the Victorian notion of continuous progress through *self*-help,[139] property acquisition through individual ownership, and the pursuit of wealth underpinned by the certainty of the superiority of Western nations. Such notions evolved across a wide section of aspirant, middle-class societies in Europe and the US from the 18th century. The nascent US sought to create the world's largest private-property-owning society through a then lionized blend of personal endeavour and nonconformist ethics. Sadly, much of their economic foundation was based on slavery and genocide. These conquerors gave themselves the legislated right both to own people and to sequester others' property in order to stabilize national boundaries and legal rights. Such rights are found throughout recorded history, as much in China, Africa, South America and the Muslim world as in the UK or US. What can be done to counter such ownership values?

Ownership moves to a more inclusive capitalism

Our present commercial society is built on the selfish ownership foundations of enforceable laws of property and contract, coupled with the ability to have rapid redress in the courts in the event of a dispute. This is still the dream for many emergent economies, who see such a commercial system as the jewel in the crown of the advanced economies – a move towards fairness and equality under commercial law. A fundamental and hard-won political principle here is that the law is more powerful than either the state or any group or individuals within it – the rule *of* law, not *by* law. This differentiates it from the current dodgy range of autocracies, plutocracies and kleptocracies. By continuously demonstrating the supremacy of the law of property, public trust has underpinned our commercial system, and reinforced the belief in property ownership as a right. However, this hard-won public trust has been squandered by the 2008 financial crisis, which destroyed so much personal wealth that this aspect of "ownership" is now reopened for public debate. The question now asked increasingly of those who own and manage our wealth is: "Surely you must have duties to your fellows, just like directors?"

The changing concepts of ownership

Three converging trends

Despite the clarity of the legal concept of ownership, its limits are becoming increasingly fuzzy as globalization, digitization and social communications grow. This confusion is being driven by three converging influences:

- Growing questioning of what ownership now means across diverse communities and cultures
- Rethinking the time-frames of "ownership" (the confusion between "patient" and "impatient" owners)
- Accepting the growing power of "psychological/emotional ownership" by acknowledging the "stakeholders"

Despite much loose talk about such issues as "shareholder owner-ship", "stewardship", "public ownership", "employee ownership", "social ownership" and "community ownership", there are some encouraging signs of progress. For example, corporations are now being pressured into acknowledging the rights of some "stakehold-ers"; the concept of inclusive capitalism is becoming more popular; and the internet has ensured that company activities are more trans-parent so that wrongdoers are increasingly being held accountable for their actions. However, before we get carried away by visions of the sunlit uplands of ownership's future values, there is a messy secret, created by English politicians in the Victorian period that needs to be addressed. This secret comes as a great shock to the public and to many of the existing players.

Shareholders are not the owners of companies

The public is unaware of a legal fudge that confounds the very base on which organizational ownership and governance thinking has been built over the past 125 years. This focuses on a major miscon-ception over shareholder property rights. During my interviews, I was very surprised to find that few individuals were willing to admit, or even knew, that in the UK and many of the 54 Commonwealth countries, the "shareholders" do *not* "own" the companies in which they invest. This came as a great shock to the majority. What share-holders do have is a right to a proportion of any dividend streams, a right to vote on board decisions in prescribed circumstances, and a right to any residual assets if the company goes into liquidation.

But shareholders are *not* the ultimate beneficial owners of a com-pany. I had been taught the exact opposite. The superstructure of much business practice has been built on the working assumption that the ultimate owners are the shareholders. Much business and political rhetoric is built on this. So what has gone wrong? And who benefits from this often-concealed fact?

The limited liability company was created as a legal *fiction* to limit the liability of shareholders by creating a "separate legal personality" (the company) that can sign contracts and formally make deals beyond the capacity of the directors and the shareholders. It is a remarkable product of human ingenuity and has fuelled the impressive development of business throughout the 20th century. But why do the legislators allow us to live with a fiction? I must give a little history here, as this fiction has shaped our modern world but is still little understood by those working under it.

Towards the limited liability company

I focus here particularly on the ownership of shares in multiple ownership companies and trusts – the default position of most who talk about "shareholdings" – rather than the "ownership" of goods and chattels like houses, cars and clothes, which tend to be owned 100% by individuals. Since the beginning of the 17th century, company law has driven and developed our concepts of ownership and capitalism in three distinct ways, in order to suit our evolving economic and social needs. First, there was a move away from the "Royal Charter" companies (whose incorporation and dissolution was by royal decree, often more of a whim). Then there followed a move away from partnerships, with their unlimited personal liability of the individual partners, towards the creation of a totally new legal concept, seen now as the basis of our current financial system: the joint stock company, created by the Joint Stock Company Act of 1844.[140]

By then, the Industrial Revolution was in full flow and so there was great need for more capital and liquidity, especially for infrastructural developments in railways, ports, bridges and roads. The legislators had assumed that this 1844 Act would mitigate the risks for individual shareholders and their personal wealth. The 1844 Act made it easier for investors to pool their commercial gains and losses rather than rely on a single investor. But the owners still had unlimited liabilities for their actions, and there was great political pressure for the government to limit owners' liabilities.

So the Limited Liability Act of 1856[141] was passed to great rejoicing. However, this Act was not effectively combined with the 1844

Act, despite Prime Minister Gladstone's continuing warnings and his efforts to resolve the contradictions in Parliament. He predicted that there would be great negative economic consequences if the anomalies were not resolved. They were not, and, being unresolved, they led to the current continuing disputes as to *where and with whom* the limitations of liability lie. At the time of the Act, the general legal opinion was that joint stock companies were an "aggregate entity", with *the shareholders* constituting that entity and so enjoying some limited liability up to the limit of their paid-up share capital (as the position is today). Yet the directors were still viewed as having unlimited personal liability.

Confusion reigned. In the end, Gladstone and others managed to get a Court resolution. It was hoped that the Salomon Judgement of the House of Lords in 1897 would clarify matters.[142] It stated that, lawfully, the corporation was *an entity in itself*. It had a separate legal personality and, as such, a corporation could sue and be sued, and make contracts on its own behalf. The company was now seen as owning its assets, and these assets were now *separate* from the shareholders who were no longer seen as having any controlling ownership. Shareholders could still own a share of the company, have a small say in the control of the company, have a right to dividend streams and the residual assets, but did *not* own the legal entity that is the company. This is the current position – much to the surprise of most "owners", directors and politicians when they are made aware of it. Moreover, the corporation as a legal entity never enters into a separate contractual agreement with its shareholders, contrary to the beliefs of the public and many directors.

It is a classic case of legislators not understanding governance issues and subsequently creating laws that then demand legal fictions for people to be able to continue with their daily business. Yet work they must, even if the ultimate ownership of a corporation now resides in a mindless and directionless legal entity without a moral compass. No-one now "owns" a company. This legal void is now filled by the directors (usually part-time and often untrained) being given responsibilities, liabilities and accountabilities often beyond their competences. Only the directors, rather than the executives, have unlimited personal liability. Many directors are shocked by such a revelation, especially the "accidental" ones. Politicians are happy about it as they have someone to blame if things go wrong. Indeed, directors can have the worst of both worlds. They often find that, because the executives are in the company full-time, they tend to control the direction of the firm, thus unofficially taking both the governance roles from the directors – direction-giving and prudent control. Oddly, there is surprisingly little law around the executives' roles, liabilities, responsibilities and accountabilities. There is so much more law for directors that they tend to take the brunt of public criticism. Even odder is that the role and duties of the *shareholders* in relation to this mindless legal entity are hardly questioned or understood by the public. In the public's mind, shareholders and their agents are usually assumed always to be the innocent victims. Wrong. Their lack of a duty of care can do serious harm to the companies in which they are invested.

Resolving the shareholders' role

It is now up to the public to ask politicians how the future ownership of a corporation should be resolved. Should not the shareholders become the ultimate owner and, therefore, the directing mind of the corporation? And, if we are moving towards acceptance of inclusive capitalism, how then can we bring the law into line so that accountabilities, responsibilities, liabilities and duties between the directors, the owners and the stakeholders are clearer and shared more equitably?

The public must keep questioning how a company, "incorporated" under the Companies Act, cannot be owned by the shareholders. How can it stay a mindless and inanimate legal fiction without values or, as Professor Dawkins might say, seem to act as a blind watchmaker?[143] Who should form the legal "membership" of the corporation? As the politicians have not grasped this nettle for over 120 years on the grounds that "there is no political will to do so" and "it's too hard to tackle anyway", it has been left to the judges, and their development of Common Law in England and the Commonwealth, to try to resolve this unsatisfactory situation. They have not succeeded – yet.

As the position of the corporation as an independent legal entity became established, the board of directors were charged with delivering the director's dilemma, and so shareholders have become more distant from the policies, strategies and values of the business. This is especially true of those shareholders that use fund and asset managers as intermediaries. This governance distance is reinforced when the focus of the politicians moves, in times of crisis, from conceptual ownership issues towards intervening directly in the *prudent control* of the business. This has brought the directors firmly to centre stage, as the only body with a mind who can give both direction and prudent control to a corporation. But I always warn directors not to attempt to micro-manage the business from the boardroom table. Management is the job of the executives and staff. If the directors subvert this managerial role, they abuse the company's use of its scarce resources, and it always ends in tears. If politicians try to subvert both, as we see currently in the NHS, it ends in chaos.

So I stress again that, in the private sector, if current corporate "ownership" exists at all, it resides in a mindless and directionless legal entity without a moral compass. Nobody "owns" a registered company . . .

The public sector

In this book on corporate governance I shall not linger long on the wider notion of the "public ownership" of a nation's land, capital and means of production for the people and by the people. That is for the politicians to argue over interminably. But I do want to focus here on the often ineffective governance of state institutions created in the UK following the Beveridge Report of 1942 on proposals to create a post-war system of "social security" through taxation-funded, free-at-the-point-of-use health, education and social services.[144] These led to the development and expansion of the public sector and public entitlement, which is now under discussion with regard to whether it is a failed political experiment or just one in need of a massive amount of new funding.

In the public sector, I was equally surprised that the concept of "public ownership" was so emotionally powerful that it blocked much rational discussion, yet it was built on an equally unstable legal base. For example, I asked who "owns" an NHS Foundation Trust. The answer, after a year of questioning many of those involved at the top of the NHS and the legal officers of government, was "no-one, as NHS FTs do not exist as a legal entity". This is despite some of them having a turnover of up to £1 billion a year of public money, being treated by the public as though they are incorporated with high degrees of autonomy, being a major employer and economic generator for their area, and seemingly being able to both sue and be sued. Yet, despite the rhetoric of them now "being businesses", their boards cannot provide systematic and effective corporate governance because they are still directly and indirectly influenced by national and local political control. NHS Foundation Trust boards cannot say "no" to the political expediencies of their major source of funding (the Department of Health) and so cannot truly govern in their own right. They are not free agents. As the NHS costs the nation some 6.7% (around £140 billion annually) of UK GDP, this conscious governance mis-design is typical of the muddled thinking on ownership and stewardship in the public sector by politicians and civil servants. These seem desperate to intervene in operational control issues to please their voters, yet demand "business-like" efficiencies without giving the directors the discretionary powers to deliver them. This dilemma runs throughout the public sector. I shall return to this point later in this chapter.

The importance of the choice of legal entity

Equally surprising was that, in both the private and public sectors, the directors, governors, fund managers, regulators, civil servants and politicians failed to understand the importance and consequences of their original choice of an appropriate legal business form, the legal entity, for the enterprises they are creating. Yet this choice determines the constitutional and legal framework for their organizational ownership, and their subsequent ability to perform effectively. This point is so fundamental, and yet so underappreciated, that corporate rot is often built in from the start of an organization's life. It will be interesting to see if the likely failures of, for example, such legal entities as LLPs (with their hidden beneficial owners), "social interest companies" and "community companies" occur quickly, as their founding political rhetoric gives way to legal and operational reality and the likely public scandals are then tested by the courts.

The UK's range of choice of legal entities include:

- Companies limited by share capital (LLCs)

- Publicly listed companies (PLCs)

- Companies limited by guarantee

- Partnerships

- Limited liability partnerships (LLPs)

- Mutuals and cooperatives

- Employee ownerships

- Private equity ownerships

- Public sector mutuals

- Social enterprises

This failure of appropriate choice in creating the legal entity seems especially messy in the public and not-for-profit sectors where a mixture of political ignorance and arrogance ("we are the masters and we know better than the law") prevails. It is only when an instigator's pet project or charity gets into serious trouble that they may learn the importance of their choice of legal entity and their directoral and managerial liabilities. I am reminded of both Winston Churchill's comment on the rebuilding of the Palace of Westminster after the war – "first we shape our buildings, thereafter they shape us"[145] – and the previously mentioned Clifford Geertz's "webs of signification which we spin and then are trapped by".[146] The same is true of the legal entities and constitutions we choose or, even worse, are imposed on us by ignorant superiors.

A sketch map of private ownership rights and duties

First, let us look at the boundaries between, and within, the basic ownership categories of individuals, corporations and the state. These categories are becoming ever fuzzier, especially between the private and public sectors, as politicians seek to capture and blend the entrepreneurial power of the private sector with the community service power and ethos of the public sector. This may seem a noble endeavour but it is currently unresolved. We need each legal entity's rights and duties to be clarified for all concerned. We need to consolidate the ragged legal boundaries currently exposed. Bringing all such registered enterprises under the seven general duties of directors would be a good start.

Owners' duties and rights in ensuring the success of the business

We hear growing public demands for increasing shareholders' minority rights, but we hear little demand for increasing all shareholders' *duties*, to ensure the success of the business in which they have invested. This is particularly noticeable in the US where the alienation between executives (not directors in the UK sense) and shareholders has been clear for decades[147] through to Bob Monks's Guildhall speech of 2014.[148] And this was during an era in which shareholders tended to hold their shares for years ("patient capital", as advocated by Warren Buffett). Cyber-technology has greatly diminished this value of patient ownership. It means that 24-hour global "impatient" trading dominates and, when linked with arbitrage algorithms, it enables trawling "day traders" and multinational banks to erode greatly any concept of shareholder ownership. Investors are being pushed out by amoral traders. Who is the owner of a share if that share is only held for a nanosecond? Do such traders have any wider societal duties? Currently the markets' answer is a firm "No".

There are signs of a weak push-back. For example, in the private sector the question is being asked whether "owners" (shareholders) have to hold a share for at least a medium-term length of time before they can gain the right to vote on the performance of the company. Currently, in most countries, the shareholder's property right in a share and their ability to vote at an annual general meeting or an extraordinary general meeting are the same. But, given this 24-hour arbitrage, should we now create two classes of shares, one of which can be traded instantly but has the right to vote stripped from it? A few Dutch and Swedish companies are experimenting with this. But no politicians are advocating serious action.

Consequently, many "shareholders" now think of shares more as gambling chips rather than as serious investments. It is legal to gamble in most countries, but the financial risks and consequences of short-term, even instant, share gambling should carry a duty of care and diligence to the individual gambler regarding the long-term effects on workers, suppliers and other disempowered stakeholders. The growing split between "patient" and "impatient" capital is dangerously destabilizing our financial system. Hence the argument that stock exchanges should only be open for one day a week. Or that 24-hour automated arbitrage should be banned. Or that there should be a sanction if a share owner does not vote. It seems inequitable that shareholders are being granted increasing rights to comment on, for example, executive remuneration, diversity, business strategies, general performance and even culture and values without having to accept any increased personal or stewardship duties of oversight, due diligence, fiduciary duty and participation. This asymmetry is unhealthy for any economy because the necessary emotional tension between directors and owners is now tilted towards directors only. Given the growing "hegemony of the CEO", such blaming seems doubly unfair.

Human values beyond flash trading

Through "flash trading", a person or an agent can "own" and sell a share within a fraction of a nanosecond. There is no long-term investment in the company, and no need for due diligence. Yet such share traders are currently viewed by society as ethics-free, amoral and, unlike directors, have no duty to consider and develop the long-term health of the businesses in whose shares they trade, let alone consider the medium- to long-term effects on other stakeholders. They are distanced from the reality of productive business while revelling in its instant rewards.

The delegation of owners' powers

The muddiness of the concept of "ownership" has increased because, for over a century, shareholders have sought to avoid any increased burden of legal regulations and risks on themselves by passing these on to agents – particularly, but not exclusively, fund managers. Such delegation is becoming a major concern for the public and so widening their current focus on the complacent and self-indulgent underperformance of boards and executives. More people begin to understand the governance costs and ineffectiveness of such duty-less agents. Their version of a "duty of care" includes themselves but excludes the shareholders and stakeholders.

Stewardship

Shareholders are not treated by the courts as if they have any duty of "stewardship".[149] A few shareholders do so voluntarily but this is not sufficient for the creation of healthy businesses nationally. Among these "good guys", Hermes EOS, Standard Life, Universities Superannuation Scheme, Norges, Governance4Owners, Bob Monks's funds, and CalPERS stand out as noticeable exceptions to the current indifference on this issue. As the public's pension returns and other investments are continually eroded through quantitative easing, this issue will become an important aspect of the future debate on shareholders' powers. And, as the other "stakeholders" continue to gain stronger external and legal powers to question and block "owners'" actions and inactions, we shall see much deeper questioning of shareholders' duties.

"But where were the owners?" A new mind-set for future ownership

As I mentioned in the Preface to this book, my motivation in writing it was the constant questioning by a disillusioned public of "But where was the board?", in response to so many of the current board- and executive-led governance scandals. As I write, the massive US fines for Volkswagen, RBS and Rolls-Royce are in the news. The focus is on the boards and the executives. Yet few of the public ask, "But where were the owners and their agents? Don't they also have duties to ensure the future success of the businesses in which they invest?" It seems that this is not yet part of the public debate. This raises major questions over the whole concept of future ownership and its relationship to corporate governance.

Ownership has always contained a focus on the individual's legal rights, but we know that individuals can err easily in the direction of greed, lust, selfishness and fecklessness. This seems to be the current default mode as far as the public's perception is concerned. They tolerate it but do not like it. I argue that the issue of shareholders' duties must be of equal importance to the future success of our organizations – private, public and not-for-profit. These duties must be integrated with those of the directors and the executives. So far, the state's response has been to increase regulation a little, but only for directors, rather than owners. There has been some weak governmental encouragement for owners to increase the pressure on board decision-making,[150] by urging shareholders to vote on the issues put up at AGMs and EGMs. But there are currently no plans to introduce fiduciary duties for shareholders.

Are directors treated unfairly?

Unsurprisingly, resentment is now growing among directors over the number of costly new laws and regulations being placed on them (to the level of absurdity in UK banks), especially as these laws seem designed to have the unhealthy effect of protecting the property interests of growing numbers of irresponsible, short-term "owners". If such owners have little interest in ensuring the long-term success of the business, yet the directors have that legal duty, surely this is inequitable? It is worrying that the two main parties in effective corporate governance – the owners and the directors – are increasingly pulling away from each other. Where are the stewards needed to restore balance? What is needed is an integrated system of corporate governance where the interests of owners, directors and executives are clearly aligned and assessed systematically. It requires a simultaneous change of mind-set by all the main players. Brexit should be the trigger.

Owners and *Ubuntu*: the mind-set change needed

A few politicians have suggested integrating the interests of shareholders and boards, but little happens. Something has gone seriously wrong with our concept of governance and ownership, but there is no public forum to explore this in order to find innovative solutions. So how can we change our mind-set towards *mutually* achieving the success of our enterprises? An interesting example of mind-set change at the national level has been Nelson Mandela's strong and consistent advocacy of the South African concept of *Ubuntu,* which means simply "I am because we are".[151] This is so profound that it takes some time to think through. It accepts that individuals can only live for a limited time outside the society in which they exist. For the majority of our time, wittingly or unwittingly, we must support each other to survive. The more we recognize, tolerate and use our interdependence, the stronger our society becomes. But our current public mind-set is a long way from this, with strong elements of selfishness and zero-sum gaming especially among the elite. Too much individualism in any society leads to jealousy, rejection and splitting. Too little leads to totalitarianism. We need to develop a new ownership mind-set that, for our mutual development, accepts that to develop we are part of a wider whole. We are back to the Global Duty of Care.

The West has been dominated for three decades by the values of self-seeking businessmen who do not care about their customers, employees, suppliers and stakeholders. They formed accepted business values but put at risk the ecosystem in which they exist. When the public ask, "But where were the directors and the 'owners'?" the answer is usually "Nowhere to be seen". But the problem is not restricted to business. For example, in times of trouble in the UK public services, we see a pattern of allegedly guilty parties hurriedly resigning, taking inflated severance pay, and then either taking a similar job in a public service in a different geographic location or, even more worryingly, hiring themselves back into the same job as a "consultant" on much higher rates. Where are the public sector "owners" to stop this unethical nonsense? We now need a public oversight body that can begin to address these governance issues. We need directors, owners, civil servants and politicians to understand that they are the stewards and consciences of our national assets.

The declining ethical values of the civil service

The public used to have certainty in the public ethos values of their civil service, but now worries increasingly about the ethical values of people working in it. Few go deeper and ask, "Who exactly are these invisible public 'owners' and what are their values"? "Public ownership" is just too vague a term. Politicians are now deemed too untrustworthy to fulfil this stewardship role. Sadly, the civil servants have been increasingly politicized by governments, to the extent that even they are now seen as unreliable for this key role. Their previous value set – of the tightly held, disinterested *public service ethos* – has been virtually wiped out in the UK following Margaret Thatcher's questioning of "Is he one of us?", and Tony Blair's ruthless use of the civil service as his politically biased executive arm. The previous ethos whereby civil servants played the role of a regulator on the swing door of party policies to ensure stable national development has been lost. In Chapter 6, I shall argue that we must build an integrated learning system to deal with this gaping hole, and that public oversight must be at the centre of it.

Charities are not exempt from criticism

My comments also apply to the "uncharitable world of charities".[152] Charities are a key aspect of our community life, with the UK and Hong Kong being leading givers per head to charity. But, in corporate governance terms, they are becoming increasingly unbalanced as their fight for limited resources and their attempts to be "more business-like" conflict with their founding values of focus, temperance and modesty. I will not delve too deeply into their specific problems here, as the current cases of Kids Unlimited, the RSPCA, National Trust and many others have already been splashed across the media, involving issues of bullying weaker donors, undue emotional pressure in their advertising, and downright corporate governance avoidance – often on the grounds that "we are good people therefore we cannot do anything wrong". This tension usually reflects the emotional ownership of the founder, and their early committed supporters, and a legal entity the ownership of which has evolved into something that is in contradiction to those early strong emotional values. These early personal values and the early accepted business values, however good-hearted, can often run into trouble with corporate governance values and the legal demands of due process. So we sometimes see good people doing bad things and not understanding that they are not above the law. What I say about governance and ownership applies equally to the not-for-profits as to the private sector companies and state-owned enterprises and agencies.

The private sector: should there be a duty of ownership?

Are the public to blame?

Let us go deeper into this crucial issue.

The lack of a clear legal fiduciary duty for owners is a most shameful aspect of our current corporate governance system. But the complaining public forget that *they* are often significant shareholders in their own right. Too often, they fail to exercise their existing legal rights. But few of them seem to realize that they are owners of significant amounts of the nation's private wealth. A toxic combination of financial illiteracy and personal aversion to investments allows the public delusion that they are not a key part of the wealth generation system. Investment is often assumed to be "tainted" by its very owners.

For example, in 2015 some 10% of the shares on the London Stock Exchange comprised the pension funds and unit trusts of ordinary folk. Yet these people do not track or ask regular discerning questions about their investments, through their pension trustees or investment fund managers. Frequently they avoid the issue by assuming that the area is too difficult for them to understand, and that those to whom they have delegated must know what they are doing, will always be professional and so have their best interests at heart. Not so. As I mentioned in the Introduction, the public is often surprisingly ignorant of even where its investments are, let alone whether they have invested wisely.

Matters are not helped by the underperformance in the stewardship role of fund managers and most pension fund trustees – those selected by the ultimate owners as their representatives. Although pension fund trustees are now required to pass some modest exams, they seem happy, indeed they seen keen, to delegate their oversight role as quickly as possible to a fund manager. However, the pension fund trustees cannot delegate their legal accountabilities. The fund managers are then given a relatively easy performance mandate to deliver – for which they are paid generously. Most fund managers then just track market trends, although a few claim to be "active managers" and so claim to think on their clients' behalf. Sadly, with rare exceptions, the performance between either is difficult to differentiate. So why do trustees pay "active fund" managers? A simple answer is that, because the majority of the public and a large proportion of politicians are ignorant of even the basic elements of finance, fund management been viewed as an indecent necessity best left alone to practitioners of the dark arts of investment. These practitioners often suppress the public's interest through their alienating jargon and opaque pricing systems. Very few individuals, for example, regularly track the performance of their own pension fund, and even fewer would think of criticizing their trustees' performance.

This British fear of "finance" contrasts sharply with other national cultures. In Hong Kong, for example, one only has to go to the "goldfish bowls" of the stockbrokers to observe ordinary members of the public taking 20 minutes out, green tea provided, to track the market and buy and sell their shares. At its extreme, this is pure short-term, selfish betting – divorced from any longer-term interest in the shares. While this has inherent problems in itself, it does demonstrate that the Hong Kong public is more comfortable with the financial basics than the British public, and that they recognize the importance of creating and tracking their fragile wealth. They are capable of asking those two intelligently naïve questions of the people who are managing their funds: "How are you performing with my money?" and "How much are you charging me for this?" And they can understand the answers. These two questions are rarely even asked in the West.

The state is neither the generator nor owner of wealth

This public fear of finance has led, especially in Europe, to the totally misguided, yet comforting, delusion that governments are the major generators and distributors of national wealth rather than the entrepreneurs. This myth is welcomed, and often reaffirmed by all major European political parties. Many tax and spend the public's money, while encouraging that same public to demonize "business", especially big business, without revealing that corporate and employment tax payments are the major source of the provision of national welfare services.

It is also convenient for politicians of all parties to promote the myth that only they can control the supply of national wealth through the distribution of "their", not the public's, money. In some countries, governments have even created the myth that theirs is a state-funded state. These myths are now beginning to be seen as patent nonsense, but they survived and flourished for some 80 years until the 2008 Western financial crisis showed that the political emperors had no clothes. Now the public need to understand quickly the roots of the creation and distribution of wealth. Remember that it is individuals and corporations that pay taxes, not governments.

Should owners and directors have duties of care and primary loyalty?

Two key civil law judgements have significantly shaped the last hundred years of corporate governance practice. Neither seems well known, even by directors and owners, let alone the public. Many directors are made aware of these civil law judgements only when they are charged with an unlawful act – which is much too late as ignorance is no defence in the eyes of the law. Both civil law judgements concern the duties of the directors – and their still unlimited liabilities. Be aware that directors' and officers' liability insurance applies only to the legal costs incurred and, even then, it is still dependent on whether or not the directors have obeyed the law. Otherwise they will face unlimited liability. Without due registration, proper induction or development processes, many directors are putting their personal and their family's wealth at risk. At first sight, neither of these legal judgements seem to affect the shareholders. Yet both have a major effect on the direction, control and, therefore, the ultimate ownership of a business.

The first law concerns the previously mentioned duty of care of directors. This is reflected currently in Sections 171 and 172 of the

2006 Companies Act and its seven general duties of directors. This Act stresses how important it is for directors to "ensure the success of the company", to show "independence of thought", and to demonstrate reasonable "care, skill and diligence" and probity in the exercise of their duties. The development of the concept of a fiduciary duty for directors – a duty of care to keep the company running successfully for future generations – is now well established in law, if not always enforced in practice.

Primary loyalty and the Denning Judgement

In the UK, the public is right to question why the Department of Business, Energy and Industrial Strategy, and especially the Financial Reporting Council (FRC), pay so little attention to the enforcement of this primary duty of care. They will be surprised to find that the FRC can debar only accountants and auditors; they cannot debar directors – which reinforces my point about their accountancy focus. Of equal importance to me are the judgements concerning the primary loyalty of directors. The legal concept is simple. Once one has signed the official papers to become a statutory director, then one's primary loyalty is to the *company* as a separate legal entity, and to no-one else. A director must *not* be a representative of a third party, even if they helped in his or her election to the board. Remember that, under Section 171, a director has already agreed to ensure their "independence of judgement" so must not act as a "representative" of others. Most directors find this intellectually stretching and choose not to believe it. For me, the definitive judgement is Lord Denning's (1963):

> Or take a nominee director, that is a director of a company who is nominated by a large shareholder to represent his interests. There is nothing wrong in that. It is done every day. Nothing wrong that is so long as the director is left free to exercise his best judgement in the interests of the company he serves. But if he is put on terms that he is bound to act in the affairs of the company in accordance with the direction of his patron, it is beyond doubt unlawful.[153]

This puts into proper perspective the current disastrous trend to think it correct and lawful to appoint "representatives" to the board simply to act as a puppet of their external masters. This is as true in the public sector as the private. It is so common a practice that many assume that it must be the law. It is not. A director has a legal duty to ensure that no-one influences their decisions from beyond the board-room table. This is why the General Duties include the demand that directors use "their independence of judgement". A director must have no conflicting interests in the matters being discussed unless this conflict has been fully declared and recorded beforehand; and the board has agreed whether that they may still participate in the discussion and the vote. This makes unlawful many of the previous decisions taken by most of the boards to which I am called in to resolve issues. Initially, the Denning Judgement concerned only nominee directors, but it has been applied more widely by the courts. It should be carved on every board table and imprinted on the forehead of all directors.

The false premise, often backed by politicians, that "representation" is always needed to ensure owners' rights, has now deeply infected the public sector. It plays to a specious notion of political correctness. This premise needs to be held to public scrutiny in both sectors. I wonder why this judgement by a previous Master of the Rolls is given such short shrift? Perhaps the regulators do not know it? But the public must.

The shareholders' lack of ownership and control of a corporation can be seen, for example, in the current confusion over the UK government's holding of the majority of the shares in the Royal Bank of Scotland. The government's massive contribution to the RBS bail-out in 2008 was stated as necessary because it was judged "too big to fail", i.e. the national banking and financial systems would collapse unless RBS was hugely supported. Yet, despite the politicians' expectations, the government-appointed shareholder seems to have little say over the bonuses of its employed executive bankers. This seems odd until one realizes that shareholders have no powers to appoint directors directly. The existing board creates the proposed new slate of directors so, at an AGM, shareholders can only influence through their votes and hope that the consequent publicity achieves their ends. Nor can they influence commercial policy except by persuasion. Which is why the growing number of "stakeholders" are demanding to have more say.

The current company legislation concerning ownership and leadership is in need of a drastic overhaul if we are to rebalance the ownership–control dilemma after 110 years of muddled thinking about the roles of directors and shareholders. I argue that the best resolution is to enforce the existing law more strongly, and to clarify the consequences of the Salomon Judgement on ownership, thus reversing the concept of ownership back to one in which the shareholders have clear property rights over the corporation while accepting their new duties of care.

Political intervention: ownership and board structure issues

Without such clarified shareholder power, the directors, and especially the executives, will continue to be tempted to play fast and loose with the company's assets. Other countries, including the Nordics, Germans and French, have tried to resolve this principle–agent corporate governance problem by creating "two-tier boards". The European Commission has advocated their mandatory use. The design comprises a higher-level supervisory board which focuses on the longer-term, more strategic and major funding issues of the enterprise, while the more day-to-day issues are handled by a second-tier operational board. Structurally, this seems an elegant solution but, in practice, it has been found to work only in very limited circumstances. The law of human cussedness cuts in, backed by the worst aspects of the Seven Deadly Sins.

Members of the supervisory board are directly responsible to the owner-shareholders. However, the shareholdings of such listed companies are often not widely distributed, but tend to be major owners with large blocks of interlinked shares, so conflicts of interest are frequent. The public rarely get a look-in, let alone any chance of influence. Such "bloc owners" are able to exert powerful control over the business. However, because of the cross-shareholdings, the directors do not always focus on the future health of the business, so short-term, micro-political issues can take undue priority, as we have seen with the recent Volkswagen pollution controls example. Directors' fiduciary duty can be compromised easily, particularly if they see themselves as subservient representatives of other shareholding blocs.

Matters are made worse if politicians then intervene with legislation for two-tier boards to secure their own political agenda. For example, in Germany, politicians insisted that a proportion of the supervisory board, as much as 50%, is made up of representatives of the trades unions. Such intervention fails to ensure "independence of thought" or a duty of care, skill and diligence. It merely adds another conflicted power bloc. Although this is designed to inspire cooperation between workers, directors and owners, it can lead to major and debilitating conflicts, especially in times of recession. The timescales of the different parties can also be contradictory and so jeopardize the long-term health of the business.

A classic case was seen in Germany with the problems at Metallgesellschaft in the mid-1990s, when the supervisory board had major problems in reining in an expansionist chief executive because the two sides of the supervisory board could not agree. The "business" half of the board represented major financial institutions and investors who were increasingly worried about the financial consequences of the rapid expansion, while the "union" side of the board were only too delighted as the plans meant more work for their members, regardless of the cost–reward ratio. Matters were made worse as the chairman of the supervisory board was the finance director of a major German international bank, which had significant investment in the company. The dispute destabilized the company for many years.

Having been questioned personally by the UK's Treasury Select Committee of Parliament on their reconsideration of the future corporate governance of the Bank of England, I was pleasantly surprised by the diversity of the committee and its willingness to listen. Except, that is, for an obsessed Scottish member who kept insisting for over 30 minutes that the "only answer" was a two-tier board. He became increasingly annoyed when I kept asking him "Why?" and I politely refuted each of his points with examples of why his solution would be inappropriate. In the end, he became so infuriated with me that he claimed I "was just a typically unworldly academic", which at least proved that he had not read his brief about me. Political intervention for a predetermined answer is never wise, as I show at the end of this chapter.

Re-establishing shareholder rights, duties and responsibilities

Despite the politicians' dreams, there is no perfect structural model for guaranteeing effective governance relationships between the shareholders, directors and executives. If there were, we'd all be using it. But there is a growing international trend to re-establish the supremacy of shareholder rights, then clarify their duties and so create a covenant for "owners", a category that will increasingly include stakeholders as inclusive capitalism gathers strength. This trend has become noticeably more strident since people's investments and pension funds started taking the brunt of quantitative easing and its long-term wealth-diluting consequences. The awakening of the public from their financial torpor is just beginning. Brexit and Trump will accelerate this.

"The creatures from the black lagoon": the future of asset and fund managers

The consciously created anti-customer attitudes and structures of much of the financial services industry is becoming more exposed. The attitude of "heads I win, tails you lose" is still prevalent, despite all the negative media coverage. There is no obvious desire from fund managers to reconsider their concept of ownership, nor to encourage wider share ownership, unless it allows them to squeeze even more cash from naïve punters. But even these creatures from the black lagoon are being exposed to the sunlight, as the public realize that their faith in always trusting your financial advisor is seriously flawed.

The structure of current financial services contains a large, slothful and greedy chain of intermediaries. This chain has been so profitable that financial services are often treated by government as a privileged industry, where even junior admin staff are guaranteed annual bonuses. There is no obvious logic for this. The long chains of agents all take their cut, and so significantly reduce the investors' real returns. Because many of these intermediaries are driven by bonuses based on *quarterly* performance, the notion of thoughtful, solid, long-term investment is frequently replaced with "socially useless",[154] manic and self-serving circular trading – "churning" – to achieve the quarterly targets. Examples such as the Libor and foreign exchange court cases have brought this incestuous and profitable corruption into the sunlight, and shown the world that the concept of owners' rights and duties is too often scorned. The scorning of owners' rights has been made easier because it has become increasingly difficult to identify the beneficial "owner", as the speed of trading, the rise of limited liability partnerships and the diversity of "impatient" shareholders increase. So fighting these over-extended agency chains is key to stopping the rot. But who now has the political will to do anything about this? And where is the public forum in which it can be openly debated? I shall tackle these questions in Chapter 6.

The changing ownership trends towards "stakeholders" and inclusive ownership

It is not as though we were not warned about this. Back in 2004, Tomorrow's Company, a lively and distinguished UK think-tank, published a report on the issues of ownership entitled *Tomorrow's Owners*.[155] Sadly, its message was way ahead of its time. Had it been published after the 2008 Western financial crisis, it would have had global interest and helped the debate. As it was, the report created spirited discussion, but among too small a minority to create critical mass. However, the report introduced the idea of *integrated ownership* as the key to the future successful development of our global organizations. The term "integrated ownership" was not meant to be a communistic concept of ownership, i.e. the means of production by the people. Instead, it suggested that future global needs will demand a major reduction of CEO-hegemony-led capitalism, and a rebalancing bringing all owners, property and emotional, into a mutually cooperative whole – of shareholders and stakeholders from the employees, customers, suppliers and local communities.

This concept reinforced the need for the reassertion of the supremacy of the board of directors under the existing company law, and for the shareholders to be recognized as the legal owners of that company. If these demands are then added to the growing raft of legislation for the new "stakeholders", then we are reaching a new landscape of ownership as a key part of inclusive capitalism.

This thinking is much closer to Nelson Mandela's *Ubuntu* notion than to Karl Marx's analysis. It is argued strongly by advocates that these new "stakeholders" add diversity, curiosity, creativity, depth and reality to the board's thinking. They are responsible for opening up the board debates towards satisfying the wider interests of the three capitals – environmental, social and financial – by discussing such issues as the firm's impact on physical extraction, local communities, employees and suppliers as a way of ensuring business success and so benefiting existing shareholders. These new groupings will need also to be underpinned by new and very different laws concerning the limitation of life, size, licence and the power of companies. These will deliver strong foundations for better strategic decision-making and the building of better business models thus optimizing the board's scarce resources rather than focusing on maximizing short-term profits.

Bonuses: the antithesis to professionalism

Many directors, executives, asset and fund managers hate these developments. They are a game-changing challenge to the "animal spirits" exuberance of the financial markets pre-2008, linked directly to the bonus-driven culture that created unbounded greed. This has led to an amoral and easy-money mind-set, to fashionable yet thoughtless "investments", to slothful market tracking, and rampant short-termism killing the concept of thoughtful long-term, "patient" investment while dismissing it as a utopian dream.

Consider the point at which the bonus culture corrupted the financial system. When did it suddenly become socially and politically acceptable for only financial services to be treated as a special case, rewarded much more than other industries and able to flaunt the ethical laws by which others are bound? Currently, we have a situation in financial services (and indeed the NHS and BBC) where distinctly average people are being paid above-average salaries and then bonuses to do their ordinary job – and often for a below-average performance. The public is wise to ask at what point did professionals, civil servants and middle managers, not just bankers, need to be "incentivized"? And why? Surely this is the antithesis of "professionalism"? It is even less logical to insist that the remuneration of such rather average people is ramped up because "we have to pay top dollar for top people". By statistical definition, not everyone can be in the upper quartile. Applying a normal distribution to such folk means that at least half of these "top" people must be underperforming. Why should they be incentivized?

Towards a fiduciary duty for owners

I argue that this nonsense has been driven by the lack of sense, or legal insistence, when considering the fiduciary duty of "impatient" shareholders. They need to be considered as equal players with directors for effective corporate governance to work. They should not be absolved from their fiduciary duty to hold their company in trust.

Their shares are investments, not gambling chips. This would help wipe out "flash traders". You can hear the agents of the overly long financial chains screaming that such action would be damaging to key liquidity in the markets. But would one need such high liquidity if there were fewer traders? It seems to me that such screams are really about protecting their doubtful incomes.

You can see the present dire position in the US and, even more starkly, in large Japanese companies. Shareholders in the US are rarely seriously considered as part of the business. They are often treated with contempt, or ignored as an unnecessary barnacle on the otherwise sleek hull of the executive vessel. Board directors are treated similarly. And the US state laws usually guarantee shareholders a lack of corporate control. These passive owners seem to accept that they can only piggy-back on the aspirations of the executives and so take their rewards in the form of dividends or capital gains on share sales. Dividends are their "bonus". Shareholders' lack of critical directoral and especially executive oversight does little to ensure the long-term success of "their" business. Governance problems emerge too late – when the executives find that suddenly the company has run out of growth, has over-expanded without sufficient funds, or wildly over-paid their executives. Either way, the shareholders miss out because there is so little that they can do about it. In the US it looks as though it will get worse.

Ownership categories and the Anglo-Saxon myth

Internationally, there is a great deal of talk about the varying models of ownership, ranging from the Islamic Sharia (risk sharing), through "Asian" (Chinese and South East Asian) and African (Ubuntu-style), to "European" (socialistic) and the "Anglo-Saxon" model. These classification categories are quite loose and I do not intend to enter into a deep analysis of them here. But I do want to address the confusion over the term "Anglo-Saxon", as this model affects much thinking, both inside and outside Western borders. The misnamed "Anglo-Saxon" model of the "equity shareholder" is much more acute in the US than the UK. It sees a shareholder only as the residual claimant on the business's assets, i.e. shareholders get what they can grab from dividend and asset growth and then can claim only the residual assets. Much of the misnaming of the category is based on the international perception that the UK and US legal systems are similar, when they are in truth diverging: the rules-based and principles-based governance systems being a prime example. This category error is then enlarged if you look at hi-tech and "gig-economy" companies as they develop an increasing anti-shareholder stance in the US. How the US will cope with inclusive capitalism will be intriguing.

Gig-economy ownership issues

Shareholders wanting to encourage the development of growth companies in the gig economy, hi-tech, TED (technology, entertainment and design) and biosciences, which demand the *human* capital that creates innovation through ideas, face a particular ownership problem. These companies offer less tangible short-term returns, are more volatile because of the human factors, and they demand long-term, "sticky" investors. The entrepreneur-owners, employees and investors have far more exposure to risk. Intermediary fund managers find such companies increasingly uncomfortable and are wary of investing. They cannot guarantee predictable quarterly returns, often have huge rates of expansion, and so are frequently under-capitalized. History tells us that 80% of them will fail in the first three years. So investment is often left to family, friends or fools. Few expect major returns for such high risks and many have strong feelings of altruism in their emotional ownership.

Therefore it is astonishing that investors are lured with the promise of massive returns especially in the gig-economy companies of Silicon Valley's IPOs (initial public offerings). Some, like Facebook and Google, seem to have "made it", although whether their astronomic valuations can be sustained is still a matter for careful observation. The social media rising star Snap seeks to raise around US$4 billion and a valuation of some US$25 billion. It listed in New York in the world's largest IPO. But it is following a worrying trend. Shareholders have "curtailed voting rights" so that the founders retain control. This follows a growing number of Silicon Valley stars creating non-voting shares. This is a serious reduction in the democratic concept of shareholder control and a worrying rise in founder autocracy. When linked to monopolistic and tax-avoidance strategies internationally, this is cause for great corporate governance concern. These will not be countered by two new pieces of US code writing – Principles of Corporate Governance for US Listed Companies[156] and Commonsense Principles of Corporate Governance.[157] While both seek "the fundamental right of shareholders to elect directors whom they believe are best suited to represent their interests and the long-term interests of their company", they quickly diverge, sadly, on such mundane issues as proxy voting and executive remuneration. They never face the fundamental issue of ownership and so let the autocrats continue.

"If investing is poker, are fund managers a busted flush?"

Back in the less risky world, it is increasingly obvious that the financial system, and its many agents, needs a complete reframing of its roles and responsibilities. As the public become aware of the possibility of *their* stewardship roles and the duties that come with their invested wealth, do we still need the long chain of intermediaries? The public's wealth is usually invested through pension funds, investment trusts, insurers, mortgage companies, ISAs (individual savings accounts) and the like, so do we still need separate fund managers and the allied professions?

I was at a large asset managers' conference in October 2013 and was shocked at the whingeing and the lack of imagination of the vast majority of the 400 in the hall. "We will never be able to get back to the old days of a return of 4% net for our clients" was the moan, and it was followed by a general acceptance that there was little that anyone could do about it. They all felt doomed. Only one person pointed out that they had achieved returns of at least 10%

throughout the 2008 crisis and had done so for over 120 years by following very conservative and unfashionable long-term investment principles. This statement went down very badly, and the underperformers huddled together for warmth against such a heretical blast. As the hall was gloomy, physically and emotionally, I went outside into the sunshine at lunchtime, crossed the street and joined a guided tour of the massive, new, complex and diverse mixed-development site at Kings Cross, London – said to be the largest urban development site in western Europe.

The owners, Hermes EOS, the developers, Argent, and their "responsible investors" had taken a very imaginative long-term, even Sharia-like, project investment and risk-sharing approach for a period of some 25 years. They were not trapped by introverted thinking, fixation on quarterly returns, or spot-welded to their high-frequency trading algorithms. They were very cheerful because already residents, office workers, shoppers, arts students, intrigued members of the general public and builders swarmed over their half-finished site. Rents were being paid, asset values had rocketed and people liked being there. Pop-up food and gift stalls had appeared and street life thrived. Developers of further development phases were thrilled as the new residential properties were selling well. Google was building a million-square-foot European HQ on the site. The London University of the Arts had created a million square feet of campus there. New medical facilities, schools, housing and offices were appearing. It had already become a "hub", and other sites were appearing on its fringes, including the world-class bioscience research facility the Francis Crick Institute.

The owners and developers were immensely proud of their project: something that few fund managers can say. No whingeing about sub-4% returns here. It was so well ahead of schedule that they expected to finish most of the development five years early. The positive effect on their long-term investment returns is huge. It put the small-minded, doom-laden, risk-averse, industry-formula-following, introverted conference-goers into perspective. It made me ask why were those fund managers in the hall needed? Most fund managers seem to talk themselves into a psychological state of institutional pessimism, especially when fixated on delivering their quarterly return mandate. These mandates are frequently written by under-trained trustees with little experience of the "sticky" and "patient" world of long-term finance. I have spoken with fund managers who say that their share portfolio holds over 4,000 different shares and consider this normal. When pressed on the amount of annual analysis they can give to each share each year, they admit that, apart from their maximum 200 top-performing shares, the average time they spend on paid "analysis" for clients of all the others is 20 minutes a year. They admit also that this is "hardly time to open their annual reports and read the executive summary".

But what really worries me is that, whatever the fund managers' performance, they continue to be contracted for their overpaid services. This caused me to do some deeper thinking. This was reinforced, and much more concisely stated, when the *Financial Times*'s Merryn Somerset Webb ran a two-page spread entitled "If investing is poker, are fund managers a busted flush?"[158]

Something was definitely changing. The article poses some basic questions which beneficial owners must first ask themselves and then, given the woeful returns on their current savings, pensions and annuities, demand much more constructive answers from their fund managers. The article is worth examining as the author is an acknowledged international authority and the Editor-in-Chief of *MoneyWeek* and so deep into the awful reality of asset management.

Merryn states that fund managers claim to be nice people who buy quality goods at reasonable prices. They claim to run their funds as Warren Buffett did, ignoring "short-term noise" and focusing on long-term trends, using "strict valuation criteria". But, in reality, they do the opposite: overtrading conventional stocks in order to meet their quarterly index targets.

Merryn claims that this short-term trading is naïve as there are proven methods of making excellent returns over the long term with both stocks and bonds. For example, it is clear from "the tables of Cyclically Adjusted Price/Earnings Ratio (CAPE) . . . that if you invest when the CAPE is low, you make excellent returns over the following ten year period."

But, if it's that easy, why do most fund managers still underperform? The answer is simple. It's because large fund management companies force their managers to track their benchmark indexes, because the companies "make their profits more from gathering money than they do from making money", and because most clients grow uncertain if their stocks initially lose money and sell them on before they have a chance to rise again. The average fund manager is therefore "overly short term", tends to overtrade, prioritizes collecting fees from shareholders rather than earning large long-term rewards for existing clients, and "almost always holds too many shares in very large companies".

If you add to this damning criticism the inefficient organization structures of fund managers, especially that long chain of agents each taking a fee, then you could easily see them in terminal decline. Indeed in the UK in 2014, 136 went out of business.

But the financial illiteracy of most clients slows this Darwinian process. Currently, asset management is still highly profitable in the UK. Indeed, many in financial services see it as the best business to be in, despite the vicissitudes of the Western financial crisis. It does not face the price competition found in the US. This is mainly because of that mixture of ignorance and complacency found in the clients and the beneficial owners. The public are not inquisitive in the key area of costs, and use few benchmarks. So they lose out constantly in their pension funds and investments. McKinsey, a management consultant, published a report in 2013 which noted that asset managers in the UK in 2012 had an average return on equity of 16.5%. On average, banks returned 9% and insurers 6.1%. Profit margins are in the upper 20% and the most profitable reach above 40%.[159] It is a very good business to be in if you are not customer-focused and rarely outperform the market. The funds typically charge 1.5% a year for their services, of which at least half went on their own pay platforms and advisors. The scope for efficiencies and lower costs looks wide. But until the public, as beneficial owners, regularly ask many more intelligently naïve questions about the costs, competence and performance of their pensions and savings, asset managers will continue to offer a pricey and ineffective service.

I have a smidgen of sympathy for fund managers. They are placed in an impossible position because they are rewarded for always outperforming each other in the highly uncertain and changing conditions of the financial markets. This is a logical nonsense, as by statistical definition only 50% are likely to outperform the others and the bulk of these will not be outstanding. So why should a fund manager accept an emotionally risky mandate? Yet many choose to do so.

Fund managers and their love affairs: the odd mindset of many fund managers

The main reason seems to be a willingness to face the daily challenge of clearly winning or losing. Yet this creates great and continuing personal anxiety. A study of 50 fund managers on three continents by David Tuckett of University College London[160] suggests that they rationalize the impossible by creating convincing "narratives". However, to convince its originator such a narrative *must* ignore some (possibly helpful) information. This process is often unconscious yet it stabilizes the fund manager's confidence, and so sanity, in times of high ambiguity and uncertainty in the markets. Tuckett says, "The great thing about a story is that it can smoothly get rid of information. Stories create a believable picture of an imagined future by being attracted to the option for some gain, repelling any potential doubts about loss." This is a phenomenon seen ad nauseam on both sides of the Brexit and Trump debates.

Tuckett describes how, after fund managers have made a selection, they enter into a dependent relationship with their investment not unlike a love affair:

> Fundamentally one has to enter into an emotional relationship with one's stocks if one is going to accept the risk to invest. It's a fantasy. It's an idea of something which is more than realistically possible. A good analogy would be the way we idealize our romantic partner, which enables us to make the kind of commitment necessary to engage

and marry. Of course you start with a great love and then gradually it becomes more realistic.

To a member of the investing public this can sound truly alarming. Haven't we chosen a fund manager who will not only protect our investment but demonstrate their expertise by increasing it? Usually no: as market trackers seem to have as good, or better, performance than almost all active fund managers and they are cheaper. Indeed, I wonder if some fund managers rationalize their "narratives" by telling themselves lies? Investing is a funny old world.

Does high-frequency trading negate ownership?

The concept of ownership becomes even more complex as new digital technology, specifically high-frequency trading algorithms, has developed far enough to demolish the concept of ownership altogether. This *is* rocket science. Many of the young physicists and mathematicians writing such algorithms could have gone into space science but were seduced by the money. The rise and rise of high-frequency trading means that investment managers' algorithms are trawling the markets 24/7 for almost 365 days a year. They are seeking arbitrage – small differences in prices which other players or markets have not yet picked up – so that they can trade ahead of the herd. There is always an asymmetry of information in the markets, as even Alan Greenspan has now conceded. Does this matter? Yes. It's becoming just a "slippery" gambling game, far removed from the original notion of investment as a long-term wealth-creating mechanism. The US regulatory authorities are now investigating whether the laying of a perfectly straight 400-mile landline to the New York stock market, to gain faster information of buys and sells ahead of honest real-time orders, is a modern form of insider trading. Are these to be the new accepted business values? It reinforces the international perception that financial markets are founded on never giving the suckers a fair chance.

Socially useless churning and corruption

It is the nature of "socially useless" trading activities to turn rapidly into corrupt practices. Money market managers have already convinced many investors of the need to "churn" their money regularly "in order to beat the market". This rarely makes noticeable improvements for the investor, but guarantees a constant stream of "churn" fees for the money managers. Their industry's revenue grew from 0.24% of US GDP in 1980 to 2.44% in 2007, and is now rising even faster. We are talking hundreds of billions of dollars here.[161] And their fees for such churning are not cheap. At 1.9% on assets each year, an investor's savings could be depleted by nearly half over a thirty-year period. So what does ownership now mean in this system? And should the asset managers have a legal fiduciary duty of stewardship to their clients?

Two ways forward

We face two unresolved property ownership questions, both of which are of increasing public concern. First, should we now distinguish clearly in law between shares as longer-term investments and those shares as instruments for instant trading? Second, should we reassert the shareholders' rights of control over a company so that they, including fund managers holding shares on behalf of a client, have clear legal fiduciary *duties* as well as rights? Should future shareholders and their agents have a duty of active oversight to ensure the continuing health of the company in which they are invested?

Unless there can be a clear legal definition agreed as to types of future shares, then the second question remains an unanswered and confusing mess. The casino markets will continue, as will the rot. There have been attempts in, for example, the Netherlands to give bonus shares to shareholders who keep their shares for more than two years. In the UK, the creation of two classes of shares, "A" and "B", has been around for some time, but there has been no noticeable success on this front. These shares tend to be used much more to retain the original investors' control than to clarify their long-term and short-term contradictions. And the Silicon Valley billionaires now have a campaign to create "C" shares which give shareholders no legal governance rights at all. What could take us forward?

The UK's Stewardship Code

The UK is to be congratulated for its early attempts to focus and resolve these issues by developing the concept of "stewardship" for both directors and owners. It is the first country to launch a national Stewardship Code through the Financial Reporting Council.[162] But there are still many problems. "Stewardship" is not defined in a clear and helpful way. Given what I have said of the unresolved questions above, this is not such a surprise. But this lack of definition, coupled with the opaqueness of shareholders' duties, does little to help the public's confusion. It allows the casino markets to roll on with their socially useless products.

For me, "stewardship" is too passive a mind-set. It suggests being concerned with the maintenance of assets, rather than their development for the future health of an organization and its owners and stakeholders. Consider that the word "development" is derived from the Latin *volupe* and has two consecutive meanings: first, seeing the potential richness within and, second, making this potential manifest. So it concerns the sequential use of imagination, risk and then effective implementation. It is the lack of these qualities in many current "stewards" that worries me. Very few of the current stewards that I have met seem at all concerned with voluptuousness.

Let us look critically at what is now promulgated. The UK's FRC 2012 Stewardship Code is aspirational but contains little practical advice. It states that "Stewardship aims to promote the long-term success of companies in such a way that the ultimate providers of capital also prosper." Note the "also": this mind-set still sees shareholders as also-rans not as active owners. *Effective stewardship benefits companies, investors and the economy as a whole*, it asserts. It could, but only if the ownership of the legal entity is returned to the shareholders and their agents. Even then, the definition needs to be expanded to cover the interests of those fast-emerging "stakeholders". Then it needs to establish the future fiduciary duty of all, to exercise their responsibilities for ensuring the future health of the company.

The 2012 Stewardship Code avoids these issues by stating:

> In publicly listed companies, responsibility for stewardship is shared. The primary responsibility rests with the board of a company, which oversees the actions of management. Investors in the company also play an important role in holding the board to account for the fulfilment of its responsibilities.

Again, note the "also". But legally they cannot hold the board to account, except in specified circumstances, because of the legal fiction of the company being a separate legal personality. And why does the Code apply only to publicly listed companies when they are a tiny minority of a nation's registered companies and organizations? If this code is to have an impact, it must apply to all registered companies, and to public sector organizations and charities.

So the next three paragraphs in the Code are purely aspirational, without a firm legal basis or process for implementation:

> For investors, stewardship is more than just voting. Activities may include monitoring and engaging with companies on matters such as strategy, performance, risk, capital structure and corporate governance, including culture and remuneration. Engagement is purposeful dialogue with companies on these matters as well as on issues that are the immediate subject of votes at general meetings.

My criticism here is that the focus seems to have been written more to deliver a code, rather than to focus on the wider aspiration of developing long-term healthy companies nationally. There is no mention of engaging with companies and boards on the fundamental issue of purpose (Why does this company exist? And how will we know when it has achieved this?), nor of the ethical human values and long-term culture on which it is built, nor any acknowledgement that the future business world will have to take much greater account of the rising power of "stakeholders" (staff, suppliers, representatives of the three capitals and their impact on the communities within which they exist) and will be assessed publicly by them.

> Institutional investors' activities include decision-making on matters such as allocating assets, awarding investment mandates, designing investment strategies and buying or selling specific securities. The division of duties within and between institutions may span a spectrum, such that some may be considered asset owners and others asset managers.

My criticism here is twofold. First, the activities listed do not set any values-based context in which they are to be assessed. Second, by splitting the terms "asset owners" and "asset managers", it suggests the latter can escape ever being part of a fiduciary duty system. Any duty of care, skill and diligence for them is missing.

The Introduction to the Code ends: "Compliance with the Code does not constitute an invitation to manage the affairs of a company or preclude a decision to sell a holding, where this is considered to be in the best interest of clients or beneficiaries." I feel that this exemplifies the confusion in the drafters' minds. They have muddled directors and their clear legal duties with managers who are not so circumscribed. Their focus should be on investors ensuring that the directors, not the managers, fulfil their seven general duties of directors under the 2006 Companies Act, not the daily management of the company.

And little is said of the scandalous behaviour of, for example, many pension fund trustees, who have simply abdicated their onerous duties to fund managers by badly drafted mandates, in the hope that the consequent underperformance of their funds is not noticed or criticized by the ultimate beneficiaries.

All of this may seem harsh criticism of a well-intentioned initiative, but I feel that it is in line with my arguments throughout this book concerning the lack of an integrated national corporate governance system in the UK, and no agreed competence measures by which to assess each of the parts – ownership in this case. Nevertheless, the

FRC is to be congratulated on at least starting the debate, even if it is not yet properly in the public domain and is currently discussed quietly between consenting adults. South Africa has followed suit, and I await more feedback from their experiment with the Code for Responsible Investing in South Africa (CRISA) recommendations.[163]

More ways forward: responsible investing

The UK has gone further by developing three more ways to tackle fundamental ownership issues. First, it commissioned the Kay Review of the UK Equity Markets and Long-Term Decision Making,[164] and, second, it signed the United Nations Global Compact, incorporated into which are (third) its Principles for Responsible Investment.[165] When implemented over the next decade, these three initiatives will have a positive global impact on effective corporate and national governance by helping owners face their duties. It demonstrates that at least the UK's political heart is in the right place, even if its political brain needs some rewiring and refocusing. Let us look briefly at what I feel are significant signposts for the future of ownership, governance and capitalism.

The Kay Review 2012

This is an important building block in restoring the balance between shareholders, fund managers and boards. It was commissioned by the UK's Secretary of State for Business, Vince Cable, and published in 2012. Its most significant advance is to state that governmental and regulatory authorities need to accept the strong public criticisms and explore the radical concept of putting the client's interests first. Given the toxic greedy self-interest of the last three decades, this is a demand for seismic change. It has not gone down well with the investment industry. Good. Its proposed changes will now be implemented through the politicians and regulators – if they have the political courage. This is still to be tested fully as it may just be kicked into the long grass forever. Written by a group led by John Kay, an acknowledged independent thinker and economist, and driven by the growing national political discomfort at the lack of rectification of the scandals of the dereliction of fiduciary duties – highlighted during the Western financial crisis – it argues for both structural reforms and, most importantly, reforms to the culture and mind-sets of those involved in investment and asset management. It accepts that, ultimately, investment is a very human activity and is always subject to the values, joys and frailties of the people involved.

The Review sets out ten principles for equity markets:

1. All participants in the equity investment chain should act according to the principles of stewardship, based on respect for those whose funds are invested or managed, and trust in those by whom the funds are invested or managed.

2. Relationships based on trust and respect are everywhere more effective than trading transactions between anonymous agents in promoting high performance of companies and securing good returns to savers taken as a whole.

3. Asset managers can contribute more to the performance of British business (and in consequence to overall returns to their savers) through greater involvement with the companies in which they invest.

4. Company directors are stewards of the assets and operations of their business. The duties of company directors are to the company, not its share price, and companies should aim to develop relationships with investors, rather than with "the market".

5. All participants in the equity investment chain should act in good faith, in the best long-term interests of their clients or beneficiaries, and in line with generally prevailing standards of decent behaviour. This means ensuring that the direct and indirect costs of services provided are reasonable and disclosed, and that conflicts of interest are avoided wherever possible, or else disclosed or otherwise managed to the satisfaction of the client or beneficiary. These obligations should be independent

of the classification of the client and should not be contractually overridden.

6. At each stage of the equity investment chain, reporting of performance should be clear, relevant, timely, related closely to the needs of users and directed to the creation of long-term value in the companies in which savers funds are invested.

7. Metrics and models used in the equity investment chain should give information directly relevant to the creation of long-term value in companies and good risk-adjusted long-term returns to savers.

8. Risk in the equity investment chain is the failure of companies to meet the reasonable expectations of their stakeholders or the failure of investments to meet the reasonable expectations of savers. Risk is not the short-term volatility of returns, or tracking errors relative to an index benchmark, and the use of such metrics and models should be discouraged.

9. Market incentives should enable and encourage companies, savers and intermediaries to adopt investment approaches that achieve long-term returns by supporting and challenging corporate decisions in pursuit of long-term values.

10. The regulatory framework should enable and encourage companies, savers and intermediaries to adopt such investment approaches.

This is an exemplary set of principles, firmly in line with human values, integrated reporting and effective corporate governance. Readers will see the connections between the Kay Review geared specifically for investment issues and the wider concepts that I am advocating for corporate governance. The notions of putting the customer first, of selfless professional ethics, of the importance of long-term thinking, of human values-based behaviour, of the careful use of metrics and performance rewards, and the necessary changes in the regulatory mind-set are all present.

The National Investors' Forum

Kay goes further and argues for a National Investors' Forum, where the public can oversee and constructively interrogate all the parties involved, and learn from them on a regular basis. I pursue this idea in Chapter 6 as a component of a wider national system. Unsurprisingly, this has not had such an enthusiastic take-up from the existing players. Indeed, the UK cross-party select committee investigating the progress of the Kay Review has signalled doubts about just how much of the review will be implemented. I review their doubts in Chapter 6, and will discuss how the blocks to reform in this area are created. And I shall argue for a structural repositioning of corporate governance in the national regulatory framework, by giving it primacy.

The United Nations Global Compact: the global rise of "stakeholders" and "ESG"

The Kay Review can be seen as a fractal of a growing global movement, signalling that executive-led and financially fixated capitalism is reaching its "use by" date. In many countries, the public has reached a point beyond which it will no longer tolerate such selfish values. The Brexit and Trump electoral results are clear examples of a rejection of "the spoilt elite". This global unease with current capitalism is not so new. In 2000 it led to the United Nations creating the Global Compact. This seminal document was developed under the chairmanship of Sir Mark Moody-Stuart. Its ten principles need to be pinned on the boardroom wall of every existing organization that is serious about creating a healthy future.[166]

Happily, the document's focus is not on massive national treaties and consequential presidential and prime ministerial grandstanding, patronage and the likely later abuse of public office. It relies on the values of honesty, modesty and diligence. It is not mandatory. Boards and individual directors sign up to it publicly but without fanfares. Any publicity is for the individuals or corporations to give. It has a strong ethical base of human rights, development and cooperation.

This means that it is, by definition, slow-growing, yet made stronger by self-implementation. It is designed so that the subsequent learning is freely shared.

> The UN Global Compact is a strategic policy initiative for businesses that are committed to aligning their operations and strategies with ten universally accepted principles in the areas of human rights, labour, environment and anti-corruption ... As social, political and economic challenges (and opportunities) ... affect business more than ever before, many companies recognize the need to collaborate and partner with governments, civil society, labour and the United Nations.[167]

It is this growing recognition that businesses, public or private, can no longer assume substantial public support, or rely on indifference, to operate purely for their own ends. It challenges the maximization of profit only in the financial interests of the owners with just enough public benefit "trickle-down" to allow them to continue operating. In future, businesses will have to cultivate more diverse players to formulate their policy development and strategy – the broad deployment of their scarce resources. It is relatively easy to see future discussions with, for example, trades unions, suppliers and educational institutions. But the UN Global Compact has a wider vision, and introduces the concept of the additional future stewardship of the physical environment and local communities as well as financial capital – the full "ESG". It argues that these will become significant factors in the determination of future business strategy. Currently, this argument is manna to many, and heresy to many more. But it is happening, in both the developing and developed world. Early indications of such "triple bottom line" annual reporting and "integrated reporting" are that it is commented on favourably by shareholders and stakeholders, as the reports of Shell and Novo Nordisk demonstrate.

ESG versus CRG and stakeholders

The voluntary reporting area, now known as "ESG" (environment, social and governance), mentioned in Chapter 2, has continued to develop over the last decade. All three complementary areas of ESG accept "stakeholders" as a natural part of future business operations. They are part of the balance mechanism of those three capitals – finance, natural and people – needed now for a long-term future for any business. These "stakeholders" are not there to interfere with the daily, managerial operations of the business, unless it is breaking UN commitments. They are there to provide an agreed critical framework and to influence by widening critical comment on policy and strategy for the long term. The stakeholder role is designed to encourage intelligently naïve questioning of the strategic decision-makers.

However, stakeholders do hold some external "community" powers over any organization, such as the issuing of planning permissions, negotiating employment contracts and granting new "licences to operate". Not every corporate or politician is happy with this power shift, especially in the US, where the previously mentioned alternative to ESG – CRG (compliance, regulation and governance) holds sway. As mentioned, I feel that such wording clearly shows that the narrow-focused US legalistic and business mind-set is designed to fail. Remember that Enron was 100% compliant under US CRG-style corporate rules. It was also proven corrupt in the courts.

The UN Global Compact Principles
The UN Global Compact is built on ten fundamental principles:

Human rights
1. Businesses should support and respect the protection of internationally proclaimed human rights; and

2. Make sure that they are not complicit in human rights abuses.

Labour
3. Businesses should uphold the freedom of association and the effective recognition of the right to collective bargaining;

4. The elimination of all forms of forced and compulsory labour;

5. The effective abolition of child labour; and

6. The elimination of discrimination in respect of employment and occupation.

Environment

7. Businesses should support a precautionary approach to environmental challenges.

8. Undertake initiatives to promote greater environmental responsibility; and

9. Encourage the development and diffusion of environmentally friendly technologies.

Anti-corruption

10. Businesses should work against corruption in all its forms, including extortion and bribery.

I believe that these ten principles do help boards create a solid basis for the development of the stakeholder-oriented and more democratic organizations for the 21st century. The UN Global Compact helps open the necessary broader mind-set for boards, shareholders and stakeholders to monitor. Within it, there are more concrete principles that allow shareholders and the public to hold all three parties to account.

The Principles for Responsible Investment (PRI)

As a complement to the Global Compact and the UNEP Finance Initiative, the PRI (Principles for Responsible Investment) has developed its Six Principles. These take a strongly "ESG" approach and are designed to change dramatically future financial reporting and annual auditing. By so doing, they will bring the issue of owners' duties to the fore of the investor and ownership debate.

The principles are:

1. We will incorporate ESG issues into investment analysis and decision-making processes.

2. We will be active owners and incorporate ESG issues into our ownership policies and practices.

3. We will seek appropriate disclosure on ESG issues by the entities in which we invest.

4. We will promote acceptance and implementation of the Principles within the investment industry.

5. We will work together to enhance our effectiveness in implementing the Principles.

6. We will each report on our activities and progress towards implementing the Principles.

Although still in their early stages, the combination of the Global Compact and the PRI already provide a strong framework for each company, and country, to develop its approach to balanced wealth creation, economic and social stability, effective corporate governance oversight, and integrated reporting. They are to be applauded. Now it is up to the public to demand of politicians and corporations that these principles are adopted and implemented in a culturally acceptable way across all organizations in their countries.

Over the next decade, I can see both the Global Compact and the PRI becoming the global default position for annual corporate integrated reporting. Indeed, my only proviso is that, while we push for international cooperation on the development of effective corporate governance, we remain culturally sensitive to the history and values of the countries involved. Effective corporate governance can be developed in many ways, and so it needs a diversity-based approach. There is no single Western/US formula.

Public ownership

I have to admit that I am still puzzled by the concept of "public ownership". Is it one of those convenient phrases which, if repeated often enough, becomes established as a fact? It represents currently the sum of political initiatives by which the state owns and holds land

and other assets on behalf of the nation. The organizational assets are owned "for the national good", like the NHS or BBC, for which the public has great affection but little public awareness of its legal status. In either case, what role should the government, as "owner", play in deciding how best to balance the direction of the company and how to prudently control the deployment of its assets? Political thinking about the governance of such public bodies is muddled. The BBC has been created as a separate, independent legal entity created by the granting of a Royal Charter. The NHS is a department of state that has central control over what are notionally autonomous public bodies: for example, NHS Foundation Trusts. But the temptation for politicians to meddle in the direction, management and organization of any publicly owned body is huge. That is when the rot starts.

How should "the public interest" be best served by effective corporate governance across the wide diversity of public organizations? Our current answer is essentially procedural rather than driven by the same laws as the private sector. At the national, regional and local levels, we regularly elect our agents, the politicians, to decide this. While this is the essence of a healthy democratic process, the downside is that politicians who are not trained in corporate governance, directing or strategic thinking can intervene and wreck such organizations. To solve this issue, we need to create legal forms that allow the public to have oversight over public organizations' assets, and to which the politicians, civil servants and their appointed agents can be held accountable. Without clarity in this area, the notion of "public accountability" is invalid, so political messiness and zero-sum power battles continue.

The big battles in this area have always been portrayed in party political terms. The extreme left were for "nationalization" and total control of the means of production. The extreme right were for privatization of as many state services as possible, to fulfil their wish for "small government, free markets and maximum individual liberty". Within such rhetoric, the British have muddled on in their self-deprecating, mildly effective, compromising and wavy way. Or at least they did until the Western financial crisis of 2008.

The consequent reduction in national spending plans and the growth of medium-term austerity regimes threw into sharp relief the question of the ownership of public institutions. The public naïvely assumed that this issue must have been resolved decades before, and that it was therefore inviolable. But no-one had really tested this. For example, we still have not tested who "owns" an NHS Foundation Trust hospital, or who owns the BBC, or a government agency. I have been surprised in my research to find just how difficult it is to get an answer to these questions, even from the top governmental lawyers. Legal and emotional ownership are often in sharp conflict. The general assumption is that "we" (the public) own them. Or that perhaps they are held in trust by the government through their unelected directors and managers in some form of stewardship? Or perhaps not? But without an answer to the ownership question, it is impossible to have effective corporate governance of such institutions.

Who "owns" an NHS Foundation Trust?

As an example, I was particularly interested in the "ownership" of NHS Foundation Trust hospitals. When I started asking the question, it seemed easy to answer, as there had been two recent National Health Service Acts and the 2006 Act had mentioned the Foundation Trusts as legal entities. So, when I checked that the use of Company Law and governance codes were therefore appropriate, I was surprised to run into a wall of obfuscation. Years of rhetoric in Parliament, truckloads of papers, and continuous investigations in the media and parliamentary committees must have resolved this? I started with the obvious source, Monitor – then the regulator for the NHS Foundation Trusts. They were charming, but they could not answer this fundamental question. They could give me operational rules but could not give a definitive legal answer on ownership. Next I went to the sponsors of the recent parliamentary bills, but I could still get no hard answers. Indeed, a leading sponsor of one of the bills got very angry with me at a weekend dinner party and said that I was talking absolute rubbish when I told her there seemed to be no legal entity for an NHS FT. She promised that, first thing on Monday morning, she would send me the relevant clause in the 2006 Act to stop me asking such a stupid question. My business card was taken and the offended party would not speak to me for the rest of the evening. On Monday morning nothing arrived, nor for the rest of the week. By chance I met her partner the following week and was told that she could not respond as there was no such clarifying clause. "*Ownership had been assumed* by all sides during the writing and political negotiating of the Act, but never clarified," he explained. He went further and said that it was assumed that all must be OK because "people like us do not make such basic mistakes". You do if you are carrying that elitist mix of ignorance and arrogance in regard to corporate governance.

I then checked this out informally with a previous attorney general who confirmed my suspicion and said, "You must understand that the issue is known in government but there is no political will in any of the main parties to resolve this issue. We get political leverage out of the resulting ambiguity taking praise when we can and avoiding blame when there is trouble." At least he was honest.

So when I address foundation trusts and public sector agencies as part of my board development work, I have to start, with the agreement of Monitor, by telling them that they are not a legal entity, so no-one is sure of their board's ultimate legal accountabilities and whether company law can be applied. However, Monitor then instructed me to say that I could get round the issue by insisting that NHS FT boards must follow good practice as laid out in the general duties of directors in the Companies Act 2006 and the NHS modified version of the Code of Corporate Governance.[168] So an NHS FT is to be treated in practice as a limited liability company but without the protection of company law and without the autonomy of a board to deploy appropriately its scarce resources. This suggestion is being made to work but it is personally uncomfortable and demotivating for those volunteering as directors who work for little financial reward and are putting their family's wealth on the line by accepting unlimited liability.

Political rhetoric wrecks corporate governance

A classic example of what follows from a mixture of ignorant arrogance and political fixation rolled out before my eyes. The basic assumption among politicians was that neither company law nor the good-practice codes applied to them. Some politicians even believed that an instruction by the regulator to work "under company law as far as possible" was too much like "being privatized", which they argued the NHS must never be. So they sought to disable effective corporate governance practice in an astonishing and unwise way.

A gloriously impractical solution was created by the politicians and the bureaucrats for NHS FTs. Their solution was to add an *additional* board to oversee the first board, thus breaking the very essence of company law: the sovereignty of the single board of directors. This edict created corporate governance confusion and anger, bad practice and a guaranteed lack of trust between the two boards from the start. I expand this example later in this chapter.

The lack of a legally defined corporate entity for many state-owned bodies and the consequent devolution of appropriate powers to deliver their purpose heightens the continuing values clash between politicians and directors. Increasingly, the government demands that directors undertake onerous accountabilities and liabilities for minuscule pay (many do not even take this), but without an agreed constitutional framework by which their governance performance can be assessed or appealed. The new directors' experience of "the public sector ethos" is then strained. Many have been directors in the private sector, and therefore find it hard to grasp the legal fluffiness of the basis of an NHS Foundation Trust. The new directors' essentially pro-bono mind-set is worthy and public-spirited, yet it exposes them to great personal risk, without proper training or cover, in an increasingly litigious society. Indeed, I wonder which legal entities and individuals will be sued finally for misconduct and gross negligence in the Mid Staffs hospital debacle?

But the confusion over the relationship between government and corporate governance goes deeper. All politicians assume, and the public allows them to assume, that *they* must know what effective corporate governance is because they understand "government" and have passed the relevant laws. Why do the public assume this? Politicians are not trained or assessed in "corporate governance" and few have any experience of organizational life other than the fetid and febrile culture of their party political machines. It is sad that many still see themselves as the "heaven-born", omniscient.

This "do as I say, not as I do" attitude is intensified in the state-owned enterprises by the feeling of many of their professionals, directors and senior managers that, because they are experts in one field, this expertise must automatically transfer to such fields as corporate governance and organizational behaviour. This is not proven. My intention here is not to keep knocking the NHS as an institution, or civil servants and experts, but to highlight that this destructive thinking is endemic across the public sector. It is unwise to expect that a nuclear submariner, a pollution monitor or a cartographer will automatically be able prudently to direct and control an organization.

Following the continuing scandals in health, social care, the police, the prisons and the BBC, the public are beginning to realize that such issues will not be solved until they are both clarified legally and ring-fenced politically to avoid crass interventions. The longest life of a parliament is only five years and, with political parties deliberately designed to be antagonistic in opposition, this is too short a time-span to establish any long-term effective public investment or tested corporate governance structure. For example, just count the number of secretaries of state and health ministers there have been in the last 15 years. And then review the two major Health Act restructurings that have destabilized the NHS. This demonstrates that neither political party truly "values" or owns this institution, despite their daily rhetoric. Nor do they have a concept of how to govern it effectively.

NHS Foundation Trust boards of governors: a case study in the design of ineffectiveness

Earlier in this chapter, I presented a classic example of political and bureaucratic arrogance and ignorance overcoming effective practice, with the creation of two boards for NHS Foundation Trusts. The political driver for this was the recurring, fashionable notion – promoted by all major political parties – for there to be "more community participation" mixed with "better oversight of boards". What they are really saying is that, "despite our rhetoric, we will not let the boards be truly autonomous as we want operational control over them to take the praise and blame them for the problems". But their lack of understanding and experience of effective governance, mixed with the bullying convictions of those pushing a political agenda, has led to the self-induced chaos which resulted in the creation of *parallel* boards – a board of directors and a board of governors – in NHSFTs. It is a definitive case of what happens when a body of experts in one field decides that this gives them the right to be experts in another, without the intervening variables of humility and common sense.

Matters were made worse by the fact that Monitor, the then regulator of NHS Foundation Trusts, had already published its own detailed code of corporate governance for the trusts, based on the Cadbury Code. Few of those responsible for these new changes seemed to have understood that code's private sector context and meaning, nor did they have the humility to realize that some basic testing and rigorous learning was needed before it could be transferred to the NHS. They believed that their espousal would simply do the trick. Those involved assumed that their opinions were more important than the private sector's experience. The "public consultation" process for the proposed new structure was desultory and brief. Many of the existing Trust directors felt that the outcome was predetermined so they dreaded the consequences. Yet few spoke out.

Their corporate governance design had two main faults. First, as well as having an existing "board of directors", they felt the necessity for a parallel "board of governors" would "better ensure public oversight of the board of directors and allow deeper community involvement". Any intelligent member of the public could predict that conflict and a major loss of trust between the two boards was guaranteed with this untested and unique design. Where was the intelligence and common sense of the politicians and civil servants in even making this proposition, let alone implementing it? Why were they so determined to break the long-established sovereignty of the board? Where had this design ever worked before? And why was an untested design to be applied universally, immediately, and become part of the compliance regime? We later saw this same daft approach applied by the financial regulator to the senior management regime for UK bankers and financial services.

Anger and infighting occurred almost immediately. The boards of directors could not see why such a structural change was needed because, under the Companies Act and NHS Code of Corporate Governance – which they were asked to follow as good practice – they were already held fully accountable. Given that they were poorly paid volunteers, their altruism and competence was then also questioned by the new design. But the politicians, responding to their vague but perceived need to sate "public demand" by including "stakeholders" in the NHS FTs, felt that they were on to a winner. This feeling was reinforced by growing litigation and plenty of electronic media abuse of Foundation Trusts, especially following the Mid Staffs scandal. The existing boards of directors were not well pleased with this totally unnecessary imposition. They felt that they were being dumped on by the same bipolar politicians who were simultaneously encouraging them to take a more "business-like" approach with their Trust by demonstrating their autonomy, while better considering all the local stakeholder demands "in the interest of their locality" regardless of priorities. This is political double-speak. Local and national political pressures, especially over hospital closures, made it very difficult to say no to this political instruction, even if it went against the long-term health of the Trust. So the Trusts asked, reasonably, what was "business-like" logic of insisting on two boards?

One of the dominant and disabling accepted business values of the organizational side of the NHS is obedience, the continuous yielding to higher authority. This means also that the NHS has a strong culture of bullying. So the Trust boards of directors tried to obey. Things then went from bad to worse, in two ways. First, the politicians made the selection process of the boards of governors community-wide. Adverts went out into the communities, and the politicians basked in their early reflected glory. But there was a huge risk of potential randomness with the selection process. The politicians insisted that this would ensure better diversity; but diversity does not equal competence, and no training was offered in any serious way. The selection process was designed so that interested parties could first register as a "Member" of their NHS Foundation Trust. From these Trust Members, individuals would be elected to the board of governors at an annual meeting. The elected members would then "represent" their communities and oversee the performance of the board of directors by "holding them to account". These board of governors positions were voluntary and unpaid. Representation was meant to reflect sufficient diversity across the local community, although there was no means of assuring this. Much was left to chance. But at least the politicians could claim their job was done and move on to more important issues. Learning and feedback systems were not rigorously installed, and, because of their fast turnover, most politicians did not have to live with the local consequences.

The idea and proposed structure seemed just about possible, in theory. Although some of the Members who were elected were kind-hearted souls who wanted to give back to their community, they were not fully competent, nor were they offered effective training or induction for their new governing role. Sadly, a shadow side emerged rapidly, especially in the early days. The politicians' expectation of representation across a broad spectrum of the community often failed to materialize. Instead, new governors tended to have vested interests in and around the NHS, and many realized that this was another way of furthering their own interests. Often new governors came with a personal agenda. Instead of trying to further the success of the Trust, they attempted to right previously perceived wrongs often for previous mistreatment. They treated their new "oversight of the board of directors" role as their lever for revenge against the Trust. For example, they could be seeking retribution for the unexplained death of a relative, "proven" lack of care in their own treatment, or for a perceived misdiagnosis of their own mental health. Or they could be a disgruntled staff member pursuing a claim, or were following a party political agenda. This did not create a culture for the constructive development of the two parallel boards. I understate my case.

With conflict built in from the start, matters were made even worse by the fact that the remit for the board of governors role had been sloppily drafted, in relation to the meaning of both "community interest" and "oversight of the board of directors". Central to the governors' role were two powers guaranteed to cause continuing conflict, not least because they were areas in which elected local politicians saw that they could have unofficial leverage over the governors. Many board directors saw this as a deliberate political part of the design: to undermine their decision-making powers while still holding them publicly accountable.

First, the governors were given the power to sack the chairman of the board of directors (who, perversely, was chairman of *both* boards!). You cannot make this up. Conflict of interest, anyone? Second, the governors were to "hold the *non*-executive directors to account for the performance of the board of directors", but not the executive directors of the board. Yet the executive directors are the well-paid, full-time board members who were most likely to need to be held accountable because they are the direct link to the day-to-day operations of the Trust. This was also another extraordinary example of corporate governance ignorance, because the terms "executive director" and "non-executive director" do not exist in company law. So bad practice was being promulgated. The new edict showed no understanding of the necessity of building trust, collegiality and primary loyalty between the two boards. Once registered as a statutory director at Companies House, all directors are equal, have equal voting rights and must display their primary loyalty to the company and its success. This law does not seem to apply to NHS Foundation Trusts. So why insist on using company law as good practice? And why were they to be overseen by second board?

This new governance "system" proved to be a badly designed mess. It was driven by political ignorance and arrogance yet no-one has been held accountable for its shoddy design.

Could it have been done better? Yes. Even at the basic human behaviour level, much could have been tested more thoroughly through a pilot study. None of the "experts" responsible for designing the system that I interviewed had any knowledge of human behavioural research. For example, the designers of the boards of governors showed no knowledge of inter-group dynamics. Yet, for some 60 years, we have known that effective and diverse groups tend to be able to work well when their numbers are between eight and 12. If they are smaller, they do not have sufficient diversity to discuss matters well, and so make sound decisions. If they are larger, then too much time is spent on trying to hold the group together and trying to avoid the inevitable micro-politics.[169] And none of the designers realized that there might be significant conflict between the groups. I have seen this before in government, when I was brought in to an agency where, without consultation, two large professional, yet culturally different, groups had been relocated to the same open-plan offices. I was asked if I could stop the physical fighting.

Because the NHS code of corporate governance for directors is based closely on the national Financial Reporting Council's Corporate Governance Code, at least the number of directors is kept to a workable 12 people. However, when reviewing the size of most groups of NHS FT governors, the picture is quite different. Loose notions of "representation" have overridden any concept of group effectiveness. When reviewing a typical local board of governors, I noted that they are comprised of:

- 13 elected governors (from the wider community)
- 4 service user governors
- 2 carer governors
- 4 staff governors
- Plus appointed governors:
  - 1 from a local university
  - 1 from a local college
  - 2 from the county council
  - 2 from the local constabularies

The board is made up of a total of some 30 people (including the chairman), not all of whom attend frequently, and most of whom see their representative status as transcending their primary loyalty of ensuring the success of the Foundation Trust. It does not take a genius to realize that this is a formula for ineffectiveness, inefficiency and frequent infighting, even between themselves, let alone with the board of directors. This is the governance of the madhouse.

Can politicians learn about effective corporate governance?

Was anything learned? Well, some boards of governors changed their names to "Council of Governors" in a minor act of contrition. More seriously, what still needs to be learned is that, first, unless there is rigorous oversight and testing of any governance design, the chances of failure are high. Second, people with good intentions will try to make any structure work regardless of how bad it is. This is particularly true if those members have little or no experience of what good governance looks like. Bad governance causes an enormous loss of goodwill, emotional stress and abuse of resources. Third, a mixture of politicians and civil servants, both with their own differing agendas, can waste public money and people's voluntary time at an alarming rate by pursuing an unworkable goal. I stress that none have been held accountable even by the Health Select Committee.

And it continues

You may think that this is a one-off. But you saw similar mixes of arrogance and ignorance in the governance designs of, for example, the BBC Trust and the laughable "design" of the Network Rail Board, where some 42 [sic] "Public Members" are meant to "hold the Network Rail board to account". No description was given of what effective board structure and performance was meant to be. This "Members" group, unpaid but with reasonable travel expenses, had few powers to ensure their oversight role, had little rigorous training and were expected to attend just eight meetings a year. Need one say more? Except that a political box has been ticked. Both have now failed.

But politicians are often still trying to experiment with additional, ill-tested new legal entities to address their ill-considered solutions. I will say more about these in Chapter 6.

And finally

I leave this chapter still puzzling over the issue of "ownership". I am only partly reassured that most experts in the public, private and not-for-profit areas seem equally puzzled. As we move inevitably towards the added complexities of "stakeholders", "inclusive capitalism" and "ESG-style integrated reporting", my worry is that, unless the concept of "ownership" is clarified, we shall have learned nothing significant about effective governance. We then run the risk of creating a messy, new corporate governance version of the famed environmental dilemma, the "Tragedy of the Commons".

In 1968, Garrett Hardin discussed the problems that arise when trying to balance population and food resources. I shall not go into the detail of that argument here, but it concerns future ownership. A synopsis of his main argument applies to our current organizations but even more to our necessary mind-set for future effective corporate governance:

> But we have difficulty in choosing to limit population, and choosing between which goods to pursue in a world that cannot provide for every different good, because we have left the choice of "the good" entirely to individuals in our capitalist society. We act as if individual choices will somehow solve collective problems such as population. Adam Smith's *laissez-faire* doctrine of the invisible hand tempts us to think that a system of individuals pursuing their private interests will automatically serve the collective interest. But applying this would be disastrous.

Hardin then used the metaphor of the "Tragedy of the Commons" to demonstrate our confusion.

> When a resource is held "in common", with many people having "ownership" and access to it, a self-interested

rational actor will decide to increase his or her exploitation of the resource since he or she receives full benefit of the increase, but the costs are spread across all users. The remorseless and tragic result of each person thinking this way, however, is ruin in the commons, and thus of everyone using it.[170]

Getting the balance right between private wealth generation and the public wealth spending remains a key ownership issue. What Hardin missed is Adam Smith's acceptance of always needing to balance the invisible hand of economics and the *moral* sentiment and political economy of business, and the distribution of wealth in a healthy society. Both of these issues are still highly apposite. It is to the politicians and regulators who notionally control this that I shall turn to in the final two chapters.

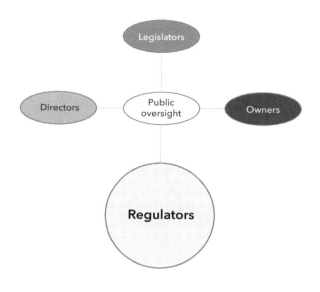

5

Regulators

Reframing governance for regulators:
fewer directives and more nudges?

Regulation is usually a downplayed, overlooked or hated part of any corporate governance system. Yet its importance is in that it publicly focuses the differences and contradictions between those accepted business values and society's expectations and aspirations demonstrated by its corporate governance values and personal values. In any organization, "corporate governance" is where the external values of accountability, probity and transparency, plus the seven general duties of directors, meet the reality of its internal accepted business values. Regulation highlights the gaps between what organizations will allow and what the state demands of them. Regulation ensures that consistent and appropriate values and behaviours are upheld on the nation's "flat playing field". Regulation comes into play when, to paraphrase C.S. Lewis, people fail to do the right thing when no-one is watching. "Regulation" is the bridge between these two value sets.

The regulator fulfils the necessary disinterested refereeing or policing role, seeking a sense of fair play on the one hand, and lawfulness on the other. The regulatory toolbox currently ranges from "a quiet word to the chairman", through the gentle "nudging" of behavioural and attitudinal changes, to the bulldozer of non-negotiable legal directives. Currently, the regulatory debate is in turbulence, because of the tension caused by the clash between "the experts'" role and "the people's" values, as highlighted by the Brexit and Trump votes.

Stopping the rot

The public now demand that the value and behavioural gaps are policed more rigorously and reduced more quickly. The fun really starts when the complexities of personal values are added to this already combustible mix. It is in these deep, unresolved dilemmas where the rot starts and where it can be stopped. Regulators hold the disputed ground between the directors, owners and the politicians. The public expects them to balance this tension continually and fairly. Yet the public, and the other players, often see regulators only as tools of the legislators, without independence of thought or action. However, regulators have become accepted in our society as a modern necessity for effective corporate governance. They will not go away. So how can we improve them? Not easily. There are still many anti-change forces working against them, as the following example shows. It specifically concerns the higher-level regulation of UK financial services, but is of much wider applicability.

Regulatory and cultural change: the Financial Conduct Authority

In October 2016, a report by the New City Agenda think-tank and Cass Business School, London University, published a damning review of the state of UK Financial Services regulation.[171] Thirty years after Big Bang and eight years after the Western financial crisis, little seems to have been learned in a rigorous and consistent manner. However, the annual public spend on such regulation has risen from £200 million in 2001 to £1.3 billion in 2015. This figure combines the spending of the Financial Services Agency/Financial Conduct Agency, the Prudent Regulation Authority, the Financial Ombudsman Service, and the Financial Services Compensation Scheme, of which around half is spent by the new UK "Financial Conduct Authority" (FCA). It does not include regulatory spending by the Bank of England.

What is most alarming is that, even after this huge spend and the massive publicity given to reforming the nature and behaviours of financial services, Justin Welby, the Archbishop of Canterbury, can state in the introduction to the report that he is still urging the financial watchdogs to "practise what they preach", because he and the authors believe that the regulations aimed at preventing another financial crisis are not strengthening the sector but weakening it. In my terms, corporate governance values have not yet transcended accepted business values. Worryingly, it looks like yet another regulator is falling prey to Stockholm syndrome, failing to use their prosecutory powers effectively in order to create precedents, and simply noting that, despite their crucial changes, following 2008, "they are already being watered down".

It also shows the Civil Service's ability to build empires without relevant performance assessment, and the way they arrogantly disregard the current company law on the duties, liability and responsibilities of company directors. While the regulators deny that they have yielded to the Treasury, the Bank of England and MPs, and that they have subsequently watered down the initial tough regulatory proposals, they are abandoning the proposed broad review of bank culture. While the report acknowledged that some improvements had been made on the consumer protection side, these were not enough. It urged Andrew Bailey, the new chief executive of the FCA, to demonstrate his independence because "leadership changes and the perception of political interference are in danger of making the FCA into a timid and cowed regulator".

The key conclusions and recommendations are worth noting here as they describe well much of the current dynamic:

- "Financial crises always lead to demands for greater regulation. We were told that the people at the top of the institutions responsible will be held accountable. This has not happened."

- "A deep seated culture of box-ticking has developed in the UK's financial regulators. Instead of concentrating on the big issues, regulators spent valuable time adding even more detailed rules and procedures and giving consumers even more complicated information. This is likely to increase confusion and cost rather than establish clarity."

- "The administrative cost . . . Is now six times greater than in the year 2000. There are now over 13,000 pages [sic] of detailed rules and guidance from the PRA and FCA. The FCA Handbook now costs £3,641 [sic] the same to buy as a second hand Mini Cooper car. Complexity and box-ticking benefit lawyers and gives a veneer of reassurance. It also distorts competition."

- "Unless we change the culture of regulators we will be sleep walking into the next financial crisis."

- "PRA and Bank of England have further to go to improve transparency and reduce group think."

- "Andrew Bailey must implement a comprehensive programme of cultural change in the FCA."

- "Politicians should support cultural change and tackle the culture of secrecy in the UK regulators."

The response from Andrew Bailey was worrying to anyone interested in effective corporate governance and regulation. He is reported in the *Financial Times*[172] to have pledged a drastic reduction in the number of its rules, and to focus on better and clearer regulation of financial services, as they try to move on from "its sorry history" of scandals and record-breaking fines, but not individual criminal prosecutions. It promises to thin out its "six foot two inches high" handbook. But the response is pathetically weak on showing a way forward. However, it is publishing a "mission statement" stating the FCA's priorities. As an example of its unworldliness, this mission statement is 50 pages long! It contains a "mission tree" which shows the subsets of its plan. No-one at the FCA seems to be aware of von Moltke's maxim that "no plan of operation extends with any certainty beyond the first contact with the main hostile force".[173] So civil servants and voluntary committees are kept busy and employed, but to what end? No-one in business will take it seriously. Half a page would have been excellent, one page just about OK; but a 50-page mission statement is just laughable.

As this book went to press, a worrying example of the FCA's accepted business values appeared. Following a *Financial Times* Freedom of Information request (6 March 2017), the FCA admitted that it had secretly censored, by "private warnings", 39 senior executives of UK financial firms, 14 of whom still hold "authorized" roles. The bulk of these related to the Libor-rigging scandals. The FCA is "currently reviewing its policy in relation to the use of private warnings and will determine our approach to future use of this tool in light of responses to this consultation". This leaves me with two worries. First, this appears to be an example of Stockholm syndrome, with the agency being too close to its regulatees to be able to play fully its publicly given purpose. Second, their value of secrecy is counter to the fundamental corporate governance value of transparency and so reinforces the public's worry that the regulator is pliable and not fit for purpose.

In this chapter I intend to go no deeper with the New City Agenda report's coruscating analysis of financial regulatory failure as I wish to take a wider view of regulation. But I do think the report is a milestone in exposing the weak, cowed and bureaucratic approaches to regulation that have failed to solve the divisive issues in society's governance. I mentioned in Chapter 1 on values my grave worries that, once regulators begin to specify accountability on such issues as "values" and "culture", then the rot really has started. This is not their territory. There are other laws that can deal with these issues. In the UK we do not need more detailed regulation but less, simpler and better-targeted.

However, we do still need much more effective *implementation* of the laws that have already been passed. Current incursions, especially by the Financial Reporting Council, the Bank of England and the Treasury, seem contradictory to other governmental initiatives, and company law, which seek to delegate much more regulation back to the companies to self-police and report more openly and with more integration as we move towards inclusive capitalism. No wonder the regulated are puzzled and rootless.

Why can't regulators act more like rugby referees?

It is human nature that both sides in any game always hate, and try to fool, the referee. Those regulated try to "game" the situation to their advantage. If the regulations are seen as too onerous, then the regulators are accused of being too draconian, expensive, bureaucratic and anti-business. If they are too lax, they are seen by the public as weak, lacking competence and dysfunctional. So why does society accept this paradoxical necessity?

A continuing international political trend is to seek to improve organizational effectiveness through competition, "the markets", in both the private and public sectors. In order to allow such competition, the majority of the previous barriers to entry in any field must be lowered significantly or demolished. "Playing fields" must become flatter and wider. The paradox is that new and often higher barriers must then be erected around the new perimeter to ensure continuing fairness. These must be then be policed externally and internally by referees – the "regulators".

In soccer, referees are traditionally derided and abused by fans and players alike, because they blow the whistle when a foul is seen, issue a penalty when the rules are infringed and move on quickly, rarely with any form of explanation. They use one-way communication, which does not encourage any *action learning* in real time. Any learning comes later, often during video feedback sessions. It is often focused more on how not to get caught next time rather than on accepting and using the rules. Compare these "strict silent policemen" with the very different approach of rugby referees. They are much more accepted in the game as a necessary evil, even respected by the players, because they focus on the real-time *learning* coming from the game as it progresses. Rather than acting as an impersonal policeman, they act as a form of running commentator, a neutral coach *and* enforcer, who clearly states the attitudes and behaviours needed by the players to play the game robustly yet fairly. How can the corporate governance regulators become more like a combined coach and enforcer? It is this rugby analogy of regulator as policeman *and* coach that I wish to expand upon in this chapter.

What is a "regulator"?

The modern term describes a means of adjusting a piece of equipment, or a system, so that it operates optimally. It came to prominence early in the Industrial Revolution. In governance history, the seminal year 1776 still shapes so much of today's commercial world. It saw the publication of three major works: Adam Smith's *The Wealth of Nations*[174] (which gave us the new mix of modern economics and social sentiment, providing us with a new framework for business values); Jean Jacques Rousseau's *The Social Contract*[175] (which gave us the new framework for the relationship between man and society and so the new framework of social values); and the United States Declaration of Independence[176] (which led us to the US Constitution in 1787, and so gave us the new model of modern democracy and clearly espoused national governance values). Each publication developed the concept of national development and welfare, based on the dynamic balance needed between markets and social good – a balance that we still seek to achieve.

Regulation as clockwork

It was realized immediately that this new US democracy needed constant vigilance and frequent adjustment – a system of checks and balances. How was this to be done for a system of national governance? This was the age of clockwork – a dramatic technological breakthrough which, at the time, was much discussed. In Boston, during the development that went from the US's Declaration of Independence, with its drawn-out debates, to the writing of the Constitution, the participants were influenced by clockwork as a very fashionable metaphor. They were especially interested in the ways in which John Harrison, discoverer of the accurate measurement of longitude,[177] and whose death in 1776 was highly topical news, had used the concept of the neutral "regulator": a device of spinning metal balls which added so much precision to a clock's accuracy. This "regulator" enabled navigators to measure accurately their longitudinal position, thus opening up much more reliable and less risky journeys, leading, ultimately, to the development of more reliable world trade. It was a heady time for capitalism. And the metaphor was used in many of the nascent US debates. It focused on ways in which the three powerful spinning forces of national power – the legislature, the executive and the judiciary – could be balanced to ensure that they span in harmony: truly a system of checks and balances. These design concepts still shape the basis of governance in many countries today.

But this solution was, by definition, mechanical. Today's world is digital, complex and interactive in real time. So a mechanical regulatory mind-set will always be out of sync with constantly changing reality. But much of the political thinking about the development of regulation is still essentially mechanical. Hence the continuing conflicts. What can be done?

The battle between executive-led and inclusive capitalism

Today the concept of "regulation" as a dynamic balancing mechanism has been weakened by politicians attempting to use it as a single "silver bullet" to resolve complex political and organizational problems by shifting their responsibilities to the regulator. They still seek that simple, binary solution that will automatically adjust the balance between markets and social justice, rather as the macroeconomists believed. Politicians also believe that, once such regulation is imposed, they are then excused from accepting further responsibility and learning from its consequences. Such an attitude conveniently enables legislators to reinforce in the public's mind that the regulator is always to blame – "our legislation is good but the implementation by the regulator is awful".

Such slippery thinking helps define the present frontline of the regulatory battle between executive-led capitalism and inclusive capitalism. In the UK, the US and the EU, this battle is being fought at the extremes between the outright "free marketeers" and the more utopian wing of the "social market activists". It is mirrored in corporate governance through the continuing "CRG versus ESG" debate. The free marketeers seem to have been winning in the short term, especially in the private sector. But, since 2008, the elitist "1%'s" dominant values of lust and greed are increasingly discredited by their lack of empathy with the public, their missing contrition over the destruction of other people's wealth, and their lack of duty of care for social cohesion. Yet, paradoxically, there is a parallel strong feeling among many of the public that too much "social" ownership – especially when state-run – leads to increasingly ineffective, anti-consumer, self-rewarding and corrupt organizations. Communism as practised in the Soviet Union is a good example of such an extreme. So can the regulators help resolve such a dilemma?

Can regulators hold the political balance?

It is becoming common parlance that the state can no longer finance all publicly demanded services and organizations. The politicians and the public have also assumed that the private sector can always deliver more effective and efficient organizations than the public sector. This is the political justification for the privatization of state, local government and community organizations. But this can prove equally unbalanced nonsense, as shown in Chapter 4 on ownership. It is well proven that such private organizations, delivering major public services will, over time, create a self-serving monopoly, start to erode services demanded by customers and communities, and become ultimately as ineffective and inefficient as state businesses. So the alert public must seek a sensible balance for their learning and create an oversight mechanism that holds their governors to account. Regulators are meant to hold this balance. But few are trained to competence, or have been granted appropriate enforcement and prosecutory powers, or have built enough public support to deliver on their role.

This is odd, as one would expect the public to be right behind them. Remember that over 250 years ago Adam Smith warned us[178] that we risked creating corporate monsters in the long term. He foresaw that, as the new joint stock companies had no regulatory mechanisms, they would become increasingly powerful because they had been granted, possibly unwittingly, by the legislators:

- Unlimited size

- Unlimited life

- Unlimited licence

- And so: unlimited power

These public fears are still strong and are debated fiercely. As the problems caused by a lack of business limitation boundaries became clearer, governments realized that, to prevent such potential abuse of power, a referee role needed to be created on behalf of the public – the regulatory function. These regulators would become both gate-keepers (having the delegated powers to agree who could enter the field of play and under which rules), and have consumer and social ombudsmen roles to keep some societal balance.

Do governments and the regulators have the courage to enforce "the walk of shame" for corporate governance abuse?

The public's touching yet often self-deluding belief that our governors are trained and competent in their roles is reflected similarly in their expectations of their regulators. The simple assumption is that they must always know how to regulate competently, and have the powers to stop misbehaviour quickly. This is not proven. Since the 2008 Western financial crisis, public anger has grown at the obvious ineffectiveness of many of our regulators. In the business world, especially the financial world, the previously fashionable political policy of "light-touch regulation" [sic] has demeaned the position of the regulators because of their perceived unwillingness or inability to pursue transgressions. They were unable quickly to set standards and punishments to which the regulated would pay rapt attention. So, many are seen as ineffective, while others are seen as having been captured by the industries they are meant to regulate. This is hardly surprising, as many new regulators themselves originate from those recalcitrant areas. It is only slightly comforting that they are now performing the function of "setting a thief to catch a thief", but their lack of solid progress fails to reassure. Hence the growing scandal that, despite examples of their lack of care, skill and diligence, no banker has been personally charged with criminal acts regarding corporate governance, as distinct from fraud. Nor have we seen personal action taken against – to consider 2016 examples – Volkswagen or Rolls-Royce. And this is despite the public outcry for retribution.

Is the US a better model?

You might think that it is different in the US, where media pictures of financiers in chains doing the "walk of shame" can be observed on newspaper front pages, TV and internet news. But these tend to be for fraud and corruption, not for corporate governance infringements, nor for directorial and managerial abuse of their fiduciary duty to ensure their business has a healthy future. They tend to be for such crimes as insider trading or security markets abuse. The US regulators do have a more feisty and pragmatic mind-set in mixing corporate and personal entities, so it is much easier to settle any charges through plea bargaining without the direct admission of guilt. This is administratively and financially convenient for both sides as it does not have to involve the courts. But is it justice? The regulators do have strong prosecutory powers to wield, but are tardy in using them. For example, no charges have been brought against Dick Fuld of Lehman Brothers, the collapse of which in 2008 is seen as the tipping point for the Western financial crisis, or the board and executives at AIG, Washington Mutual or Bear Sterns. However, Jon Corzine of MF Global will now testify in a US$3 billion PwC lawsuit. But, by 2016, fines worth over a massive $2.8 billion have been paid to the US government. Even so, with the way current laws are written in the US and the UK, it is still difficult to prove that such *individuals* broke the law, despite the fact that they drove their companies bust.

However, as reported in the US and UK financial media, in the US, by 2015, 17 bankers from smaller banks have been jailed and a mortgage broker jailed for 30 years. So much for the public's wish for "justice" for the big boys and the billionaires. For members of the public seeking retribution, the US Securities and Exchange Commission regulatory overseer has filed civil cases against some 138 companies and individuals. And the US regulators are going further and deeper. The Federal Housing Finance Agency has fined three banks

$5.2 billion over misleading mortgage securities. It is now threatening the UK's RBS bank. The Federal Deposit Insurance Corporation has fined three Washington Mutual directors a total of $64 million and has won a judgement of $169 million against three directors of IndyMac. JPMorgan Chase has paid, in addition to some $5.6 billion already agreed, an additional $1.3 billion to settle all its outstanding issues over mortgage securities. Bank of America had paid $12 billion by Christmas 2013, and Ocwen paid $2.1 billion to settle its outstanding issues over mis-sold mortgages. These substantial fines have greatly increased US federal funds, but the UK government does not seem interested in such a national source of fundraising, although I am sure that the public would be delighted by it. But the mere fining of corporations harms the shareholders and does not change the individual behaviour of the executives and directors.

Even a few small countries have taken robust criminal action against their bankers' unlawful board actions. Iceland jailed senior managers and shareholders of Kaupthing for market manipulation. Ireland has charged the former chief executive and finance director of Irish Life and Permanent, and a former Anglo Irish Bank director with a $7.2 billion fraud – in connection with window-dressing its balance sheet – and three other directors, including Seán FitzPatrick, its former chief executive, have been charged with fraud. This debacle cost Irish taxpayers some €30 billion in state support, and forced their government to beg for an international bailout resulting in years of hardship for the Irish people. With the major exceptions of the Health and Safety Acts, the Corporate Manslaughter legislation, the Anti-slavery Act and the areas of fraud and corruption, there are still few areas of law where UK directors can be brought to heel in the criminal courts. None of these legal infringements are under the jurisdiction of the corporate governance regulators. What worries me is that there has been no corporate governance prosecutions to clarify the legal position of directors, owners and regulators to concentrate everyone's minds and behaviours. So accepted business values are often still seriously out of sync with the legislated corporate governance values, and often wildly adrift from personal values. A serious issue here is that corporate fines punish the *shareholders,* not the directors and executives. We need legislation to clarify this position.

Incompetent corporate governance or showing lack of care, skill or diligence – to an extent where the future health of a business is compromised – is not usually considered by our regulators as unlawful and certainly not a crime. Remember that the Financial Reporting Council has no power to debar directors; only the Department of Business, Energy and Industrial Strategy has this power, and it uses it only for small offenders. The FRC can debar accountants and auditors but that is not corporate governance. Is this why the public are so incensed? I shall be happier when we see the "privileged 1%" beginning to feel rattled by action over corporate governance misdemeanours.

The problems with corporate governance codes

I use here the well-developed UK FRC Corporate Governance Code as a metaphor for the wider international issues. In the UK, the accepted business value has been, with the agreement of the regulators, to downplay the primacy of directors' duties in the Companies Act 2006, and for the regulators in the FRC, DBEIS (Department of Business, Energy and Industrial Strategy), FCA and Bank of England to rely heavily on the weaker, secondary system of corporate governance regulation from the FRC Code.[179] Rather than have a helpful stream of smaller, "nudging" cases to guarantee appropriate behaviour, nothing much seems to happen between crises. The now defunct Financial Services Authority tried rather halfheartedly to bring cases against, for example, Sir Fred Goodwin at RBS and Peter Cummings at HBOS, who was fined £500,000 in 2016; but there has been little progress despite the existing law and codes. Unless there is a strong political will by our legislators to follow through their own regulatory laws and codes, encourage action learning in real time, be seen to penalize wrongdoers and treat effective corporate governance as a valuable national asset, nothing much will change. Deckchairs might be rearranged on the deck of the *Titanic,* but the rot will continue.

For example, it was not until November 2015 (over seven years after the event) that the Bank of England published its report on the failure of HBOS, despite the massive taxpayer-funded bailout. The leading criticism was that the board of directors failed to install a culture of balance between risk and return – a classic corporate governance failure. Since then, little has happened so the public remain frustrated and under-informed. Few outsiders, including the politicians, have the ability to ask the really penetrating questions about these infringements. If the appointed regulators are also unwilling to do so, why do we have them?

Indeed, only six UK bankers have received fines throughout the whole banking crisis, and there have been no criminal prosecutions yet. We may see a couple from the 2017 HBOS "liquidations" trial. Even the fine on Christopher Willford, previously finance director of Bradford & Bingley, for failing to provide the board with sufficient information about the bank's eroding finances, has been *reduced* markedly on appeal to only £30,000. Only two RBS and HBOS directors have been held accountable, and Johnny Cameron of RBS agreed to ban *himself* from the world of financial services.

Delays by "Maxwellization"

Effective justice is speedy justice and builds public trust in the governance system. The huge time delays by regulators in bringing allegedly unlawful business folk to justice is a valid reason for the public's outrage against "the establishment". In the UK, this is explained mainly by a curiously British interpretation of "fairness" in the writing of official reports – otherwise known as "Maxwellization". It was why Fred Goodwin and James Crosby were not named in the RBS report, the failure of which cost UK taxpayers some £67 billion to buy shares in a failed bank which continues to run up huge deficits. "Maxwellization" is a process agreed by the legislators by which those criticized in an official report can have (seemingly unlimited) time for themselves and their lawyers to comment on and try as far as possible to neutralize any critical draft findings. Few heads of governmental enquiries set any enforceable time limits on the responses from those in the Maxwellization process. Unsurprisingly, they have no wish to respond quickly. This abuse of the timeliness of a legal process raises the issue of fairness for society. I argue that it is an abuse of legal process and should be treated as such. The consequent nitpicking, long delays and counter-threats of legal action go directly against the concept of timely justice. The public see the allegedly guilty continuing life freely, as they have not been tried, and view this as highly unfair. They feel instinctively that justice delayed is justice destroyed. It is particularly ironic that the process is named after one of the UK's biggest *convicted* corporate criminals, Robert Maxwell. Time for a political rethink?

The UK's weaknesses in corporate governance

It is a paradox that the UK is seen externally as world-class in corporate governance[180] and yet seen internally as having many weaknesses, especially due to its lack of a rigorous enforcement and monitoring regulatory system. I argue that this shows just how bad effective corporate governance is in the rest of the world. So why is there such indifference in the UK? It's partly due to the lack of political will in all the main political parties. The "lite regulation" mind-set created internationally under Labour by Tony Blair, Peter Mandelson and Gordon Brown, established the UK as a good place for any financial services firm to do business. But it also fed the values of rapacious exuberance and greed in the incoming players. This, in turn, contaminated the values of the majority of the incumbents. Tragically, there is still little national political will to take responsibility for what happened, whether by design or negligence. The legislators continue their Faustian contract with the public, whereby "we deliver (short-term wealth) and you obey us or avoid your gaze about the long-term consequences". What is worse is that the main regulators have done so little proactively to plug the dangerous hole into which the financial and social stability of the country has been led.

The politicians are not using those corporate governance values they created and now espouse.

Regulators have two golden get-out clauses. Few members of the public know about either of these and so regulators aren't challenged about them. First, regulators still behave as if the only group that can pay any fines are the *shareholders,* not the directors and executives. Why? Shareholders have the legal right to demand that directors fulfil their fiduciary duty to "ensure the continuing health of their company" through their personal use of care, skill and diligence. The company as a legal entity is "mindless", so surely the directors and executives, not the shareholders, must fulfil this mind function? There must be an "overseeing mind" within them? So why are their consequent liabilities and accountabilities not enforced by the regulators? Second, it is rarely possible to identify an individual responsible for what is often a group decision – either board or top team. This has been such a well-used excuse, originally in corporate manslaughter cases, that the public now believe that it must be true. It is not.

So have we now reached the point where, for example, the bankers could get their comeuppance and become the model for future successful individual prosecutions? Is public anger sufficiently strong that the legislators must fulfil their enforcement responsibilities? It is here that some truly intelligently naïve questioning by the public should yield results. The City has created a rod for its own back. For example, in consistently pushing the notion that City bonuses have to be welded to the individual performance of supposedly unique "talent", does this not mean that it is now much easier to link the specific decisions and actions of an individual with specific results and consequent liability? If so, then surely they must be pursued for failing in their individual directoral or executive duties and made to pay individual fines and, if they are found to be corrupt, then jailed? If not, why do we pay these bankers so much? In what other realm of corporate life can individuals profit so well from "success" and yet pass on to the owners the consequences of their failure?

What is the corporate governance regulatory system?

Who are these regulators of corporate governance? In the UK, prime responsibility for initiating regulation lies with the Department for Business, Energy and Industrial Strategy, yet another new name for yet another reshuffling of the governmental "business" deckchairs. The DBEIS is the primary sponsor for corporate governance legislation and enforcement and so supervises Clauses 171 and 172 of the Companies Act 2006, covering the seven general duties of directors. It is lax. If it were run on an annual public oversight basis, it would have at least provided an early warning system of governance and financial crises to which the regulators would then have to pay attention. It is not.

Instead, taking the UK as an example that is being copied elsewhere, the legislators have delegated many of their powers of supervision over corporate governance to other regulators. Corporate governance does not have a focus in central government. So a combination of the Bank of England, the Treasury, the Financial Conduct Authority, and the Financial Reporting Council, among others, are able to divide and misrule the key wealth generators in the UK – including our key economic generator, the financial services industry. By contrast, it is interesting to note that, by 2016, London has become the unofficial global capital for "design" (from architecture and structural engineering through TED to fashion and graphics). Their combined economic output may now have reached around 30% of that created by the financial City. Yet they do not pay guaranteed bonuses or silly salaries, neither do they seem to need an overabundance of regulators. Let us hope that the legislators do not spot this and impose regulation on them.

A mixture of lax supervision, through conscious governmental under-resourcing, conflicts of boundary interests and middling-quality staff, has ensured that continuous effective regulatory supervision is not yet possible. Nor is there any systematic process to create the necessary learning for a more effective system. Since the 18th century, the City of London has been the international hub of finance. Yet, since Big Bang in 1985, the combined output of these regulators is weak, unsystematic, unfocused and lacking in imagination and the personal courage to reinforce the City's ancient ethos of "My word is my bond". But without such trust the City is dead. Currently it is rotting. This is a clear case where accepted business values clash with corporate governance values and where personal values come a very poor third. This helps explain the poor personal psychological condition of many City folk. Yet still regulators do not see themselves either as police with teeth or educative coaches with a duty to speak out, even after the Public Interest Disclosure Act 1998[181] – the "Whistleblower Protection Act" – was enacted to help them: and despite the fact that the media is increasingly critical of the quality of UK corporate governance regulation.

In Chapter 6, I discuss my ideas for changing this current non-system into a national action-learning system for effective corporate governance.

The Financial Reporting Council

The Financial Reporting Council (FRC) is the lead regulator for corporate governance in the UK. It is an odd agency, with limited effectiveness over the regulation of corporate governance nationally. The biggest problem is that corporate governance does not have a separate, autonomous agency for its regulation. Instead, it is effectively a mere *sub*committee of the FRC. Which raises the immediate question: why? Why should accountants have control over the UK's corporate governance system? They are just accountants, after all, and accountancy and audit have already enough problems with their future roles. This unsatisfactory situation needs addressing quickly if we are to resolve the nation's governance issues. In regulatory terms it is worth noting that the FRC cannot debar directors and has weak links with the Department of Business, Energy and Industrial Strategy, which can.

A better future for corporate governance regulation

The need for a Corporate Governance Reporting Council

We need a separate Corporate Governance Reporting Council to build the professionalism of directors and to ensure the protection of the public, by clarifying the levels of directoral competence they can expect. Currently, directors do not have a dedicated professional body to represent and discipline them. The London Institute of Directors has never resolved the splits in its personality between being a political representative body for medium-sized businesses, being a social club with some nice premises scattered around the UK, and being a professional body for directors' standards – through the Chartered Director scheme that it administers as a national award but does not own. Its energies are split between tasks that are often contradictory. It is impossible for it to be taken seriously as a professional body if it still offers six bottles of champagne to every new member. Their main focus is not effective corporate governance.

This proposed Corporate Governance Reporting Council will focus firmly on delivering the seven Duties of a Director under the Companies Act of 2006. It should operate using the values of accountability, probity and transparency, should be regulated through its own mix of professional directors and laity, backed by the rigorous enforcement of existing law, and it should be answerable to the public. We shall see a major change in mind-set when we find politicians who are willing to create such a national asset.

What, then, is the future role of a corporate governance regulator? One possibility is found in the troubled and publicly derided financial services markets, where a structural change is being attempted. In 2013, the Financial Services Agency was replaced by the Financial Conduct Authority, whose purpose is very different, and more outwardly focused:

> Our strategic objective is to ensure that the relevant markets function well and our operational objectives are to:
>
> • Protect consumers – we secure an appropriate degree of protection for consumers.

- Protect financial markets – we protect and enhance the integrity of the UK financial system.

- Promote competition – we promote effective competition in the interests of consumers.[182]

It is noticeable that the statement is more proactive, much more consumer-focused, and is designed to allow less "industry capture" than the statements of its predecessor. It is also less geared to box-ticking, and tries to be more shaping of appropriate values and consequent behaviours by putting much more emphasis on developing appropriate *personal* behaviours, based on those well-tested, but often forgotten, corporate values of accountability, probity and openness. It is a conscious aspiration to align accepted business values, corporate governance values and personal values. It has the added advantage of making it more difficult for compliance departments to standardize and so dilute their processes and objectives. It is worth noting that the advocacy of the new City Values Forum,[183] with its "City Obligation" personal oath of "My word is my bond" is a noble step forward here in striving to restore the professional reputation of the City of London, through personal commitment within a values-based framework.

Attestations

The Financial Conduct Authority says that it is attempting to refocus its mission so that directors and senior management will be more open to civil and legal action in the future. But they have yet to demonstrate this by improving their own behaviour, especially towards consumers. Their current fail-safe position is to use the independent Financial Ombudsman Service. We need much stronger signals of the FCA's position. There may be some hope, as we begin to see the growing use of "attestations" – a response to a request from the FCA that the board members *personally* vouch that the activity for which they are responsible is fully compliant with the existing rules. This is a notable move towards better self-regulation, through a focus on board morality rather than simply economic values. It is being resisted strongly and the politicians seem indifferent.

The curse of the Cadbury Report's consequences

Remember that the seminal Cadbury Report of 1992[184] was commissioned by the International Stock Exchange, London, and the Institute of Chartered Accountants in England and Wales. Although there are many accountants on boards of directors – and the specialist role is always useful on a board – many accountants have little generalist boardroom experience. Accountants are necessary, but by no means sufficient, for effective corporate governance. Why does the FRC not actively support at least the growth of directoral professionalism, by encouraging the Chartered Director certification across *all* registered organizations in the UK – private, public and not-for-profit? It is an historic coincidence that the FRC, as distinct from the Department of Business, Energy and Industrial Strategy, regulates UK corporate governance. The nation became aware of the phrase "corporate governance" following the Cadbury Report, but note by its title that it was on *"The Financial Aspects* of Corporate Governance". Both sponsors had a legitimate interest in keeping the report financially focused and only on listed companies. In the popular imagination, the notion that corporate governance is accountancy-dominated has stuck. But this is slowing the public understanding of the value of corporate governance in all organizations. The FRC has never had the imagination or motivation to see its role as helping the nation by widening its scope to incorporate private companies, charities, state-owned enterprises and government bodies. We are poorer for it.

In the public's mind, accountancy is not famed for its imagination, entrepreneurialism or farsightedness. Indeed, some would say that those accountants who possess too much imagination and entrepreneurial ambition need careful regulation themselves. The public do not appreciate "creative" accountants. So the current FRC governance focus is not on boards ensuring a proper balance of the director's dilemma but more on reporting the present, and the past, "prudent control" aspect. Such over-concentration means that things can go horribly wrong especially by avoiding the ESG areas. If too much emphasis is placed on the regulatory compliance aspects of corporate governance, it turns rapidly into a neutral box-ticking exercise, as the 2016 New City Agenda report illustrated.[185]

Taken to the extreme, such board debates turn into questions like "How many angels can stand on the head of a pin?"; "Can a director serve for more than ten years?"; or "Can a managing director ever become a chairman directly?" – rather than sticking with balancing the director's dilemma. These are issues of good practice but not of primary law. Yet they are seductive issues for FRC regulators looking to assert their reach and can easily be translated into boxes for ticking. Everyone will have an opinion on them and much publicity can be generated, publicity that will suggest that the regulator is doing its job. But if a regulator pushes too much for prescription, it destroys the very basis of the principles-based approach and its self-policing component.

The FRC Governance and Stewardship Codes

In September 2014, the FRC published amendments to its Corporate Governance and Stewardship Codes. It was followed with minor amendments in 2015 and 2016, but with a message that few changes would occur until at least 2019 in order "to allow changes to embed". Such amendments reinforce my argument that they are not interested in corporate governance as a *national* asset but merely in dealing with issues for listed companies, and that they are driven more by accommodating the demands of warring political parties and financial services than expanding national wealth and social capital. The areas in which the amendments are codified show this:

- Remuneration

- Shareholder voting

- "Going concern" and risk management (as accounting procedures)

This is not to decry the amendments as unhelpful to listed companies, but they do demonstrate the narrow perspective of the current FRC. They show that the "CRG" mind-set is still uppermost, with "ESG" as an also-ran.

The FRC did include a nod in the direction of long-termism. Unfortunately, it rather ham-fistedly asked that companies present a "viability statement" to their shareholders, which sets out the various risks faced over a period *"significantly further ahead"* than the usual 12 months. This is a worthy but fuzzy aspiration, while being of little utility to the shareholders (how would they interpret it?) and potentially onerous and costly for boards and executives. The FRC does not seem to understand the mathematical differentiation of the terms "risk" and "uncertainty" and tends to use them interchangeably. If companies developed a more concise description of their specific business model, stated their aspirations, gave some metrics for their consequent trends, and reported to their shareholders and stakeholders more regularly (rather than annually) on the probabilities of such, it would help enormously.

Deeper issues of corporate governance regulation

It is unwise for any board to refuse a reasonable request from a regulator, especially when the public is angry and you have shown no contrition for your past actions. Notice that it is now a *written* attestation that is requested by the FCA, and the FCA has stated clearly that it will not accept qualified statements. There has been an inevitable City abreaction about such unusual FCA regulatory conduct. Indeed, a Freedom of Information Act request has been made to get the FCA to explain when it will ask for attestations as part of its supervisory oversight toolkit, and how they would be used as part of its enforcement mechanism. At present, the FCA has said that "it is not in the public interest to answer the requests" [*sic*]. This is very curious if the regulator is trying to re-establish basic values of honesty and transparency yet is relying on secrecy to create a more constructive national climate for the oversight of future business. This is very odd.

Regulatory demands needs to be matched by an acceptance of higher professionalism in the regulators themselves. Very few politicians are arguing for the rapid creation of a cadre of well-trained regulators. There were two major assumptions which are yet untested by these politicians. First, there is a ready supply of intelligent, decent, honest, courageous, professional, experienced, independently minded and altruistic people who could play the regulator role effectively. Second, the politicians would willingly cede their powers of intervention and party-political point-scoring to such paragons of virtue. Neither assumption has been proved. I feel that a major part of the reason is that the politicians and the public have confused two types of regulatory approach: the moral/social, and the economic/ legalistic. So the battle for more effective corporate governance regulation continues.

Can you ever legislate for people to be good?

Today, most emphasis in corporate governance is still placed on the economic/legalistic aspects, with the moral/social values either assumed or not considered. So whether one is regulating energy, communications, trains, water or financial services, the focus has been on improving the short-term efficiency of the existing systems rather than delivering the values-driven, long-term effectiveness and purpose of the regulated organizations. Superficially, the values may seem the same for both types of regulation – accountability, probity and transparency – but the interpretation of each, in the short and long terms, can be quite different dependent on the economic and moral perspectives.

Probity versus compliance

Accountability and transparency can mostly be handled through specific regulation. The really difficult value for regulators is dealing with probity. A regulator can never ensure that honest dealing occurs around a boardroom table, or in the letting of a contract, or in ensuring that an organization has a sustainable future. But there is some hope here, as both regulators and economists begin to realize that behavioural economics are much more important than algorithms; and that human "values" determine those beliefs-in-action which trigger emotions and learning – positive or negative – from directors, owners, consumers and politicians. Values and their consequent culture are not a vacuous social concept but are observable and measurable, as shown in Chapter 1. Probity can be tested.

Compliance as a reductionist mind-set

However, the major focus of today's regulatory approach is still defined, sadly, by that one word: "compliance". If regulators only take a short-term view, then it is usually interpreted that the maximum outcome needed is strict compliance to the existing rules. The spirit of the values and laws that originally determined those rules is often rapidly forgotten because they are not designed into the delivery of the codes. Nor is there easy access to "rugby-style" refereeing and open learning. The consequence is quickly to force the regulatory system into a reductionist, box-ticking fixation. In Chapter 2, I mentioned the global intellectual directoral fight between "ESG" and "CRG" values and behaviours, and principles-based and rules-based corporate governance systems. These different world-views are reflected and continually fought out in the regulatory world.

The intellectual poles are easily defined. On the one hand is the previously mentioned *"rules-based"* approach to regulation. This relies on two main concepts. First, people are not to be trusted, and therefore must be made to comply totally with the prescribed rules. Second, the regulators are omniscient and therefore know, or have prescience for, everything that people will do to subvert the rules. This is not proven. On the other hand, there are those *"principles-based"* regulations that spell out what is both legal and what is considered good practice; but which accept that unique circumstances require unique solutions, provided that the owners are kept informed, consulted and agree within the law. Under this latter "comply or explain" system, if the organization cannot or does not wish to comply, then it must get formal agreement of the shareholders to deviate within the law. The principles-based approach relies on a mixture of common sense and pragmatism for its effectiveness. Interestingly, comply-or-explain has been developed in South Africa as "comply *and* explain".

The "rules-based" approach – as used in the US and, through "extraterritoriality", any country unwise or unfortunate enough to deal with the US – is based on mistrust, and the doubtful ability of the regulators to second-guess all the necessary rules and all the likely infringements. This nonsense means that the US codes have to be frequently extended, which adds extra costs and inconvenience, and decreases the owners' entrepreneurial options. This diminishes the purpose of ensuring the long-term health of the business and devalues the importance and credibility of regulation in the minds and hearts of the majority of parties involved. Let us not forget that Enron was 100% compliant under a rules-based system when it crashed. It was criminal, but the regulatory system did not pick this up.

The US's subsequent Sarbanes–Oxley Act of 2002 is a classic case of what happens when a rules-based approach to regulation is then implemented to ease noisy political demands. The main driving idea was that, because US corporate governance and accounting practice were lax, they needed standardization at the federal level. However, as pragmatic implementation was not agreed at national level, a sizeable and profitable compliance industry has sprung up globally, simply to ensure that organizations can tick all the many boxes. A worrying side effect of this helpful process is that, once the boxes are ticked, then, by definition, everything else is possible. The game then becomes outfoxing the box-setting regulators and we are back in dubious acceptable business values territory. This descends quickly into the regulators feeling that they must create more and more boxes to regain control. This is countered by the companies pushing for more creative avoidance strategies and the whole process collapses into a reductionist spiral of increasing expense, litigation and frustration. One thing it does not do is progress effective corporate governance or entrepreneurship.

The one time that I saw the legalistic/economic regulatory approach work, almost alarmingly well, was at the creation of Hong Kong's Independent Commission Against Corruption (ICAC) in 1976, a commission dedicated to stamping out rampant illegality in business, including the financial services. These financial services were not famed for their probity. The plutocratic Hong Kong government had given the new commission one draconian special power – the ability to enforce the immediate house arrest of any suspected perpetrator

– and they used it immediately. The effects were dramatic: a few big names were arrested, charged, or kept out of contact with others at home for up to three months. Some were later found guilty by the courts, who were seen as honest and efficient. After this, there was a noticeably rapid disappearance of various dubious business practices. I know regulators in many countries who crave the power of house arrest, even for a year, so that they could reset the values and mind-sets of those they regulate. However, few politicians possess the political will even to consider this measure, despite popular opinion. So we must progress by more subtle means.

We struggle on with the present regulatory confusion, mixing moral/social and economic/legislative regulation in unwise combinations. The politicians seem divided into two political camps over regulation, backed by warring and publicly discredited macroeconomists, without being aware of the reality of the basic law concerning directoral duties.

In the UK we see, for example, competition policy and future energy industry investment in turmoil. What is the role of a regulator here? The arguments all seem economic and nothing to do with the directors fulfilling their legal duties to their shareholders *and* their stakeholders. Similarly, the rail regulator was meant to bring in long-term investment to renew the infrastructure and efficient customer-friendly pricing. But we see costs per passenger-kilometre at 40% higher than other EU nations. The long-term investment "strategy", including the interminable public spats on, for example, High Speed 2, leave the customers furious at rising fares, faulty notions of "encouraging competition", low customer satisfaction and scandals of hidden governmental subsidies, with little long-term vision of the purpose and future of the railways. The regulators of the NHS or the airports could be similarly charged. Again, what is the role of the regulator here and how do we measure their cost-effectiveness and accountability? And can the lessons learned be applied to corporate governance?

Uncontrolled regulatory spending by government

It seems that, in a time of declared "austerity", "regulation" is, ironically, one of the fastest-growing arms of government. This is despite the fact that David Cameron declared that the opposite was happening in his "Bonfire of the Quangos" speech in 2010.[186] In 2014, there were 60 UK central-government-linked regulators, despite efforts to reduce the number. In addition, there are many NGOs, professional associations, local authorities, consultancies and auditors now playing active regulatory roles. Sadly, this is usually only by encouraging box-ticking while collecting substantial fees. The OECD has recently described regulatory spending as "the least controlled and the least accountable" of all government costs.[187] Increased regulation has not led businesses to the politically promised land of wise policy formulation, implementable strategy and publicly agreed, technocratically led long-term planning and operational delivery; with the exception of the 2012 London Olympics. But that had strong selection and performance criteria, a fixed timetable and budgets, a very high international profile and, after a difficult start, remarkable freedom from the politicians who would be globally humiliated if it went wrong. There is a strong message here but few signs of the politicians learning from it. So, again, it is up to the public to keep asking those intelligently naïve questions, to keep their governors' feet to the fire.

We often see the reverse: politicians neutering any public respect for the regulators' role by trying to micro-manage operational detail directly from their ministries. Far from the regulators becoming a strong, independent force for the nation's balanced development, and answerable to the public, they are increasingly the whipping boy in party political debates. As I write, ministers have intervened via their civil servants and personal advisors on such varied operational details as cigarette packaging design, obesity targets, train pricing, reduction of sugar in children's cereals and GPs' opening hours. These interventions, and the consequent changes, seem continuous, debilitating and often just plain wrong. They may make the minister feel good because he or she can claim action on an issue of public concern, but they neutralize the principles-based, independent regulatory system that they claim to support. This is a major issue: how do ministers deal with an "independent" board that they have created if they then say no to their ministerial interference?

Regulators and the Stockholm syndrome

Professor John Kay, in his thoughtful 2012 report, describes the gut reflexes of regulators and legislators to continuing public disquiet about the lack of effective regulation:

> Dysfunctional structures . . . give rise to behaviour we don't want. We respond . . . by identifying the undesirable behaviour, and telling people to stop. We then find that the same problem emerges, in a slightly different guise. So we construct new rules. And so on. And on.[188]

He notes that the growth of regulation is both extensive and intrusive, yet also ineffective and prone to "regulatory capture". "Industry capture" of the regulators takes the following route: at first, the regulators begin to acclimatize to the industry mind-set; then they accept and follow this industry mind-set; and eventually they become apologists for dysfunctional businesses – a regulatory version of the Stockholm syndrome. Once captured, the regulatory system becomes increasingly bureaucratic. The primary law is weakened by expanded secondary legislation. Codes are developed which then gain the power of secondary legislation. What were once helpful guidelines, which left the business risks and moral judgements to the directors, are now seen as the core of the system for which compliance and risk reduction is the only objective. The regulators grow in size and power. Companies then respond by forming departments just to ensure compliance – for example, "corporate governance" or "risk management" – and an unholy alliance is created to generate jobs and costs on both sides of this new divide. A new cottage industry of "compliance" is born.

What started as "principles-based" regulation can easily degenerate into a form of "rules-based" regulation, and a growing number of people then have a vested job interest in keeping it that way. Then regulators take away the discretionary judgement power of boards, as they specify not just what has to be done, but how to do it and which targets to set. A classic example of this has been seen in the NHS. Can you imagine an NHS Foundation Trust saying no to a minister or the Department of Health? Yet their boards are meant to be designed to do exactly that – to deliver their unique *local* community needs in an increasingly competitive world. The wisdom of Michael Porter's axiom of "regulate for outcomes, not methods"[189] is easily lost in the micro-politics of such regulations. And, when it is forgotten, the drive to find new, better and cheaper ways of delivering services and products is also lost. Then the regulator becomes a blockage to innovation and erodes the very purpose of any wealth-creating organization.

As economists are the priesthood of executive-led capitalism, so regulators are becoming the priesthood of corporate governance. They can easily lead us astray from their original guardian and balancing roles to the minor and false god of unthinking compliance. It is for boards, owners, managers and the public to combine to fight this. On the public's behalf they must fight the politicians to assert the spirit and purpose of the primary law and reduce the growth and costs of secondary legislation and codes. There is currently little political will to do this. The Labour government's 2005 Better Regulation Task Force[190] warned us of the unintended consequences of regulation, because the government has automatically assumed that regulation is always the answer and, therefore, always "good". This is not proven. "Solutions that give stakeholders the flexibility to solve problems themselves are often preferable to imposing rules on them."[191] Note the early nod to "stakeholders" here. They also realized that the alternative was to do nothing. But, as politicians can only influence through laws and taxes, this is an option rarely considered by them.

Two ideas to help

What can be done to stop the rot in corporate governance regulation and turn it into an integral part of a national learning and development system for organizational effectiveness – private, public and not-for-profit? I suggest two simple actions:

1. Increase public oversight of corporate governance effectiveness

Currently the UK's regulatory system for corporate governance is a confused mess derived from six main sources:

- Those regulations derived from the Companies Act under the sponsorship of the Business, Energy and Industrial Strategy Department

- Those regulations derived from the Financial Reporting Council's Code of Corporate Governance

- Those regulations derived from the Financial Conduct Authority and the Bank of England

- Treasury interventions

- Those regulations derived from the London Stock Exchange listing requirements

- Parliamentary oversight

This last one is reinforced by such national organizations as the National Audit Office for governmental spending and the (disgracefully) soon-to-be-abandoned Audit Commission for local authority spending. The parliamentary select committees are beginning to have some bite, especially the Treasury and Public Accounts select committees – but is often these who end their reports with comments like "this organization's corporate governance must be made more effective" without offering any help as to how.

This is such a diverse mix of regulators that it is not surprising that public frustration continues. Accountability, probity and transparency are needed within the regulators. I shall go into more detail on this in Chapter 6.

2. Extend corporate governance law and codes to all registered organizations

Readers will notice immediately that, despite the generic nature of the Companies Act, the current national corporate governance regulatory system is not just heavily weighted towards listed companies but is designed only for them. This is nonsense, as less than 5% of companies registered in the UK are listed. Surely corporate governance laws and rules should apply to all registered companies? I go further and argue that the primary laws and revised secondary codes for corporate governance must apply to cover *all* registered organizations in the UK – private, public and not-for-profit – if we are to have effective organizations as a continuing national asset. The public need note that non-listed, not-for-profits, limited liability partnerships, mutuals, cooperatives and social interest companies are outside the regulators' current mind-set of "normal" businesses. This is dangerous nonsense and a key part of the rot. It is assumed also that, as far as the not-for-profit sector is concerned, the unsatisfactory Industrial and Provident Societies Act 1965 and the Charities Acts will just have to make do for them. The governmental assumption seems to be that any deficiencies can be made up by grafting on untested bits of company law and codes to hide the problem. I shall also deal with this in greater detail in Chapter 6.

The problem for charities

The public often assume that, in the altruistic world of charities, corporate governance is better ordered. They are often wrong, very wrong. It is true that the vast majority of directors and executives of charitable organizations are driven by the value of altruism – especially with a desire to right wrongs and to "give back". They are usually well-meaning people but often organizationally and legally naïve, especially in terms of corporate governance. As with politicians, a motivation to "do good" guarantees neither effectiveness nor organizational efficiency. There are too many intervening variables. I have seen too many examples of "the uncharitable world of charities" to dismiss this pungent phrase as a myth. So what effect is the main regulator, the Charities Commission, having on the corporate governance of this "not-for-profit" sector?

The answer is very mixed. There are undoubtedly good charities out there doing a magnificent job. We see this frequently in relation to distressed people, animals and emergencies. The British people, like those of Hong Kong, are renowned for the generous personal post-tax contributions they make to charity. But, as I write, the role of the charity regulator is under heavy scrutiny over two current cases in which the regulator is accused of being slow to act. One involves the Cup Trust – a company accused of allowing financiers to use their registered charity as a legal entity to create an offshore tax avoidance scheme. Such action goes against the very ethos of being a charity. It is alleged that less than 5% of the Cup Trust's turnover went towards charitable work. The other 95% went to the beneficiaries of the tax avoidance scheme and the creators' other companies Charitable misconduct also hit the headlines in 2014, when Lord Bhatia was accused of misappropriating £600,000 from the Ethnic Minority Foundation, the charity he formed and ran.

When such charges are made public, alongside reports of the elderly being harassed to keep giving to charities to which they once subscribed, the credibility of all charities is brought into question. An angry public has accused the Charities Commission of being supine, naïve, lacking in rigour and complacent. In 2015, the astonishing behaviour of the Chairman and Chief Executive of Kids Company became public. The media carried stories of a teenager being flown first class to the US to see his girlfriend, of youth club members asking and getting presents without much discretionary questioning, and the government giving emergency funding of £4 million without due diligence. When the crisis erupted, the chairman went on television and stated angrily that they were well governed and that they must be as they had an annual external audit. The alleged lack of board oversight is now under deep investigation. These are very worrying examples for an altruistic public who still want to give but need assurance that the maximum amount of their charitable giving goes to legitimate and well-governed causes.

But the heavier, most informed criticisms are directed toward the Charity Commission itself. These criticisms come from the National Audit Office,[192] following questioning by the government's Public Accounts Committee (a good example of two agencies working together for improved public oversight). They include the following strong statements:

- There is a gap between public expectations of the Commission and what it actually does

- It continues to make little use of its statutory enforcement powers

- It can be slow to act when investigating regulatory concerns

- It does not take tough enough action in some of the most serious regulatory cases

- It relies heavily on trustees' assurances

The growing doubts about the weak corporate governance of charities is exposed here – in their regulator. Both need rectification.

The need for three major changes to the corporate governance regulatory system

In conclusion, I would like to reinforce the need for three major changes to the present UK national corporate governance context and framework.

The first is that the Companies Act's seven general duties of directors apply to and are enforced for *all* registered organizations in the country – private, public and not-for-profit. This is already the case in South Africa and such legislation is slowly transforming the mindsets there, as much in government and the not-for-profit sectors as in family-run and start-up companies. For me, it is blindingly obvious that this is a foundation stone upon which the whole must be built.

Second, corporate governance regulation needs to be broken out of the Financial Reporting Council's grip and become an autonomous reporting council in its own right. It seems illogical, given the public anger over the current Western financial crisis and the greed that led us there, that – as the world moves towards ESG, integrated reporting and stakeholder-led capitalism – corporate governance regulation should still be held hostage by accountants. Effective corporate governance is so much wider, deeper and creative than accountancy. It needs to be freed.

Third, the government needs to establish a national *forum* for the continuous learning, development and regulation of effective corporate governance. This public oversight body would link boards of directors, owners and their agents, regulators and legislators into a crucial national dialogue; and so increase learning about organizational effectiveness and efficiency while relieving the current unhealthy stand-off with the public. The International Integrated Reporting Council (IIRC)[193] already attempts this for regulators, investors and other interested parties, so we have an example to work from.

Quis custodiet ipsos custodes?

Ultimately, who will guard the guards themselves? This question echoes through history since its writer, Juvenal, first penned it in his 1st-century "Satires".[194] The public's trust in their guardians rests on a "noble lie", as writers as diverse as Socrates, St Augustine and Karl Popper have suggested. It was raised again in the Nobel Memorial Economic Science Prize acceptance speech by Leonid Hurwicz in 2007.[195] This question must be asked frequently in a healthy society, even if it may be unanswerable at a given time. In a democracy, our legislators are ultimately accountable to the public. But, if there is no national oversight system of corporate governance regulation, then we have no means of assessing the performance of our key organizations. For for how we might solve it we must now turn to Chapter 6.

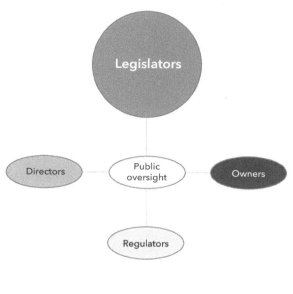

6

Does government know what "governance" means?

Reframing corporate governance
to stop the rot

Context

At the start of this book, I stated that the public are increasingly estranged from their governors, national and corporate. This is an international phenomenon. And the public's reactions to such issues as Brexit, Trump and the turbulence in the European Union have reinforced my view. This growing divide is apparent economically, politically, socially and culturally. I argued that neither the public nor their current governors, political and directoral, have yet to develop the intellectual and practical tools to resolve this phenomenon. Because the necessary words and frameworks are neither debated nor agreed, there is a dialogue of the deaf between the five main players: directors, owners, regulators, politicians and the public. Each finds it very easy to blame the others and none seems to have taken a "helicopter view" to look at how all five might work together to create a whole – a national system of governance.

The public's ignorance of "governance" leaves them feeling especially angry and helpless. I argue that a change of public understanding of how we need to govern our organizations effectively will have faster, more beneficial and longer-lasting effects on our societies than any political rhetoric. And it will counter many "post-truth" stories. This is the focus of this concluding chapter.

'Twas ever thus. The selection of quotes below illustrates the range of cynicism, scepticism and desperate humour that has existed in regard to the public's views of politicians for over two millennia.

> Those who are too clever to engage in politics are punished by being governed by those who are less clever.
>
> Plato, *Republic*

> An honest man in politics shows more there than to the world elsewhere.
>
> Mark Twain, *A Tramp Abroad*

> The seven Social Sins are Wealth without Work, Pleasure without Conscience, Knowledge without Character,

Commerce without Morality, Science without Humanity, Worship without Sacrifice, Politics without Principle.

Frederick Lewis Donaldson, Sermon in Westminster Abbey, 20 March 1925

Since a politician never believes what he says he is quite surprised to be taken at his word.

Charles De Gaulle

A politician needs the ability to foretell what is going to happen tomorrow, next week and next year. And the ability afterwards to explain why it did not happen.

Winston Churchill, 1902

There comes a time when one has to take a position that is neither safe, nor politic, nor popular, but he must take it because conscience tells him it is right.

Martin Luther King, *A Testament to Hope*

It is a well-known fact that those people who most want to rule people are, ipso facto, those least suited to do it . . . anyone who is capable of getting themselves made President should on no account be allowed to do the job.

Douglas Adams, *The Restaurant at the End of the Universe*

The legislators' role in creating a corporate governance learning system

This chapter will not spend long on a critical analysis of the role and values of politicians. Instead, it will be more constructive, proposing an integrated national action-learning system for the continuing development of corporate governance. This chapter places the final two players – politicians and the public – into my proposed five-role design. The design ensures that the politicians must always be overseen by, and accountable to, the public to ensure those fundamental governance values of accountability, probity and transparency. This system will give the public sufficient information to constructively criticize and develop both their governors and themselves.

Legislators lack a duty of care for governance

Within this new national system, each of the five players needs to be much better organized, effective and efficient, within their own spheres, in order to ensure that they then have the ability to integrate successfully with the other players. A precondition of such integration is that *all* nationally registered organizations are brought into the protection and discipline of the existing legal incorporation framework. That this has not already been done is my major criticism of the current legislators' lack of a duty of care towards developing effective governance. It is the role of our legislators to protect and develop our society by creating the national conditions for effective corporate governance. These legislators create our legal framework and have a duty to enforce and monitor it. Sadly, they rarely fully implement, nor live by, their own laws. Few politicians recognize this.

In Ed Straw's thought-provoking book *Stand and Deliver: A Design for Successful Government*,[196] he neatly summarizes my position in relation to our legislators:

> A key issue for democratic politics, in the UK and many other nations, is what to do about voter disengagement? The faith that the electorates have in government – of whatever party – to make their lives better is dramatically decreasing, while the incompetence of our political structure and of those elected to office becomes increasingly apparent. The problem is now so acute that many believe we are in danger of losing an entire generation from the political process.

He highlights the blockages, and argues that government does not have to be this bad, but that nothing will improve until we understand the present *system* as a whole: "Governments are 'organizations'

– bigger, more complex and more important than most, but organizations nonetheless." His prescribed resolution, through a national Treaty for Government, is well worth debating. I stress here my conviction that becoming competent at effective governance, especially corporate governance, in all of our organizations will lead to a more stable society without any loss of creativity. I am seeking a paradox: a structural system that delivers creative contentment. I outline my design for this towards the end of this chapter.

This chapter reminds us of the purpose of government, and then reviews all five key players as the essential structural components of an integrated national system of dynamic corporate governance, created through continuous mutual action learning. Do remember that I am a Chartered Designer with a background in architectural education. I believe that the architectural education process is a useful model for future director and governor development. Architecture must integrate science and the arts, technology and economics, ecology and anthropology to create a sustainable design. Such integrated thinking development is the future for politicians and directors. It is the antithesis of current, exclusive, discipline-based, reductionist "business education".

Does government know what "governance" means?

In talking with politicians and finally giving evidence to a parliamentary select committee, I was increasingly surprised at how little many of them had seriously considered "governance". They seemed much more interested in "politics". So I had to go back to its historic roots.

The prime purpose of any government is to provide a system of governance that protects and develops its people. This concept embodies the classic director's dilemma – *the tension of how do we create a healthy future for our organization while keeping it under prudent control* – but writ large at the national scale. Effective national governance requires our legislators to have the competences to think long-term, about policy formulation and national sustainability; strategically, to prioritize the careful deployment of a nation's scarce resources; short-term, to ensure prudent control; and, holistically, to ensure that its executive functions optimally to implement those scarce resources and reduce the risks of unintended consequences. None of these thinking processes are part of the selection or development of a politician. Nor of that of directors, managers, owners or regulators. It needs to be developed consciously at the national level as part of governance learning.

Most politicians will automatically concentrate on the short term because their political tenure is usually four years. So it is unsurprising that continuously balancing the "director's dilemma" with long-term national needs is not their core mind-set. Indeed, in party politics this mind-set is usually regarded as "too challenging" and so avoided. A good example of this is the messy exploitation of the wealth generated in the UK by North Sea oil. Both Norway and the UK suddenly had vast wealth to deploy. The Norwegians acted as a nation rather than as a political party, creating a sovereign wealth fund, and investing their money wisely for the long term. By mid-2015 they had generated $7.1 trillion to fund their citizens' economic and social security. Singapore and the Gulf states have had similar long-term national investment plans and are benefiting from them. The UK governments did not think long-term. Instead, they fought along party political lines over how to quickly spend the new wealth rather than invest at least some of it. We suffer economically and socially as a consequence.

Even South Africa, a country relatively poor in relation to the UK, realized that, to provide a sustainable national pension scheme, it could not rely on annual taxes alone. It has therefore created the Public Investment Corporation Fund to provide its national pension scheme. This fund represents good, long-term, non-adversarial, national governance, even as the country wallows in increasing corruption. The UK has not done this; it funds national pensions and health from direct taxation and, as a result, suffers from a growing governance deficit, and the public's perception of a lack of duty of care. The annual political question for the UK is therefore how much to spend next year on pensions. But with a rising dependency ratio, due to the "baby boomers" creating a top-heavy national demographic pyramid not underpinned by a healthy profile of taxable succeeding generations, this is a fiscal time bomb waiting to go off.

It is the conscious integration of both long- and short-term thinking that delivers effective "governance". Unfortunately, most politicians seem arrogant enough to assume that they automatically know how to resolve these governance dilemmas. Some even feel that they do this well. What is worse is that the public's ignorance of effective governance means that this fallacy continues, and the estrangement gap widens. How can we stop this rot?

Ensuring that effective governance is valued as a national asset

The current bitter distaste, and occasional hatred, of politicians by the public is as old as recorded history. For example, in 1726, Jonathan Swift's *Gulliver's Travels* has the King of Brobdingnag saying:

> Whoever could make two ears of corn, or blades of grass, grow upon a spot of ground where only one grew before, would deserve better of mankind, and do more essential service to his country, than the whole race of politicians put together.[197]

Nowadays he might have included economists, lawyers and accountants. But before this becomes a rant, let us look rationally at what governments are designed to do.

What do governments do?

The public's fundamental expectation of their governors is of national defence and financial and social stability. Beyond that, the government's permanent dilemma is to balance national direction-giving with prudent national control. This breaks into three distinct activities:

- Service provider   (through directly or indirectly employed labour)
- Service purchaser (from suppliers in the private and public sectors)
- Regulator   (of agreed service standards and delivery processes)

These roles, and the quality and quantity of their delivery, are designed to be balanced at national level by the continuous and critical interaction between the legislature, the executive and judiciary. All are buffeted daily by regional, national and international events and by querulous media and unpredictable public opinion. In a democracy, the legislature is the main regulator of national progress through its power to pass laws and so influence public opinion through its political judgements. The judiciary and the executive power blocs are designed to act as conscious counterbalances. The system is designed to work like clockwork. Sadly, it does not. We are now in a digital age where real-time ideas and information are demanding more interactive approaches to governance. How can that be achieved?

Raising corporate governance above party politics

To progress as a nation we need to get all political parties to agree that effective corporate governance is a key national asset and should therefore be above party political debate. Can they accept that our organizations, our institutions, the very cement of our society, need mutually agreed long-term commitment? If so, can we embed this within a national Covenant for Corporate Governance? We have already achieved this with the Military Covenant, which evolved from pressure groups and Parliament debating the military's future roles in times of spending cuts. So why not do the same for our governance systems?

We need to create a national corporate governance oversight and *learning* system which regularly holds boards, owners, stakeholders, regulators *and* legislators to public account. In a digital age, this does not mean the creation of expensive new agencies and buildings, but rather the establishment of interactive learning systems open to public access and comment. In my many discussions over the last four years while preparing this book I have found that no-one was against such an ideal – in principle. Yet few had any idea of how this could be achieved. Can we stop the rot by working towards a National Corporate Governance Covenant, where the quality and competences of our organizational, financial and especially corporate governance processes are upgraded continuously as part of a national development process? Post-Brexit, we need it.

The rotting of old-style governance allows a new framework to be developed

The good news is that times are changing. There are a growing number of seemingly unconnected initiatives already under way, which will transform the governance scene as experienced by the public within the next couple of decades. These initiatives reflect the convergence and interaction of those four international trends I outlined in Chapter 2: the desire for the rise of inclusive capitalism, the acceptance of more "people values" in organizations, the need to rethink "professionalism" and the global effect of the rising middle classes.

Behind these trends lies a growing public awareness of the combined failure of modern economics (macro and micro), party politics and public ethics. This refocuses the need to rebalance the competing demands for all three types of capital – financial, people and physical – to create a more humanely constructive context for our national and global development. This is not sufficiently appreciated by parties used to bipolar adversarial systems. Yet it is through these continuing public demands that we can ensure the future quality, competence, development and governance of our organizations.

Facing down current party politics

First we need to recast our current issues in effective governance terms, to break those "webs of signification" that we have spun. For centuries we have dug ourselves into a political pit in the name of "democracy": a pit from which we are now struggling to escape. The major cause of this descent is not the loss of the democratic ideal but rather irrational idolization of a consciously adversarial political system. The rise of the global electronic media, with its wide and uncritical dissemination of data, has diluted the public's awareness of both the priorities of political issues and their ability to ask discriminating questions of the data. "Fake news" thrives in these conditions. The media has frequently overplayed the Yahoo behaviours and thoughtless loyalties of the party adversaries to the point where the public has switched off, just as Ed Straw warned that they would. So has the business community. Hopefully, this era of the "big lie" will not last long, and people's discernment can be developed to sift the truth from the chaff – a prerequisite for good governance by the people.

Alarmingly, the mantra of many current directors and executives is that "we must always keep out of politics". In a world where the rise of stakeholders and inclusive capitalism continues apace, it will be impossible to be completely apolitical. Scarce resources still have to be prioritized. But this does not mean that a corporation must, therefore, always be party-political. Single-issue problems arise frequently beyond party politics. It is possible for directors and active owners to rise above such binary politics to ensure a company's continuity by understanding, integrating and riding the energies of political trends while still balancing their corporate interests. I see this as *the* major directoral skill in the future.

We must demand that our current politicians, directors and owners review their whole approach to the meaning and importance of corporate governance and then commit to a consensual view of progress. While politicians always talk about great visions, sunlit uplands and glorious futures, it is as well to remember, as Enoch Powell reminded us, that "all political lives unless cut off at a happy juncture . . . end in failure".[198] It is a paradox that good people, entering politics with the intent to help their society, regularly seem to end up achieving the reverse, and at great personal cost. The reality of bipolar politics, the political compromises needed to pass legislation and taxation, often conflict with their vision and their personal values. Then, via constant media exposure, these conspire to diminish their public image or even ruin them. No wonder many MPs are enthusiastic for the "law to forget" internet legislation, yet paradoxically being publicly in favour of free speech. This is a classic and very public example of the clash between politicians' espoused values (accepted business values), legislated values (corporate governance values) and their deep beliefs (personal values).

Matters are made worse by the noticeable rise of the "career politicians" and their unelected, unaccountable and often inexperienced "special advisors". These frequently display the arrogance of ignorance. Political careers often now start straight from university via "internship" and political research. They then move on as political "advisors", and finally to a safe Parliament seat with little experience of their constituents' working lives, issues and values. In many countries, the fetid, enervating and ultimately corrupting world of government is now effectively hermetically sealed against the wider world. So many politicians have insufficiently diverse experience or independence of thought for their personal rate of learning to be equal to, or greater than, the societal changes around them. They are then trapped by those webs of signification that they themselves have spun. The public is estranged from them, and them from the public. It is not just the metropolitan elite that are now distanced from their electors but the vast majority of politicians.

There are some counter-moves. For example, the rise in the power of parliamentary select committees in the UK is a welcome way for the public to get at least some of its questions asked of politicians and civil servants. But the membership of many committees is of very mixed competence. In many countries, wisdom generated through diversity of personal experience is not valued in government. Moreover, party loyalty, especially in the selection of ministers, is put firmly above independence of thought or long-term national interest. This prioritizing of party loyalty to maintain existing power sits uneasily with the growing public demand for more multidisciplinary, experienced, wiser and more thoughtful long-term leaders.

Can politicians ever be competent at corporate governance?

As mentioned in the Introduction and in Chapter 3, few politicians have any concept of what effective corporate governance is, or the role they need to play in delivering it. They certainly do not expect to be personally trained to govern, so even the basics are not appreciated and developed. This is particularly odd, as, given the peculiar nature of the Westminster timetable, they should have plenty of "spare" time in which to learn while biding their time on the backbenches, aspiring to become ministers. There is currently no mandatory induction to political competence nor is there any suggestion of regular personal evaluations of competence – except by the voters at the next election, and even that depends more on demography than competence. So, unlike any corporate leader, politicians cannot be expected to know, let alone obey, such fundamentals of corporate governance as the seven general duties of directors. Currently, the notion of them having a parliamentary version of these duties seems beyond hope. So "ensuring the success of their nation", "ensuring care, skill and diligence" in what they propose and deliver, ensuring their "independence of thought", and "declaring conflicts of interest" are currently unfulfilled public demands.

Yet such competence *is* increasingly demanded by the public. So it is up to them to keep asking these intelligently naïve questions of their politicians, and to demand the establishment of a national learning system for effective corporate governance for our mutual development. Only then can our directors, owners and regulators have the opportunity to move towards national progress through the development of such true "professionalism" as spelled out in Chapter 2.

A basic demand of governments

I am determined to increase public debate in order to ensure that effective corporate governance is accepted as a national asset that creates those effective organizations – public, private and not-for-profit – that cement our society. We need a new theory of government. This demand goes beyond party politics. It will need little new legislation in the UK as the public have put most of the necessary corporate governance elements in place over many years, especially the laws. But it does demand that we now both enforce those laws rigorously at the level of directors, owners and regulators, personally and through our courts, and that we have the nationally agreed system of oversight and learning for the whole. How would one do that? I see two stages of national development to achieve this.

Two proposals for a new system of corporate governance

Throughout this book I have used the symbol:

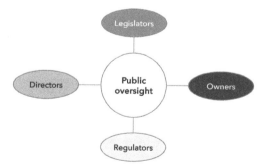

Now I wish to make two concrete proposals to ensure that each group plays its part in stopping the rot.

Proposal 1: Six key steps for immediate political agreement and enforcement

I have listed below six areas in which the government, directors and owners can implement immediate amendments (not radical changes) to the existing structures and laws in which the UK has already invested. These amendments will help stabilize our institutions, private, public and not-for-profit, lead to more effective corporate governance and therefore stop the rot. I have used the UK as an example of what could be for other nations. This proposal uses human values and digital communications to create an action-based interactive learning system within and between each of the five main players. Public oversight is at its apex. It is *not* an argument for the founding of a government-led ministry or agencies, nor for more civil servants or quangos, but for a much more creative rethink about using the existing resources to design a better national system.

Step 1. Bring all registered organizations in the UK within the corporate governance laws and codes

I start with a fundamental demand for government: that they ensure that the company and corporate governance laws and rules are applied to *all* publicly registered organizations in the UK – private, publicly-owned, PFIs, state-registered, cooperatives, mutuals and not-for-profits. This will require enforcement of the current general duties of directors under Sections 171 and 172 of the existing Companies Act and its clear extension to state-owned enterprises, charities and government agencies. It will require little investment, but a lot of "nudging" to change behaviours. South Africa has already done this, so why can't the UK? This gives a common national foundation from which all incorporated organizations can build their competences, their evaluations and share their learning. Our current messy legislative fudges are built on the ridiculous premise that corporate governance is important and enforceable only to listed companies, financiers and accountants – everyone else is excluded. This myth needs to be killed if the government and the public are to understand that the effective governance of our organizations is the cement that holds our society together. This is an obvious and simple start. It alone would be a national symbol that the process of stopping the rot has started.

We must also ensure that within this change the seven general duties of directors under the Companies Act are mandatory as the building blocks for *all* nationally registered organizations. These duties would focus their directors' attention on their personal and group roles and liabilities and so give more confidence that their organizations are assessed on the values of accountability, probity and transparency.

Step 2. Redesign direct governmental oversight

This would then demand some basic reforms of the various agencies of government that are making such a half-hearted attempt to even manage, let alone develop, the national approach to corporate governance. We need much better public scrutiny of these agencies to ensure that *their* governance duties are delivered competently and evaluated by the public on the same regular and rigorous basis that they wish to impose on others. For example:

Department of Business, Energy and Industrial Strategy (DBEIS)

In many countries, the "business" ministry is usually a mess: political aspiration meets intellectual confusion and vested interests, resulting in a ragbag of indicatives and rules. These are often reshuffled frequently depending on the president's or prime minister's whims. A good example is the UK's Department of Business, Energy and Industrial Strategy, recently rethought in 2016/17 under the new Theresa May government. To give some idea of its current range, it includes business regulation, energy, corporate governance, innovation, intellectual property, climate change, company law, trade, science and research, and outer space. It is difficult to spot a unifying theme or even some basic values and political priorities.

This is a problem because they are the main sponsoring department for business legislation, but they do not give effective corporate governance high priority. It is not seen as "sexy" and does not hit the media, as other issues like investment and employment frequently do, until it is too late. Yet without it neither of those issues can be addressed long-term. Despite growing public demands, there is no evidence that DBEIS will grasp the corporate governance issue and seek to transform the effectiveness and efficiency of our organizations. The department has become a party-political football. I argue that the long-term goal of developing effective corporate governance must be removed from such short-term games and raised to the level of a super-political national asset. This will demand a much stronger focus on the rigorous scrutiny and enforcement of the existing Companies Act 2006 and the Bribery Act 2010, acts that are specifically designed to include public oversight. The primary duty of all directors is "to ensure the success of the business"; if applied to DBEIS, such continuing oversight and enforcement will help them deliver the generation of enterprise, the wise assessment of risk, innovation, and the consequent creation of new wealth and employment. Given Brexit, this would seem a national no-brainer. But it is not prioritized – yet. These acts are within the political remit of DBEIS, but have never been delivered in a systematic way. The public must ask why not.

To be effective, the new version of DBEIS needs much stronger corporate governance links to the National Audit Office, the Treasury, the Bank of England, and the Treasury and Public Accounts Select Committees, to create a mutual, governmental national learning system that can then better instruct the regulators. After all, they are the very bodies that demand "much stronger corporate governance" following their many enquiries. Why do they not follow through?

Step 3. Resolve the faulty Salomon Judgement in favour of the shareholders

As mentioned in Chapter 4, the government could do everyone a major service and resolve a century of ownership confusion by clarifying legislation and reframing the Salomon Judgement of 1890 so that "patient" shareholders *do* own the assets of a company, and thus have the democratic right to be informed of, and vote on, strategic directoral decisions. "Ownership" should be according to the percentage of the shares held by "patient" shareholders only (no short-term chancers and churners), subject to the present protection of minority shareholder rights legislation. The company would remain a separate legal personality and the directors would still be its delegated agents and so take ultimate responsibility for their, and their executives', actions on its behalf. But the directors would be directly answerable to the shareholders for the care, skill and diligence, and independence of thought, they show in addressing the director's dilemma through their policies, strategies and espoused business model. The company would thus have its "corporate mind", and the personal accountabilities and liabilities of its directors and managers, clarified. In addition, the shareholders would employ the auditors and so accept their duty of care. This would be a major step towards breaking the stranglehold of executive-led capitalism, reasserting the sovereignty of the board and establishing stakeholder-led inclusive capitalism. This would give a clear fiduciary duty for both "patient" shareholders and the directors to act as mutual stewards to ensure the success of their organization. This would leave the "impatient" shareholders, the churners, excluded from any voting rights over the direction and control of the company. They would merely have the right to trade their shares as short-term bargaining chips.

Step 4. Parliamentary scrutiny: the need for a select committee on corporate governance

It is a puzzle to me that the rise in public accountability, through the effective scrutiny of parliamentary select committees, has not focused specifically on the importance of effective corporate governance. After all, the lack of corporate governance is mentioned so often during their own enquiries: usually as a key recommendation to answer the nagging question of "but where was the board?" I suggest that a new parliamentary select committee should be created, to focus exclusively on corporate governance issues across all UK registered organizations. This would highlight corporate governance as a valuable and developable national asset in the minds of both the politicians and the public. The lack of such a committee currently allows much political buck-passing between departments, the Bank of England and the regulators. It would hold public bodies, not-for-profits and the private sector to account, and force them to assess their boards' knowledge, skills and diligence with particular questioning of the duty of care exhibited by the directors and senior executives involved. When this select committee chose to examine an organization, it would be able to explore the organization's espoused purpose, vision and values, strategies, business model and operational processes, and longer-term success – as well as being able to comment publicly on the differences between espoused and accepted behaviours.

Step 5. Rethinking the corporate governance regulator

I argued in Chapter 5 that the government must remove corporate governance regulation from the control of the Financial Reporting Council and create a national Corporate Governance Reporting Council in its own right. Accountancy and finance are a necessary but not sufficient part of effective corporate governance, while areas such as behavioural economics, anthropology, strategic thought, business models, and old-fashioned entrepreneurial nous are not currently considered important or measurable. But this is beginning to shift despite the current accountancy capture, with its focus on compliance and box-ticking. If you look only a little way into the future, you can see that integrated Reporting, Long Finance (as a radically different and more useful method for auditing environmental, sustainability, social and human rights issues), and community stakeholder involvement are increasingly relevant in shaping the future of businesses and so corporate governance. These are the future disciplines on which the public, the business schools and the management consultancies need to build. The current regulator, the Financial Reporting Council, needs to gracefully concede its dominant role in regulating corporate governance to a more appropriate body.

Step 6: Creating a profession of directing

Following the 2013 Davies Report on UK Banking,[199] the government has finally put its weight behind ensuring that banking, at least, is now closer to becoming a regulated profession. It is astonishing that it never was. Nor was insurance, although the insurers have shown a little contrition for their previous anti-consumer actions and a slightly faster turn of speed in creating a profession.

Public demands for more "professionalism" and customer focus across our business and services sectors are deafening, yet politicians of all parties still do not appreciate that the public is serious, and that there are votes in it, as shown by the Brexit and Trump polls. Instead, politicians seem puzzled and frightened about what to do to achieve more professionalism. There is recent history in this. Margaret Thatcher set out to destroy the professions in the UK, particularly the legal and medical professions, as conscious policy on the heels of "defeating the unions". She saw them as a major constraint to trade because they were the antithesis of her free-market philosophy. But she was never a social historian, and her knowledge of the history of the professions and the reasons for their existence did not concern her. She was convinced that "the markets" alone would protect the public and that independently minded professionals were redundant. We are still suffering the consequences of the partial destruction of the professions and their public service values. We need to form a new national social contract with them.

I would like briefly to review their history to explain what has been lost. The "old professions" – the Church, Medicine, Law and Architecture – were reinforced in mid-Victorian times by the rise of the "new professions", especially accountancy, audit, actuarial surveying, banking and insurance, in order to reinforce the growing business class and its commercial and social interactions.

A national consensus was agreed, and reinforced by law. This granted each profession a monopoly in its discipline so long as they ensured that they would be disinterested, and that their clients' interests came first, even if the professional lost out in the short term on a transaction. This was the professions' version of "My word is my bond". The professions were therefore granted the sole rights to control entry and training, plus the ability to set and police fixed fees and professional conduct. In return, and to ensure client protection, they guaranteed a code of conduct which would bring members to account, discipline and fine them, and – in extreme cases – expel wrongdoers. Mrs Thatcher put an end to restricted entry to the professions and destroyed fee scales, but did little to maintain the quality of education or customer service, especially the ethos of "client first". She preferred to leave all of this to the markets, and introduced only light consumer legislation which was too narrow for modern needs. This action demeaned the professions in the public's eyes, even law and medicine; in an age of "light-touch legislation", self-interest now tends to be seen as having been substituted for ethical values. This helps explain the current public demand for the restoration of a more "professional ethos" to fight the many "customer last" accepted business values. But there is a quiet and growing counterculture against the values of Greed and Sloth in many of our organizations.

The quiet rise of the professional director: towards a Royal College of Chartered Directors

What astonishes me is that, despite all the public condemnation of ineffective corporate governance and the consequent media hand-wringing from public enquiries and select committees, there has hardly been any focused public demand for the professionalization of *directors*. It is as though they are untouchable and undevelopable. Not so. Their invisibility does not mean that they are undevelopable.

An even bigger surprise to many is that a strong foundation for this profession of directing already exists in the UK, and in a growing number of other countries. It has been growing quietly and effectively for over a decade. It is called the Chartered Director initiative.[200] It is still relatively small but highly committed. This is because, from the mid-1980s onward, the Chartered Director initiative has been driven by *individual directors* and not as a sponsored government or industry initiative. Although it has received little publicity, it is very robust as it is driven by the personal commitment of peers, of practising directors, rather than legislation and regulation. When I became involved in the professionalization of directors back in the 1980s, the then Department of Education was strongly against any such initiative outside their bailiwick. It fought a long fight to bring it into its national award system and to constrain it within the bureaucratic confines of its National Competences framework. This was strongly opposed by the small band of directors on the Education and Professional Development committees of the Institute of Directors, London, who were determined to create a profession-led process. In the end, the DES (Department of Education and Science) was bypassed by the directors who went directly to the Privy Council, effectively cutting out government oversight.

The Privy Council was strongly in favour and granted, through Her Majesty the Queen, a Royal Charter for the status of "Chartered Director" to be awarded to suitably qualified people – a national award to be administered, but not owned, by the Institute of Directors, London. This is still shamefully under-publicized, even within the IoD, let alone to the general public. Yet some 1,400 existing directors have submitted themselves to two onerous written examinations and one gruelling oral, practice examination by peers. There is a strong continuing professional development aspect and a code of conduct which allows for dismissal. Directing is becoming a modern profession almost by stealth. It is a much more pragmatic response than the "evening MBA and a tiny touch of ethics" alternative. It is much needed. The intellectual framework is developed partly from my "learning board" model in *The Fish Rots from the Head*. Of the over 1,400 Chartered Directors in the UK, many are from a noticeably younger generation and include a small but growing number of directors from the public sector and not-for-profits as well as the private sector. This highlights the growing passion of such committed folk for the professionalization of directing and the good work of Sharon Constançon to keep the flame alight despite seas of indifference.[201] There are now sister organizations offering locally created Chartered Director awards in South Africa and Australia, and many more are evolving, particularly in the 54 Commonwealth countries.

As Chartered Director status already exists, this qualification needs no new legislation, but it does need to be scaled up by

BOB GARRATT

existing directors, coupled with public and governmental advocacy and acceptance that professional directing is a crucial future national asset. It is an obvious response to the current public criticisms. Any new funding should come from the bloated regulatory budget of the Financial Conduct Authority.

I now argue strongly that its Part 1 examination – on the rights and duties of a director – should be mandatory for any director of a UK registered company, however small. I am astonished that it is not. However, I argue also that Parts 2 and 3 should be voluntary, provided that the public can access this information easily. The majority of the nationally registered companies aspire to stay small, as do charities. But it should become a national initiative that over, say, a decade all listed companies, private enterprises above a modest size, NHS Foundation Trusts, state-owned enterprises, cooperatives and charities would strive to have a *majority* of Chartered Directors on their boards. This would encourage simultaneous professionalism and increased diversity. To me, this seems a modest proposal.

The need for two new categories of "director"'

The immediate objection is that, legally, anyone can become a company director if they go through the very simple process of nationally registering a company and declaring at least one person a "director". This is true. But what is not often understood is that, by declaring yourself a director, you bring yourself under the Companies Act and the seven general duties of directors, with its consequent liabilities and personal exposure. So I argue for the government to acknowledge legally two levels of director: a "Registered Director" – a vanilla-flavoured director who is only minimally registered under the Companies Act; and a "Chartered Director", who is professionally accredited and developed and who obeys a higher code of conduct which allows the public to have much higher levels of trust in their likely competence. This is also why I want the Chartered Director award to be completely decoupled from the Institute of Directors' "ownership". The Chartered Director award sits uncomfortably in the IoD as it is not an independent, dedicated professional institute in its own right. This is what the Royal College of Directors should be. Funded separately, and with the active cooperation of the IoD, it should become a powerful national institution. Indeed, I can see it becoming as socially useful and influential as the medical Royal Colleges.

Despite all the current criticism of UK corporate governance, there are positive signs of a revival and growth. What is remarkable is that this has not been through governmental initiatives, or the funding of vast schemes by business as a sop to their conscience, but through the commitment by active practitioners, who recognize that only they can make the changes for the better, that they should fund it themselves, and that ultimately self-regulation is the best way forward.

London and Johannesburg are key creative hubs in this renaissance. When added to the remarkably creative and increasingly prolific work by such think-tanks as Tomorrow's Company, the City Values Forum, PIRC and Business in the Community with its push for a "Business Covenant" – plus the four powerful King Commissions in South Africa (with their strong effect on creating change) – it is obvious that the present situation is untenable, and that there are growing international forces to create the necessary changes.

Proposal 2: Towards a national framework for continuous learning and development of corporate governance as a national asset

A Standing Commission for Corporate Governance

What is therefore needed is a clear cross-party agreement on the national priority of effective corporate governance. I have argued that it does not need massive new legislation, just small amendments and clarifications to existing laws. However, in order to go up a gear and rise to the creation of a sustainable nationally agreed learning system, we need a new design. My proposal is that the government agrees to the creation of a Standing Commission on Corporate Governance. My wish is that, in parallel, the politicians agree to keep their party-political hands off the hopeful current developments in effective corporate governance, and that they promise to generate *less* legislation and fewer codes while learning to trust these new-style Chartered Directors to become a self-regulating profession willing to work within tough, agreed and monitored national competence and ethical frameworks.

Creating the national corporate governance fora of interactive networks to feed the Standing Commission

I have argued throughout this book that there are five parties needed to deliver a national system of effective corporate govern-ance: boards, owners, regulators, legislators and public oversight. I have also argued that it is unnecessary to go to the time and expense of forming a centralized body to control their learning. Centralized bodies are slow to learn, prone to organizational amnesia[202] and bad at disseminating development rapidly. Their rate of learning is always unequal to, or less than, the rate of environmental change. Which is another way of saying that they are bound to rot. As we live in a world of increasing connectivity, it seems wiser to design a series of decentralized fora where the ideas and issues can be discussed quickly and mutually, action can be taken, learning codified, and then dis-seminated through rapid feedback across the whole system – with the whole process open to public oversight.

This would take the notion of a continuing Investors' Forum – as suggested in the Kay Review – and create similar fora for boards, regulators and legislators. They would be consciously designed to always put the users' interest first. To progress Kay's idea, they must always have open access to the public. As they become more used to social media, searching, debating and deciding online, this opens up new ways of communicating the strengths and weaknesses of corpo-rate governance at national and international levels.

Above all, there would be a government-created Standing Com-mission on Corporate Governance – the national focus of pub-lic oversight. This would operate for the public good by bringing together the outputs of the four specialist fora to inform and develop

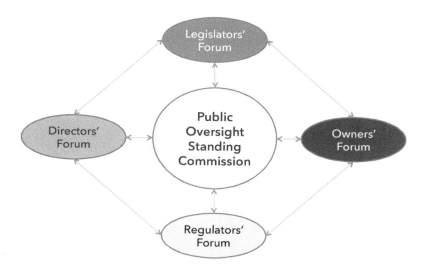

Figure 7: The proposed learning system

the wider public debate. This is where the sunshine works as the best disinfectant to stop the rot.

The design of the fora for the four main players

Each forum would form part of the wider interactive national, and international, action-learning network in continuous contact with each other and with the wider public digitally through the Standing Commission. They would be self-funding and self-governing, and the quality of their learning will be determined by both peer and public criticism. My draft design for each forum is as follows:

1. Boards of Directors' Forum

This would have real-time inputs from practising directors from, for example:

- The Chartered Director initiative (the Royal College of Directors)

- The Institute of Directors
- The Institute of Company Secretaries and Administrators
- The company lawyers
- The accountancy and audit professions
- The listed companies
- Private businesses
- Mutuals and cooperatives
- The not-for-profits and charities
- State-owned enterprises
- Government agencies
- Community interest companies
- The NGOs

Its purpose is to collect and disseminate good and best practice, to monitor trends and to pass on to the owners, legislators and regulators information for their consideration before reporting on a regular basis to the Standing Commission.

2. The Owners' Forum

This would have continuous inputs from directors, regulators, legislators and the public and include, for example:

- The Investors' Forum – pension and investment fund trustees, asset managers, individual investors and traders
- Members of cooperatives and not-for-profits
- Stakeholder groups – which would include the ESG interests of local communities, the workforce, suppliers, and environmental stewards

The purpose of all four forums is the same as that of the Directors' Forum.

3. The Regulators' Forum

This would include inputs from directors, owners, the public and legislators, and include, for example:

- Members of the new Corporate Governance Reporting Council
- Members of the professions with disciplinary codes
- Lawyers dealing with business issues and rights issues
- Governmental departments
- The Bank of England
- The Financial Conduct Authority

4. The Legislators' Forum

In addition to the independent Standing Commission, this is where the three national-level fora inputs mentioned above will take proposed ideas, and take feedback, on proposed legislation. In addition, The Legislators' Forum would have inputs from, for example:

- The new Parliamentary Select Committee on Corporate Governance
- Other parliamentary select committees, especially Treasury and Public Accounts
- Governmental and public enquiries
- International agreements
- Consultancy and educational research
- The United Nations Global Compact and Principles for Responsible Investment
- The UK's Department of Business, Energy and Industrial Strategy
- The Bank of England
- The Treasury

The proposed learning process

- These form a focus on the development of continuous "horizon-scanning" activities (nationally and internationally) to record changes, trends and issues arising in each forum. These are to be passed on in real time, if urgent, but otherwise at least monthly to the other three fora.

- At six-monthly intervals, the main issues and learning are consolidated by all four fora into a half-yearly *public* statement by the Standing Commission; which will include examples of good and best practice, as well as any individuals and corporations needing to be "named and shamed" for non-compliance or bad practice.

- A yearly public review by the Standing Public Commission for Corporate Governance. This will hold all the four major players – boards, owners, regulators and legislators – accountable for their duty of care and effectiveness in their roles in developing effective corporate governance on behalf of a healthier, wiser and wealthier nation.

I have no doubt that such a national learning system is now demanded, and that it will help the estranged public to become re-engaged, as it is *their* duty to maintain vigilance by continuously questioning the effective governance of their institutions. But there will always be dangers, as Niccolò Machiavelli warned us over 500 years ago:

> We must bear in mind that nothing is more difficult to set up, more likely to fail, and more dangerous to conduct than a new system of government: because the bringer of the new system will make enemies of everyone who did well under the old system, while those who do well under the new system still won't support it warmly.[203]

Above all, we must not slip back into the seductive comfort of a rules-based, compliance-dominated and personal-responsibility-avoiding slothful national mind-set. We must strongly pursue the essence of our principles-based system of corporate governance, building on human values, accountability, probity and openness. We all have a duty of care to each other in our organizations and must live more openly by it. Otherwise, we shall continue the current governance imagination paralysis, just getting by and condemned only to hope. This is an unacceptable position for any nation seeking effective corporate governance and a wealthy, healthy and sociable future.

We must combine to stop the rot!

Bob Garratt
London
March 2017

Notes

Introduction

1 Cadbury Committee, *The Financial Aspects of Corporate Governance*. London: Gee & Co., 1992.

2 Gillian Tett, "An interview with Alan Greenspan". *Financial Times Weekend Magazine*, 25 October 2013. Retrieved from https://www.ft.com/content/25ebae9e-3c3a-11e3-b85f-00144feab7de

3 Bob Garratt, *The Fish Rots from the Head: Developing Effective Board Directors*, 3rd edition. London: Profile Books, 2010.

4 Cardinal Vincent Nichols, Blueprint for Better Business Initiative Speech. Catholic Bishops' Conference of England and Wales, 2012. Retrieved from http://catholic-ew.org.uk/Home/News/2012/July-Sept/Archbishop-s-Speech/Archbishop-s-Address

5 Winston. S. Churchill, Speech in the House of Commons, London, 11 November 1947.

6 Jan Techau, "Sophisticated states are failing: Politicians need to take risks". *Financial Times*, 19 April 2016.

7 Hillaire Belloc, "Jim: Who ran away from his nurse and was eaten by a lion". In *Cautionary Tales for Children*. London: Eveleigh Nash, 1907.

8 Jean-Claude Juncker, *Financial Times*, 20 April 2016.

9 Techau, "Sophisticated states are failing".

10 Sir Adrian Cadbury, personal letter to Bob Garratt, May 2015.

11 Sections 171 and 172 of UK Companies Act 2006. Retrieved from http://www.formacompany.com/en/uk/uk-companies-act-2006/companies-act-2006-notes-171-181.php

12 Daniel Malan, "Global Agenda Council on Values: A new social contract". World Economic Forum, 23–27 January 2013. Retrieved from http://www3.weforum.org/docs/WEF_GAC_Values_2013.pdf

13 Dave Francis and Mike Woodcock, *Unblocking Organisational Values*. London: Pearson Scott Foreman, 1990.

14 Matthew Arnold, "On Dover Beach" (1867). In *New Poems*. London: Oxford University Press, 1988.

15 C.K. Prahalad and Allen Hammond, *The Fortune at the Bottom of the Pyramid: Eradicating Poverty through Profits*. London: Prentice Hall, 2005.

16 Adam Smith, *An Inquiry into the Nature and Causes of the Wealth of Nations*. London: W. Strahan & T. Cadell, 1776.

17 Section 171 of UK Companies Act 2006.

Chapter 1: The value of "values"

18 Oscar Wilde, *Lady Windermere's Fan* (1893). In *The Importance of Being Earnest and Other Plays*. London: Penguin, 1940.

19 Milton Rokeach, *The Nature of Human Values*. New York: Free Press, 1973.

20 Smith, *Wealth of Nations*.

21 The source is anonymous but frequently attributed C.S. Lewis.

22 Arnold Kransdorff, *Corporate Amnesia*. London: Butterworth Heinemann, 1998.

23 The "Walker Report": *A Review of Corporate Governance in UK Banks and Other Financial Industry Entities: Final Recommendations*, 26 November 2009. Retrieved from http://webarchive. nationalarchives.gov.uk/+/http:/www.hm-treasury.gov.uk/d/walker_review_261109.pdf

24 United Nations Office on Drugs and Crime, United Nations Convention Against Corruption, 2004. Retrieved from https://www.unodc. org/documents/brussels/UN_Convention_Against_Corruption.pdf

25 United States Department of Justice, US Foreign Corrupt Practices Act, 1977, amended 1998, 15 USC. Retrieved from https://www.justice. gov/criminal-fraud/foreign-corrupt-practices-act

26 United Kingdom Bribery Act, 2010. Retrieved from http://www. legislation.gov.uk/ukpga/2010/23/contents

27 Mervyn King, King Reports on Corporate Governance, South Africa, 1994–2017.

28 Financial Reporting Council, Final Draft: The UK Corporate Governance Code (April 2006). Retrieved from https://www.frc.org.

uk/Our-Work/Publications/Corporate-Governance/Final-Draft-UK-Corporate-Governance-Code-2016.pdf

29 See note 11.

30 Michael Reddy, *Bad Apples with Shiny Skins. Personality Disorders at Work: A Guide for Business Leaders. A Special Report.* Watchman Publishing, 2014.

31 Stanley Milgram, *Obedience to Authority: An Experimental View.* New York: Harper & Row, 1974.

32 Roger Steare, *Ethicability.* London: Roger Steare Consulting Ltd, 2009.

33 Sir Michael Jackson, *Soldier.* London: Transworld, 2007.

34 See note 25.

35 See note 26.

36 Centre for Policy Studies, *Big Bang 20 Years On: New Challenges Facing the Financial Services Sector* (2006). Retrieved from https://www.cps.org.uk/files/reports/original/111028101637-20061019EconomyBigBang20YearsOn.pdf

37 See note 23.

38 For information, visit http://www.cityvaluesforum.org.uk/about_city_values_forum.html.

39 For information, visit http://wcomc.org.

40 Francis and Woodcock, *Unblocking Organisational Values.*

41 Deuteronomy 5:4-21.

42 1 Corinthians 13:1-13.

43 Aligherie Dante, *The Divine Comedy* (1320). Trans Robin Kirkpatrick. London: Penguin Classics, 2006.

44 Steare, *Ethicability.*

45 Malan, "Global Agenda Council on Values: A New social contract".

46 Clifford Geertz, *The Interpretation of Cultures.* New York: Basic Books, 1973.

47 Lou Solomon, "Two-thirds of managers are uncomfortable communicating with employees". *Harvard Business Review*, 9 March 2016. Retrieved from https://hbr.org/2016/03/two-thirds-of-managers-are-uncomfortable-communicating-with-employees

48 Michael Hammer, "Reengineering work: Don't automate, obliterate". *Harvard Business Review*, July 1990. Retrieved from https://hbr.org/1990/07/reengineering-work-dont-automate-obliterate

49 Bob Garratt, *Twelve Organisational Capabilities: Valuing People in Organisations.* London: Profile Books, 2000.

50 Cornell University Law School, "Fiduciary duty". Retrieved from https://www.law.cornell.edu/wex/fiduciary_duty

51 Garratt, *Twelve Organisational Capabilities.*

52 Cadbury Committee, *The Financial Aspects of Corporate Governance*

53 Investor Stewardship Working Party, *2020 Stewardship: Improving the Quality of Investor Stewardship* (2012). Retrieved from https://www.icsa.org.uk/assets/files/pdfs/Policy2/2020_Stewardship_Final_L.pdf

54 Financial Reporting Council, UK Corporate Governance Code.

55 Kurt Lewin and Martin Gold, *The Complete Social Scientist.* Washington, DC: American Psychological Association, 1999.

56 Garratt, *Twelve Organisational Capabilities.*

57 Simon Chapman, "Implementing strategy: What the military have learned about strategy into action". In Bob Garratt (ed.), *Developing Strategic Thought: A Collection of the Best Thinking on Business Strategy.* London: Profile Books, 2003.

58 Geert Hofstede, *Culture and Organisations: The Software of the Mind.* London: Profile Books, 1994.

59 Fons Trompenaars and Charles Hampden-Turner, *Riding the Waves of Culture.* London: Nicholas Brealey, 1993.

60 *Riding the Waves of Culture.*

61 Charles Handy, *The Second Curve: Thoughts on Reinventing Society.* London: Random House, 2016.

62 Alan Greenspan, *The Map and the Territory: Risk, Human Nature and the Use of Forecasting.* New York: Penguin Press, 2013.

63 Gillian Tett, "An interview with Alan Greenspan". *Financial Times Weekend Magazine*, 25 October 2013. Retrieved from https://www.ft.com/content/25ebae9e-3c3a-11e3-b85f-00144feab7de

Chapter 2: Towards human values-based governance

64 Gillian Tett, "An interview with Alan Greenspan".

65 Bob Monks, "The end of the beginning". Speech at the International Corporate Governance Network conference, ICGN London, June 2014.

66 Daniel Snowman, *The Long March of Everyman.* BBC Radio 4 series, 1970.

67 Prahalad and Hammond, *The Fortune at the Bottom of the Pyramid.*

68 Mervyn King, Financial Statements 2014. The International Integrated Reporting Council. Retrieved from http://integratedreporting.org/wp-content/uploads/2015/06/IIRC-FINANCIAL-STATEMENTS-2014-FINAL-signed.pdf

69 Geertz, *The Interpretation of Cultures*.

70 Speaking at the ICGN Conference, London, June 2014.

71 Michael Lewis, *The Undoing Project*. New York: W.W. Norton, 2016.

72 Pew Research Centre, "A global middle class is more promise than reality", 8 July 2015. Retrieved from http://www.pewglobal.org/files/2015/07/Global-Middle-Class-Report_FINAL_7-8-15.pdf

73 The ten principles of the UN Global Compact. Retrieved from https://www.unglobalcompact.org/what-is-gc/mission/principles

74 Shanghai Academy of Social Sciences: http://english.sass.org.cn:8001/introductionOoverview/index.jhtml (accessed 14 March 2017).

75 Warren Buffett: http://www.berkshirehathaway.com (accessed 14 March 2017).

76 The Good Friday Agreement (Belfast Agreement) between the United Kingdom and Irish governments, 10 April 1998. Retrieved from https://www.gov.uk/government/uploads/system/uploads/attachment_data/file/136652/agreement.pdf

77 UK Office for National Statistics, Average income figures for January 2017. Retrieved from https://www.ons.gov.uk/employmentandlabourmarket/peopleinwork/earningsandworkinghours

78 Thomas Piketty, *Capital in the Twenty-first Century*. Boston, MA: Harvard University Press, 2013.

79 "Piketty's 'Capital' summarised in four paragraphs". *The Economist*, 5 May 2014. Retrieved from http://www.economist.com/blogs/economist-explains/2014/05/economist-explains

80 Kate Allen, "Hans Rosling, physician and statistician, 1948–2017: The dean of data who brought life to world trends". *Financial Times*, 10 February 2017. Retrieved from https://www.ft.com/content/df4af260-eece-11e6-930f-061b01e23655

81 Melvin I. Urofsky and David W. Levy (eds.), *Letters of Louis D. Brandeis. Volume II: 1907–1912: People's Attorney*. New edition. New York SUNY Press, 1972: 688.

82 Monks, "The end of the beginning".

83 Geertz, *The Interpretation of Cultures*.

84 Henry P. Sims and William Lafollette, "An assessment of the Litwin and Stringer Organization Climate Questionnaire". *Personnel Psychology*, 28(1) (December 2006): 19-38.

85 Garratt, *Twelve Organisational Capabilities*.

86 Revans, Reg, *The ABC of Action Learning*. London: Gower, 2011.

87 Deng Xiaoping, Four Modernizations speech to the Supreme Council of the Communist Party of China, Beijing, 1980.

88 Transparency International, Corruption Perception Index 2015. Retrieved from https://www.transparency.org/cpi2015; Bribe Payers Index. Retrieved from http://www.transparency.org/research/bpi/overview

89 Mervyn King and Leigh Roberts, *Integrate: Doing Business in the 21st Century*. London: International Integrated Reporting Council, 2013.

90 Stockholm syndrome is a condition that was formally named in 1973 following the kidnapping of four people in a Stockholm bank and which was reaffirmed in the kidnapping of Patti Hearst in 1974. First the victim is terrified, then infantilized, but over time following small acts of kindness the victim can begin to empathize with the kidnappers and even end up supporting them. For more information, see http://www.history.com/news/stockholm-syndrome.

91 Marc Flandreau and Joanna Kinga Slawatyniec, "Understanding rating addiction: US courts and the origins of rating agencies' regulatory license (1900–1940)". EHES Working Paper No 44, 2014. Retrieved from http://www.ehes.org

92 Mike Mainelli and Ian Harris, *The Price of Fish: A New Approach to Wicked Economics and Better Decisions*. London: Nicholas Brealey Publishing, 2011.

93 For information, visit http://wcomc.org.

94 Woolf Committee, *Ethical Business Conduct in BAE Systems plc: The Way Forward*, May 2008. Retrieved from https://www.icaew.com/-/media/corporate/files/technical/ethics/woolf-report-2008.ashx

95 GlaxoSmithKline, "GSK publishes 2010 Corporate Social Responsibility Report", 28 March 2010. Retrieved from http://ca.gsk.com/media/537223/gsk-publishes-2010-corporate-responsibility-report-28_03_11-eng-final.pdf

96 "GlaxoSmithKline says China executives have broken law". BBC News, 22 July 2013. http://www.bbc.co.uk/news/business-23402154

97 Rob Davis, "Starbucks pays UK corporation tax of £8.1m". *The Guardian*, 15 December 2015. Retrieved from https://www.theguardian.com/business/2015/dec/15/starbucks-pays-uk-corporation-tax-8-million-pounds

98 Vodafone Group Plc, *Annual Report 2014*. Retrieved from https://www.vodafone.com/content/annualreport/annual_report14/downloads/additional_information.pdf

99 FT Remark and State Street, *Frontline Revolution: The New Battleground for Asset Managers*, June 2014. Retrieved from http://www.

statestreet.com/content/dam/statestreet/documents/Articles/Asset%20
Manager%20-%20Executive%20Summary%20Deck.pdf

Chapter 3: The directors' role in stopping the rot

100 Gareth Morgan, *Images of Organizations.* New York: Sage, 2007.

101 *Henry IV, Part 2,* Act 3, scene 1, 26-31.

102 Such as Garratt, *The Fish Rots from the Head,* and Bob Garratt, *Thin on Top: Why Corporate Governance Matters and How to Measure and Improve Board Performance.* London: Nicholas Brealey Publishing, 2003.

103 Cadbury Committee, *The Financial Aspects of Corporate Governance.*

104 Earl of Halifax, Lord Edward Frederick Lindley Wood. *Fullness of Days.* London: Dodd Mead, 1957.

105 Norbert Weiner, *The Human Use of Human Beings: Cybernetics and Society.* New York: Da Capo, 1950.

106 Revans, *The ABC of Action Learning.*

107 Stafford Beer, "Designing freedom". Canadian Broadcasting Corporation Massy Lectures, 1973. Retrieved from http://www.ghbusinessonline.com/designing-freedom-cbc-massey-lecture.pdf

108 W.R. Ashby, "Self-regulation and requisite variety". In *An Introduction to Cybernetics.* London: Wiley, 1956.

109 Garratt, *The Fish Rots from the Head.*

110 Malan, "Global Agenda Council on Values: A New social contract".

111 Klaus Schwab, "World leaders reckon with a global rebalancing". *Financial Times,* 17 January 2017. Retrieved from https://www.ft.com/content/04523434-d8da-11e6-944b-e7eb37a6aa8e

112 King Reports on Corporate Governance.

113 Revans, *The ABC of Action Learning.*

114 J. Rhodes, *I Wonder: The Science of Imagination.* London: Clink Street Publishers, 2017.

115 Hermes Investment Management, "Hermes launches the Hermes Global Equity ESG Fund", May 2014. Retrieved from https://hermesinvestment-dev.kurtosysweb.com/uki/blog/news-article/hermes-launches-the-hermes-global-equity-esg-fund

116 The Co-operative Group, *Our Ethical Plan 2013–2015: Because good things can happen when we work together* (2013). Retrieved from http://www.all-energy.co.uk/__novadocuments/2962 2?v=635043980035330000

117 Greenspan, *The Map and the Territory.*

118 "Mid Staffs hospital scandal: The essential guide". *The Guardian*, 6 February 2013. Retrieved from: https://www.theguardian.com/society/2013/feb/06/mid-staffs-hospital-scandal-guide

119 Cardinal Vincent Nichols, Blueprint for Better Business Initiative Speech.

120 Edelman Popularity Ratings. Retrieved from http://www.edeleman.com

121 Cadbury Committee, *The Financial Aspects of Corporate Governance*.

122 C.P. Snow, *The Two Cultures*. Cambridge, UK: Cambridge University Press, 1959, reissue 2012.

123 J.M. Keynes, "Alfred Marshall, 1842–1924". *The Economic Journal*, 34(135) (1924): 311-372.

124 F. Scott Fitzgerald, *Tender Is the Night*. London: William Collins, 1934, reissue 2012.

125 Frank Knight, *Risk, Uncertainty and Profit*. Boston, MA: Houghton Mifflin, 1921.

126 Investor Stewardship Working Party, *2020 Stewardship*.

127 Ibid.

128 Adolf Berle and Gardiner Means, *The Modern Corporation and Private Property*. New York: Harcourt Brace, 1932, rev. edn 1967.

129 Ayn Rand, *Atlas Shrugged*. New York: Random House, 1957.

130 Charles Handy, "What is a company for?" *RSA Journal*, 1991: 139.

131 John Elkington, *Cannibals with Forks: The Triple Bottom Line of 21st Century Business*. Oxford, UK: Capstone, 1997.

132 US Congress, Sarbanes–Oxley Act (SOX), 30 July 2002. Retrieved from https://www.sec.gov/about/laws/soa2002.pdf

133 King, Financial Statements 2014.

134 Michael Mainelli and Bob Giffords, *The Road to Long Finance: A Systems View of the Credit Scrunch*. New York: CSFI, 2009.

Chapter 4: Owners and their responsibilities

135 Warren Buffett, "Back to School: Questions and Answers. Sessions with Business Students", 12 December 2008. http://www.bnpublishing.net.

136 A.H. Maslow, "A theory of human motivation". *Psychological Review*, 50(4) (1943): 370-396.

137 Andro Linklater, *Owning the Earth: The Transforming History of Land Ownership*. London: Bloomsbury, 2014.

138 *Wall Street* (1987), directed by Oliver Stone.

139 Samuel Smiles, *Self Help*. New York: Seven Treasures Publishing, 1859, reissue 2009.

140 UK Government, Joint Stock Companies Act 1844. Retrieved from http://hansard.millbanksystems.com/acts/joint-stock-companies-act-1844

141 UK Government, Limited Liability Act 1856. Retrieved from http://hansard.millbanksystems.com/lords/1855/aug/07/limited-liability-bill#S3V0139P0_18550807_HOL_4

142 House of Lords, Salomon's Judgement (1896), UKHL 1, AC22. Retrieved from http://corporations.ca/assets/Salomon%20v%20Salomon.pdf

143 Richard Dawkins, *The Blind Watchmaker*. London: Penguin, 1986.

144 UK Government, The Beveridge Report. Social Insurance and Allied Services (1942). See http://www.psi.org.uk/publications/archivepdfs/Victims/VV2.pdf

145 Winston S. Churchill, Speech in House of Commons, 28 October 1944). Retrieved from http://hansard.millbanksystems.com/people/mr-winston-churchill/1944

146 Geertz, *The Interpretation of Cultures*.

147 Berle and Means, *The Modern Corporation and Private Property*.

148 Monks, "The end of the beginning".

149 Tomorrow's Company, *2020 Stewardship: Improving the Quality of Investor Stewardship* (2012). Retrieved from https://www.icsa.org.uk/assets/files/pdfs/Policy2/2020_Stewardship_Final_L.pdf

150 Investor Stewardship Working Party, *2020 Stewardship*.

151 President Obama, Speech at the funeral of Nelson Mandela, 10 December 2013. See https://www.youtube.com/watch?v=SgtXy1vTcGY

152 Jenny Harrow, "The charity world: Governance at its most uncharitable". Conference paper. London: Cass Business School, May 2006.

153 The Denning Judgement (1963). Boulting vs Association of Cinematograph, Television and Allied Technicians. 2 QB 606.

154 Lord Adair Turner, "City is too big and 'socially useless'". *Daily Telegraph*, 29 August 2009.

155 Tomorrow's Company, *Tomorrow's Owners* (2009). Retrieved from http://tomorrowscompany.com/wp-content/uploads/2016/05/Tomorrow_s_Owners___Defining__Differentiating_and_Rewarding_Scholarship__52ef86c12aa78.pdf

156 Investor Stewardship Group, Corporate Governance Principles for US Listed Companies (2017). Retrieved from https://corpgov.law.harvard.edu/2017/02/07/corporate-governance-and-stewardship-principles

157 Commonsense Principles of Corporate Governance (2017). Published in major newspapers in the US and the *Financial Times* in London by a concerned group of US business leaders of whom Warren Buffett is a leading name. Retrieved from http://www.governanceprinciples.org/wp-content/uploads/2016/07/GovernancePrinciples_Principles.pdf

158 Somerset Merryn Webb, "If investing is poker, are fund managers a busted flush?" *Financial Times*, 17 May 2013.

159 McKinsey, Wealth and asset management reports. New York: McKinsey Insights, 2013. Retrieved from http://www.mckinsey.com/.../mckinsey%20offices/.../global_wealth_management_survey_2...

160 David Tuckett, *Minding the Markets: An Emotional Finance View of Financial Instability*. London: Palgrave Macmillan, 2011.

161 Robin Greenwood and David Scharfstein, "Calculating free cash-flows". Harvard Business School Background Note 206-028, October 2005.

162 Investor Stewardship Working Party, *2020 Stewardship*.

163 Institute of Directors Southern Africa, Code for Responsible Investing in South Africa (CRISA) (2011). Retrieved from https://www.icgn.org/sites/default/files/South%20African_Code.pdf

164 Department of Business, Innovation and Skills, The Kay Review of UK Equity Markets and Long-Term Decision Making (July 2012). Retrieved from http://blog.manifest.co.uk/wp-content/uploads/2012/07/Kay-review-Final-Report-July-20121.pdf

165 Principles for Responsible Investment: https://www.unpri.org

166 https://www.unglobalcompact.org/what-is-gc/mission/principles

167 *UN Global Compact Communication on Progress 2016*. Retrieved from: https://www.unglobalcompact.org/system/attachments/cop_2017/357481/original/Duba-B8-COP2016_final.pdf?1485785422

168 Monitor, NHS Code of Corporate Governance (July 2014). Retrieved from https://www.gov.uk/government/uploads/system/uploads/attachment_data/file/327068/CodeofGovernanceJuly2014.pdf

169 Lewin and Gold, *The Complete Social Scientist*.

170 Garrett Hardin, "The Tragedy of the Commons". *Science*, 162(3859) (13 December 1968): 1,243-1,248.

Chapter 5: Regulators

171 New City Agenda and Cass Business School, *Cultural Change in the FCA, PRA and Bank of England: Practising what they preach?* (25 October 2016). Retrieved from http://newcityagenda.co.uk/

wp-content/uploads/2016/10/NCA-Cultural-change-in-regulators-report_embargoed.pdf

172 "UK financial regulator vows to slash FCA rules". *Financial Times*, 26 October 2016. Retrieved from https://www.ft.com/content/0de65fea-9b61-11e6-b8c6-568a43813464

173 *Essays, Speeches, and Memoirs of Field-Marshal Count Helmuth von Moltke* (1882). See also Martin van Crefeld, *The Art of War*. London: Cassell, 2000.

174 Smith, *Wealth of Nations*.

175 Jean-Jacques Rousseau, *Of the Social Contract, or Principles of Political Right* (1762). See also Christopher Bertram, *Rousseau and the "Social Contract"*. London: Routledge, 2003.

176 US Declaration of Independence. Retrieved from https://www.archives.gov/founding-docs/declaration-transcript

177 Dava Sobell, *Longitude: The True Story of a Lone Genius Who Solved the Greatest Scientific Problem of His Time*. London: Harper Perennial, 1995.

178 Smith, *Wealth of Nations*.

179 Financial Reporting Council, UK Corporate Governance Code.

180 Sir Win Bischoff, Chairman of the Financial Reporting Council, Speech on the 25th Anniversary of the Cadbury Report. Mazars, London, 2 March 2017. Retrieved from https://www.frc.org.uk/Our-Work/Publications/FRC-Board/Speech-Sir-Win-Bischoff-25-years-since-the-Cadb.pdf.

181 UK Government, Public Interest Disclosure Act 1998. Retrieved from http://ukpga_19980023_en.pdf

182 Financial Conduct Authority, "About the FCA". Retrieved from https://www.fca.org.uk/about/the-fca

183 See note 38.

184 Cadbury Committee, *The Financial Aspects of Corporate Governance*.

185 New City Agenda and Cass Business School, *Cultural Change in the FCA, PRA and Bank of England*.

186 David Cameron, Speech to House of Commons, 23 May 2010.

187 Claudio Radaeli and Oliver Fritsch, "Measuring regulatory performance: Evaluating regulatory management tools and programmes". OECD Expert Paper, No. 2, July 2012. Retrieved from https://www.oecd.org/gov/regulatory-policy/2_Radaelli%20web.pdf

188 Department of Business, Innovation and Skills, The Kay Review of UK Equity Markets and Long-Term Decision Making.

189 Michael Porter, "America's green strategy". *Scientific American*, 26(4) (April 1991).

190 Better Regulation Commission, *Risk, Responsibility and Regulation: Whose risk is it anyway?* (October 2006). Retrieved from http://www. regulation.org.uk/library/2006_risk_responsbillity_regulation.pdf

191 Ibid.

192 Comptroller and Auditor General of the National Audit Office, *The Regulatory Effectiveness of the Charity Commission* (December 2013). Retrieved from https://www.nao.org.uk/wp-content/uploads/2013/11/10297-001-Charity-Commission-Book.pdf; Comptroller and Auditor General of the National Audit Office, *Follow up on the Charity Commission* (January 2015). Retrieved from https://www.nao.org.uk/wp-content/uploads/2015/01/Follow-up-on-the-charity-commission.pdf

193 http://integratedreporting.org/the-iirc-2

194 Juvenal, "Quis custodiet ipsos custodes?" *Satires* (1AD): Satire VI, lines 347-348.

195 Leonid Hurwicz, "But who will guard the guardians?" Nobel Prize lecture, Oslo, 8 December 2007. Retrieved from http://www.nobelprize. org/nobel_prizes/economic-sciences/laureates/2007/hurwicz_lecture.pdf

Chapter 6: Does government know what "governance" means?

196 Ed Straw, *Stand and Deliver: A Design for Successful Government.* Layerthorpe, UK: York Publishing Services, 2014.

197 Jonathan Swift, *Gulliver's Travels* (1726). London: Penguin Classics, 2003.

198 J. Enoch Powell, *Joseph Chamberlain*. London: Thames & Hudson, 1977.

199 Lord E. Mervyn Davies, CBE, The Davies Report on Women on Boards (2013). Retrieved from https://www.gov.uk/government/uploads/system/uploads/attachment_data/file/31480/11-745-women-on-boards.pdf

200 Institute of Directors, Chartered Director initiative. See https://www.iod.com/training/qualifications/chartered-director

201 See http://www.geniusmethods.com.

202 Kransdorff, *Corporate Amnesia*.

203 Niccolò Machiavelli, *The Prince* (1532). London: Penguin Classics, 2011.

About the author

Bob Garratt is a "pracademic": a practitioner of effective corporate governance who has always kept a link to academia to test his practice against evolving theory, and vice versa.

His work has developed through integrative disciplines: from architectural education through management, to board and director development. All involved learning to take strategic decisions in times of uncertainty while cross-pollinating from seemingly unrelated areas. His practice was honed through live projects at the Architectural Association School in London and Ulster College in Belfast. His introduction to business was through the seminal Developing Senior Managers Action Learning Programme at the General Electric Company in the UK led by the redoubtable Professor Reg Revans. His work has taken him to over 40 countries including China where, with his wife, Sally, and Professor Max Boisot, he helped establish the first China MBA programme in 1983 for the China-EEC Management Programme. In 1992, they helped create the ASEAN-EU Management Centre in Brunei Darussalam.

His board assessment and development work is well known through his long-selling book *The Fish Rots from the Head: Developing Effective Directors* (Profile Books, 2010). He has worked with the International Monetary Fund in Washington, DC on rethinking its corporate governance, and governments in Australia, Hong Kong, India, Saudi Arabia, Singapore and South Africa.

He was on the visiting faculties of the Judge Institute of Management, University of Cambridge; Imperial College London, and is now a Visiting Professor at Cass Business School, City University, University of London; and Professor Extraordinaire at the University of Stellenbosch, South Africa, where he is Chairman of the Centre for Corporate Governance in Africa. He is a Past Master of the Worshipful Company of Management Consultants, City of London.

As well as *The Fish Rots from the Head*, his books include *The Learning Organization: Developing Democracy at Work* (Harper-Collins Business, 1987); *Twelve Organisational Capabilities: Valuing People at Work* (Profile Books, 2000); *Developing Strategic Thought: A Collection of the Best Thinking on Business Strategy* (as editor; Profile Books, 2nd edn 2003); and *Thin on Top: Why Corporate Governance Matters and How to Measure and Improve Board Performance* (Nicholas Brealey Publishing, 2003).

204

Index

accepted business values 14, 29, 30-1, 32, 71; amorality/shadow side 34; disjointed values 33; erosion of positive values 35-6; of the FCA 235-6; myth of "our business values" 30-1; personal values and 38-40, 64; statements of values 39; two sides of 33-4; whose values? 32-3

accidental directors 52, 120, 122

accountability 15, 31, 34, 36; regulators 255, 262

accountants 97-8, 101, 252; real-time accounting 97-8

action learning 5, 60-1, 131, 237; legislators' role 269-70

Adams, Douglas 269

Africa 36, 40, 108; middle class 73, 78-9

agency-based system 150, 154, 164, 167-8; duties of agents 169

AIG 242

Airline Safety Reporting System 109

alternative truths 63

Amazon 110

Anglo Irish Bank 243

annual reports 31, 61, 106, 154, 157, 202; business models 157; company values statement 30; integrated reporting 214; real-time reporting 97-8; triple bottom line 154, 214

anthropology 48-50, 59, 66, 147

anti-business bias 80

anti-corruption 106-9; Hong Kong 257-8; UN Global Compact 216, *see also* corruption

Apple 110

arbitrage trading 18, 181

architecture 271

Argent 201

Arnold, Matthew 14

Ashby, W.R. 125

Asia 36, 108; directoral competence 137; middle class 73, 78-9

asset managers 203; future of 194-5

Atkins, Jill 169

attestations 251, 254

Audit Commission 262

auditors 96, 98; business model 99-100; employed by shareholders 99-100; internal audit 100-1

Augustine, St 266

Australia, Chartered Director award 287

authoritarianism 70, 152

BAE Systems 61, 106, 108

Bailey, Andrew 234, 235

Bank of America 243

Bank of England 110, 234, 236, 248, 262, 282, 284, 293; audit 96; HBOS report 245; regulatory spending 233; select committee on 193-4; senior management regime 121

banking: Co-operative Bank 137-9; Davies Report 2013 285; graduate recruitment 145; investment banks 144; partnership banking 144; professionalism and 19-20, 285; public attitude to 145, 247;

sub-prime mortgages 41, 96, 141-3; Walker Report 41

Banking Act 2015 101

Barings Bank 34

Battle of Britain 60

BBC 105, 197, 218; bonuses 197; emotional ownership 167, 219; ownership 218, 219; Trust 228

Bear Sterns 242

Beer, Stafford 125

Berle, Adolf 150

Bhatia, Lord 264

Big Bang 16, 41, 64, 94, 144, 248

Bill & Melinda Gates Foundation 73

Bischoff, Sir Win 58

Blair government, regulation 104, 246, 261

Blair, Tony 94, 185, 246

board of directors 22; chairman see chairman of the board; directoral competence 136-7; operational board 192; structure 192-4; supervisory board 192-3; two-tier boards 192-4

Boards of Directors' Forum 291-2

Boisot, Max 87

bonuses 109, 197, 247

Bradford & Bingley 245

Brandeis, Louis 86

Brexit 2, 29, 38, 106, 156, 167, 184, 194, 204, 213, 268

bribery 36, 40; Bribe Payers Index 94; company policies 108; gifts 108; GSK 107; inducements 107, see also corruption

Bribery Act 2010 37, 40, 86, 107-8

Bribery Act Working Group 108

Britannia Building Society 138

British Army, action learning 60-1

Brown, Gordon 246

Buffett, Warren 68, 81, 168, 180, 202

Business in the Community 289

business models 3, 157; annual reports 157; audits 99-100; behaviourally based models 3; Corporate Governance Code 157; definitions 157; failure of 3, 65, 68; financial crash 2008 and 3, 65, 68; get-rich-quick 142; learning board 157, 158; management consultants 102; sub-prime mortgages 142-3

business values see accepted business values

Cable, Vince 210

Cadbury Code 150

Cadbury Report on the Financial Aspects of Corporate Governance 1992 1, 55, 120, 124; consequences 252-3

Cadbury, Sir Adrian 9, 124, 127, 146

call centres 83-4

CalPERS 182

Cameron, David 94, 259

Cameron, Johnny 245

capital: finance capital 70; three types 17, 69-71

capitalism 7; emerging economies 152; executive-led 151-2, 196, 239-40, 283; flaws in current model 68; inclusive see inclusive capitalism; stakeholder capitalism 151

Carney, Mark 68, 76-7, 96

Cass Business School 145, 233

CEOs see chief executive officers

chairman of the board 122; role in inclusive capitalism 159-60

charities: criticism of 186, 264-5; regulation 263-5

Chartered Director award 161, 252, 286-9

Cherokee Nation 171

chief executive officers (CEOs) 6, 69; hegemony 69, 72, 130, 144, 151, 156, 181, 196; managing directors compared 129-30; United States 129, 130

China 46; business schools 87; capitalism in 94; Communist Party 79, 80, 87, 89; corruption 89, 107; Four Modernizations 87; middle classes 79-80, 89; raw material price cycle and 8

Churchill, Winston 179, 269

churning 17, 195, 206, 283

City of London 6, 121, 138, 145, 248-9, 251; bonuses 247; Livery companies 41, 77, 88, 145-6; personal values and 40-1

City Values Forum 41, 251, 289
civil service 185-6, 234
class: five new classes 7-9; "unequals"
    7, 18, see also middle classes;
    working classes
Co-operative Bank 137-9
Co-operative Society 92, 137-8
Code for Responsible Investing in South
    Africa (CRISA) 210
codes of corporate governance 21, 37,
    58, 61; Corporate Governance
    Code 148, 149, 157, 227, 244,
    253-4, 262; Development in
    Corporate Governance and
    Stewardship 58; extension to all
    registered organizations 280-1;
    Stewardship Code 149, 207-10,
    253-4
Commonwealth 46, 129; Chartered
    Director awards 287; corporate
    governance values 38, 54, 55;
    director's dilemma 123; ESG
    reporting 155; general duties
    of directors 5, 125; meaning of
    "director" 119, 120; shareholders
    173, 177
Communism 170; China 79, 80, 87, 89;
    Soviet Union 239-40
Companies Act 2006 8, 19, 120, 263;
    drafting of 38; extension to all
    registered organizations 280-1;
    general duties of directors 10, 21,
    121, 125-6, 220, 244, 248, 265,
    280-1; incorporation under 176;
    public oversight 282; regulations
    262
company secretaries, role 103-4
competence: assessable 4; developing
    governor competence 15-16;
    directoral see directoral
    competence; of national leaders,
    defining 11-12; of senior executives
    92
complaints about bosses 50-1
compliance, risk and governance (CRG)
    reporting 155-6, 214-15, 239
Connors, John 110
continuous learning 4, 28, 119, 147,
    266, 289-95

corporate governance 1, 127-8;
    Cadbury Report 1; Co-operative
    Bank 137-9; codes 21, 58,
    61; cultural differences 155-6;
    development as a national asset
    289-95; directoral competence 136-
    7; experts 127; failure, examples
    of 137-44; lack of national system
    146; as a learning system 131;
    meaning of "governance" 4;
    meaning of 123-4; as national asset
    273, 274-5; National Corporate
    Governance Covenant 21-2, 274-5;
    ownership and 165-6; party politics
    and 8, 94-5, 274-5, 276-8; political
    rhetoric and 221-2; politicians and
    9-11, 130-1, 276-8; principles-
    based approach 55-6, 256; rules-
    based approach 54-5, 256-7; select
    committee on 283-4; six key steps
    280-9; stakeholder-based approach
    57; Standing Commission on see
    Standing Commission on Corporate
    Governance; stewardship-based
    approach 57; values see corporate
    governance values
Corporate Governance Code 148, 149,
    157, 227, 244, 253-4, 262
Corporate Governance Reporting
    Council, need for 250-1, 284
corporate governance values 14, 29,
    36-8, see also accountability;
    probity; transparency
corporate lawyers 55, 101-2
corporate memory 35
corporate social responsibility (CSR) 75
corruption 36-7, 40, 64; anti-corruption
    106-9, 216; China 89, 107;
    financial services 195; Hong Kong
    257-8; limit on gifts 108; lobbying
    86-7; middle classes 86-9; UK
    legislation 37, 40, 86, 107-8; UN
    definition 36; UN Global Compact
    216; US legislation 37, 40, 86, see
    also bribery
Corzine, Jon 242
credit rating agencies 96, 143
CRG see compliance, risk and
    governance reporting

CRISA *see* Code for Responsible Investing in South Africa
Crosby, James 245
cross-cultural mapping 62-3
CSR *see* corporate social responsibility
culture 28, 31; assessment tools 60-1; complaints about bosses 50-1; cross-cultural mapping 62-3; emotional climate 59, 60; learning culture 52, 54, 60; malicious obedience 51; meaning 49-50; national *see* national cultures; personal values as key organizational asset 52-3; societal values 42
Cummings, Peter 244
Cup Trust 264
customer loyalty 34
Cuthbert, St 132
cyber-technology 180
cybernetics 4, 50, 51, 125, 147

Dante 45
Dark Matrix 68-9
Davies Report on UK Banking 2013 285
Dawes, Henry 171
Dawkins, Richard 176
De Gaulle, Charles 269
democracy 6-7, 20, 87-8, 276
Deng Xiaoping 87, 94
Denning, Lord 190-1
Department for Business, Energy and Industrial Strategy (DBEIS) 190, 244, 248, 249, 252, 262, 281-2
Dickens, Charles 80
directoral competence 136-7; decision-making in uncertainty 148-9; NHS practitioners 141
directoral learning 146; blockages to 146-7; divergent thinking 147-8; long-termism 147-8
directors 19, 22; accidental directors 52, 120, 122; accredited directors 101; approved directors 120, 122; board *see* board of directors; careerist directors 35; chairman of the board of 122; Chartered Director award 161, 252, 286-9; collective responsibility 121;

debarring 244; direction-giving 124; directoral competence 136-7; director's dilemma 5-6, 123-4, 131, 134, 140, 272; duty of care 189-90; duty of primary loyalty 190-2; executive directors 120, 122; feedback function 125; fiduciary duty 52, 190, 193, 247; general duties 5, 10, 21, 101, 121, 125-6, 147, 191, 220, 244, 248, 265, 280-1; independence of judgement 190, 191; induction 128-9; learning *see* directoral learning; managers compared 125-7; managing directors 123, 129-30; meaning of "director" 119-20; new categories 288-9; non-accredited directors 101; non-approved directors 120, 122; non-executive directors 120, 122; professional directors 285-6; public attitude to 6; Registered Directors 288; registered/statutory directors 122; registration 141, 226; "representative" directors 122; role 5; senior management regime 121-2; shadow directors 122; unlimited personal liability 119, 120, 125, 128-9, 175, 176, 220
disruptive economies 36
Donaldson, Frederick Lewis 268-9
Dunkirk 60
duty of care 2, 164, 167, 168; directors 189-90; Global Duty of Care 3, 8, 185; owners 182; shareholders 181

economic crisis 2008 *see* financial crisis 2008
emerging economies 152
emotional climate 46, 49, 51, 59, 60
Enron 128, 215
entitlement 8, 55, 71, 92-3
environmental, social and governance (ESG) reporting 37, 75, 76, 136, 155-6, 239, 266; UN Global Compact 214-15
equity markets: Kay Review 2012 210-13, 260, 290; Principles for Responsible Investment (PRI) 210, 216-17

ESG reporting *see* environmental, social and governance reporting
ethical leadership 131
Ethnic Minority Foundation 264
European Union 38, 57, 268; auditors 96; director's dilemma 123; inclusive capitalism 76; stakeholders 155, *see also* Brexit
Eurozone 17
extraterritoriality 152-3; United States 56, 57, 156, 256-7

Facebook 199
fake news 276
FCA *see* Financial Conduct Authority
feedback mechanisms 51, 58, 61, 125, 225, 290; wash-up sessions 61, 147
finance capital 70
finance fixation 89
Financial Conduct Authority (FCA) 121, 233-6, 248, 262; accepted business values 235-6; administrative costs 234; attestations 251, 254; criticisms of 234-5; Handbook 234; mission statement 235; private warnings 235; purpose 250-1; secrecy 235-6; spending by 233, 288
financial crisis 2008 6, 8, 50, 55, 63, 94, 189; accountants and 97; auditors and 96; austerity regimes 218-19; CEO hegemony and 72; duration 140; failure of models 3, 65, 68; failure to learn from 76; lack of contrition 3, 6, 66, 76, 145, 239, 254; lack of professionalism 19; ownership and 171; public anger 74, 75, 118, 143, 156, 266; sub-prime mortgages 142
Financial Reporting Council (FRC) 236, 248, 249, 266, 284; codes 37, 58, 150; Corporate Governance Code 148, 149, 157, 227, 244, 253-4, 262; *Development in Corporate Governance and Stewardship* 58; human values 12, 55; powers 244; primary loyalty and 190; Stewardship Code 149, 207-10, 253-4; viability statements 254

Financial Times "Inclusive Capitalism" conference 76
Fitzgerald, F. Scott 148
FitzPatrick, Seán 243
flash trading 76, 112-13, 182, 198; flash crashes 18, 33, 80
Flowers, Paul 138
Foreign Corrupt Practices Act 1977 (US) 37, 40, 86, 108
foreign exchanges 18, 33, 195
Fox, Kate 48
Francis Crick Institute 201
Francis, Dave 43
FRC *see* Financial Reporting Council
free markets 3, 17, 19, 57, 70, 74, 150, 239, 285
Freedom of Information Act 105, 112; requests 254
Fuld, Dick 242
fund managers 187-8; future of 194-5; mind-set 204-5; pessimism 200-2; underperformance 202-4

Garratt, Sally 87
Gates Foundation 73
Geertz, Clifford 49, 61, 73, 89, 180
Germany 9, 110, 193
gig economy, ownership issues 199-200
Gladstone, William 175
GlaxoSmithKline *see* GSK
Global Compact *see* UN Global Compact
Global Duty of Care 3, 8, 185
Goodwin, Sir Fred 244, 245
Google 110, 199, 201
Governance4Owners 182
governments: basic demand of 279; extension of laws/codes to all registered organizations 280-1; public attitude to 273; public expectations 273; roles 273-4, *see also* legislators; parliamentary select committees; party politics; politicians
Great Crash 1929 5
Greenspan, Alan 3, 50, 65, 139, 205; *The Map and the Territory* 65, 66
group dynamics 59, 157, 227
GSK 107, 108
Gulf states 36, 272

Halifax, Lord Edward 124
Hampden-Turner, Charles 63
Handy, Charles 153
Hardin, Garrett 229-30
Harpham, John 161
Harrison, John 238
HBOS 32, 41, 98, 144, 244, 245
Hermes EOS 182, 201
Hermes Fund Managers 136-7
Hierarchy of Human Needs 170
high-frequency trading 70, 201, 205; as
   insider trading 205
Hobbes, Thomas 72
Hofstede, Geert 62
honesty in business 139-40
Hong Kong 188; charitable giving 186,
   264; Independent Commission
   Against Corruption (ICAC) 257-8
human behaviour 12, 68, 128, 226-7
human resources 52-3; HR
   professionals 104; rethinking
   human metrics 90-1
human values 73-4, 139; demand for
   2, 71; NGOs 155; rebuilding 3, *see
   also* values
Hurwicz, Leonid 266

IIRC *see* International Integrated
   Reporting Council
IMF *see* International Monetary Fund
inclusive capitalism 19, 89, 128, 170,
   176, 275; chairman's role in 159-
   60; emerging economies 152;
   executive-led capitalism and 239-
   40; *Financial Times* conference 76;
   nature of 151; ownership and 172,
   173, 196; rise of 72, 75-7, 151-5,
   276; stakeholders and 194, 283;
   for sustainability 72; taxation 109,
   111; three capitals 17-18, 69-71;
   United States and 199
inclusive ownership 195-6
India: call centres 83-4; middle classes
   83-4
inducements 107
Industrial and Provident Societies Act
   1965 263
Industrial Revolution 174, 237
IndyMac 243
inequality 8, 72, 82, 85-6

information technology 65, 78, 79, 82,
   92, 180
insider trading 76, 242; high-frequency
   trading as 205
integrated ownership 196
integrated reporting 19, 72, 109, 156,
   157, 212, 214, 217, 229, 266, 284
international business values 14-15;
   culture and 54; US rules/UK
   principles clash 54-7
International Corporate Governance
   Network conference 2014 68
international cross-cultural mapping
   62-3
International Integrated Reporting
   Council (IIRC) 266
International Monetary Fund (IMF)
   78, 79
internet 112, 118
investment banks 144
Investors' Forum 213, 290, 292
Ireland 243, *see also* Northern Ireland
Irish Life and Permanent 243
irrational exuberance 3, 16-17

Jackson, General Sir Michael 39-40
Jesuits 42
John Lewis Partnership 139
Johnson & Johnson 110
joint stock companies 153, 174
JPMorgan Chase 243
Judge, Barbara 161
Juncker, Jean-Claude 8
Juvenal 266

Karran-Cumberlege, Gillian 169
Kaupthing 243
Kay, John 211, 260
Kay Review 2012 210-13, 260;
   National Investors' Forum 213,
   290; Principles for Responsible
   Investment (PRI) 210
Keynes, John Maynard 148
Kids Company 264-5
Kids Unlimited 186
King Commission, South Africa 289;
   Reports 37, 131
King, Martin Luther 269
King, Mervyn 95
Knight, Frank 149

Kosovo Campaign 39
KPMG 96
Kraft Corporation 20

labour force: cheapness 81; growth of
   globally 79
labour rights, UN Global Compact
   215-16
Lagarde, Christine 68, 76, 96
lawyers, corporate lawyers 55, 101-2
leadership 70-1, 118-19; ethical
   leadership 131
learning: action learning 5, 60-1, 131,
   237, 269-70; continuous learning
   4, 28, 119, 147, 266, 289-95;
   directoral see directoral learning;
   as fundamental resource 91-2; as
   human values-based culture 131;
   national framework 289-95; nature
   of 132; rate of 91, 132; value of 74
learning board 132, 134-6, 287; basic
   model 135; full model 157, 158
learning culture 52, 54, 60; feedback
   mechanisms 51, 58, 61, 125, 225,
   237, 290; wash-up sessions 61, 147
learning leaders 136
learning organization: basic model 132;
   complex model 133; learning board
   see learning board
Leeson, Nick 34
legal entity, types of 104-5, 178-80
legislators 19, 22; corporate learning
   and 269-70; duty of care for
   governance 270-1, see also
   governments; parliamentary select
   committees; politicians
Legislators' Forum 293
Lehman Brothers Bank 143, 242
Lewin, Kurt 59
Lewis, C.S. 232
Lewis, Michael 77
Libor 33, 34, 86, 195, 235
Limited Liability Act 1856 174-5
limited liability companies 173-6, 220
limited liability partnerships (LLPs)
   104-5, 179
Linklater, Andro 171
Litwin and Stringer Organization
   Climate Questionnaire 90
Livery companies 41, 77, 88, 145-6

lobbying 86-7
local laws 152-3
London Olympics 2012 259
London Stock Exchange 77, 187, 262
London University of the Arts 201
long finance 156, 284
Luxembourg, tax system 110, 111

Machiavelli, Niccolò 294
Mainelli, Mike 99
Malan, Daniel 12, 47-8
malicious obedience 51
Mallin, Chris 161
management consultants 102-3, 139-40
managers, directors compared 125-7
managing directors 123; chief
   executives compared 129-30
Mandela, Nelson 184, 196, 246
Mandelson, Peter 94
Mannesmann 2000 110
marginal trading activities 70
markets: irrational exuberance 16-17;
   professionalism and 16-20
Marx, Karl 196
Maslow, Abraham, Hierarchy of
   Human Needs 170
Masters of the Universe 65-6, 80, 145
Maxwell, Robert 246
Maxwellization 245-6
Mazars 95
McKinsey 203
Means, Gardiner 150
Melvin, Colin 161
Metallgesellschaft 193
MF Global 242
Microsoft 110
Mid Staffordshire hospital scandal 141,
   221, 224
middle classes 7, 19; anti-business bias
   80-1; China 79-80, 89; corruption
   86-9; hollowing-out of 7, 18, 73;
   IMF definition 78; India 83-4;
   inequality and 85-6; Northern
   Ireland 82-3; rise of global middle
   class 72-3, 77-89; shadow side
   81-2; South Africa 83; stabilizing
   effects 82-4, 152; values 78, 81-2
Military Covenant 274
Moltke, Helmuth von 235

"Monetary Assets" Working Group 110-11
money market managers 206
Monitor 219, 220, 223
Monks, Bob 56, 68-9, 86-7, 180; funds 182
Moody-Stuart, Sir Mark 213
MoralDNA 39, 47
mortgages: self-certified applications 140; sub-prime mortgages 41, 96, 141-3
MSCI World Equity Index 136-7
mutuals 139
"My word is my bond" 40-1, 77, 140, 249, 251, 285

National Audit Office 73, 262, 265, 282
National Corporate Governance Covenant 21-2, 274-5
national cultures 40, 53; cross-cultural mapping 62-3; dilemmas 63; individualism/collectivism 62; male/female 63; power distance 62; truth, concept of 63; uncertainty avoidance 62; US/UK clash 54-7
National Health Service (NHS) 105, 109, 218; boards of governors 221, 222-8, 261; bonuses 197; Code of Corporate Governance 220, 224, 227; costs 178; emotional ownership 167, 219; market-based practitioners 140-1; Mid Staffordshire hospital scandal 141, 221, 224; ownership of NHS Foundation Trusts 178, 218, 219-20
national investment plans 272
National Investors' Forum 213, 290, 292
national leadership, major players 22-3
national political leadership 20-1
National Trust 186
nationalization 218
neoclassical economics 65, 66
Network Rail Board 228
New City Agenda 233, 236, 252
NGOs see non-governmental organizations
NHS see National Health Service

Nichols, Cardinal Vincent 6, 145; "Blueprint for Better Business" 145
Niemoller, Martin 68
Nine Virtues of Effective Governance 113
Ninja mortgages see sub-prime mortgages
non-governmental organizations (NGOs) 155, 259
Norges 182
North Sea Oil 272
Northern Ireland: inequality 82; middle classes 82-3; peace process 82-3
Novo Nordisk 100, 154, 214

oath: Hippocratic Oath 141; "My word is my bond" 40-1, 77, 140, 249, 251, 285; of professionalism 113
Obama, Barack 66
Ocwen 243
OECD 259
offshoring 83, 84; call centres 83-4
Olver, Dick 61
organization amnesia 35
oversight: direct governmental oversight 281; public oversight 4, 11, 22, 41, 262-3, 280, 282
owners 5, 19, 22, 37, 161; delegation of powers 182; duties of care and primary loyalty 189-92; duties and rights 180-3, 206; fiduciary duty 187, 197-8; Salomon Judgement 1890 192, 282-3; shareholders 150-1, 173-4, 175, 191, 282-3; stewardship 182-3
Owners' Forum 292
ownership 70-1; agency-based system 150, 154, 164, 167-8, 169; Anglo-Saxon model 198-9; asset managers 194-5; avarice and 170-1; board structure issues 192-4; categories 198-9; concept of 164-6; corporate governance and 165-6; duties 169; duty of ownership 187-8; emotional ownership 93, 164-5, 166-7; fund managers 194-5; gig economy 199-200; high-frequency trading 205; inclusive capitalism and 172, 173, 196; inclusive ownership 195-6; integrated ownership 196; legal

entity types 104-5, 178-80; legal ownership 164-5, 166; limited liability companies 173-6; models of 198-9; NHS 178; political intervention 192-4; in practice 169-70; private sector 167-8, 187-8; public ownership 217-19; public sector 177-8; redefining 71; shareholders 150-1, 173-4, 175, 180-3, 191, 282-3; stakeholders 154, 195-6; Stewardship Code 149, 207-10; *Ubuntu* concept 184-5, 196, 198

Palmer, Coralie 33
parliamentary select committees 15, 262, 271, 277, 286; on corporate governance 283-4, 293; on Kay Review 213; Public Accounts 262, 265, 282, 293; Treasury 138, 193-4, 262, 282, 293
partnership banking 144
party politics 8, 94-5, 274-5, 276-8
Paul, St 45, 46
pension fund trustees 187-8
pensions: South Africa 272; UK 272-3
personal values 12, 14, 29, 34, 35, 42-3; "American" values 46, 54; behaviours/words and 42; business values and 38-40, 64; City of London and 40-1; communitarian values 46; five-level hierarchy 42-3; imposition of 44-7; as key organizational cultural asset 52-3; MoralDNA 39, 47; "My word is my bond" 40-1, 77, 140, 249, 251, 285; Seven Deadly Sins 44-7, 64, 152; "Western" values 46, 47, 152; yielding under pressure 39-40
Phillips, Trevor 64
Pierce, Chris 161
Piketty, Thomas 85
PIRC 289
Pitman, Sir Brian 144
Plato 268
political elites 8
politicians 18; corporate governance and 9-11, 130-1, 276-8; failure 6-7; general duties of 9-11; political rhetoric 221-2, *see*

also governments; legislators; parliamentary select committees; party politics
Polyani, Karl 72
Ponzi schemes 88
Popper, Karl 266
Porter, Michael 261
"post-truth" 54
poverty 72-3, 78, 85
Powell, Enoch 276
PPI mis-selling 34
PRA *see* Prudential Regulation Authority
primary loyalty duty 190-2
Principles for Responsible Investment (PRI) 210, 216-17
privatization 218
probity 15, 31, 34, 36; regulators 255-6, 262; self-regulation 108; taxation and 109-12
professionalism 4, 72, 285-6; anti-corruption and 106-9; bankers and 19-20, 285; bonuses and 197; Chartered Director award 161, 252, 286-9; demolishing 18-20; financial crisis 2008 and 19; honesty in business 139-40; independence of judgement 96; markets and 16-20; national political leaders 20-1; oath of professionalism 113; re-establishing 74-5; rethinking the meaning of 94-6, 275; shadow side 104-5; taxation and 109-12; transparency and 112-13
professions 18-19; accountants 97-8, 101, 252; auditors *see* auditors; company secretaries 103-4; corporate lawyers 55, 101-2; future roles 95-6; human resources 104; limited liability partnerships (LLPs) 104-5, 179; management consultants 102-3, 139-40; nature of 95; professional directors 285-6; purpose of 96; Stockholm syndrome 96, 99, 102; Thatcher and 19, 285, 286
Prudentia 45
Prudential Regulation Authority (PRA) 121, 233, 234

Public Accounts Committee 262, 265, 282, 293
public estrangement 68, 69-71
Public Interest Disclosure Act 1998 249
public oversight 4, 11, 22, 41, 262-3, 280, 282, see also Standing Commission on Corporate Governance
public ownership 217-19
public sector ethos 40, 221
public service 185-6

rail regulators 258
Rand, Ayn 150
ratings agencies 96, 143
raw material price cycle 8
RBS see Royal Bank of Scotland
re-engineering 51
real-time accounting 97-8
recognized national development benefit 152
recognized public good 153-4
Reform Act 1832 69
regulation 70-1, 232, 274; Better Regulation Task Force 261; Blair government 104, 246, 261; charities 263-5; as clockwork 238-9; compliance 255-8, 260-1; comply-or-explain system 256; extending to all registered organizations 263; principles-based approach 256, 260; regulatory spending by government 233, 259-60; rules-based approach 256-7, 260; UK system 248-50
regulators 5, 19, 22, 232-3, 274; accountability 255, 262; Charity Commission 263-5; civil service 185-6, 234; Corporate Governance Reporting Council 250-1, 284; failure to act 241-2; get-out clauses 247; holding the political balance 240-1; IIRC 266; probity 255-6, 262; rail regulators 258; as referees 236-7; spending by 233; Stockholm syndrome 233, 260-1; transparency 255, 263; US model 242-4, see also Financial Conduct Authority; Financial Reporting Council
Regulators' Forum 293

Reilly, Mark 107
remuneration 64; bonuses 109, 197, 247; pay-offs 64
responsible investing 201, 210; Principles for Responsible Investment (PRI) 210
Revans, Reg 91, 125, 132
reward systems 46-7
rights movements 46
risk, uncertainty and 149
Rolls-Royce 107, 183, 242
Rosling, Hans 85-6
Rousseau, Jean-Jacques 72, 237-8
Royal Bank of Scotland (RBS) 183, 191, 243, 244, 245
Royal Charter companies 165, 174
Royal College of Directors 286, 289, 291
RSPCA 186

Salomon Judgement 1890 192, 282-3
Sarbanes-Oxley Act 2004 (US) 155, 257
Schröder, Gerhard 9
Schwab, Klaus 131
select committees see parliamentary select committees
self-help 91, 138, 171
self-regulation 19, 40, 108, 139, 251, 289, 290
senior management regime 121-2
Seven Deadly Sins 44-7, 64, 152, 192
shareholder value 20
shareholders: Anglo-Saxon ownership model 198-9; auditors and 99-100; gig economy 199-200; ownership of company 150-1, 173-4, 175, 180-3, 191, 282-3; regulators and 247; rights and duties 164, 180-3, 194, 206; role of 176-7; Salomon Judgement 1890 192, 282-3; stewardship 182-3; symmetry of information 112
shares, classes of 206-7
Shell 154, 214; People, Planet and Profits 100
Shermon, Richard 41
short-termism 20, 28, 34, 35, 39, 65, 83

Silicon Valley 35-6, 54, 80, 88; class "C" shares 207; IPOs (initial public offerings) 199-200
Singapore 272
Smith, Adam 17, 72, 153, 240; invisible hand 229, 230; *Wealth of Nations* 17, 237
Snap 199-200
Snow, C.P., "two cultures" 147
social contract 7, 47-8, 69, 70, 77, 237-8
social media 92, 199-200
social psychology 59
social science 147
Socrates 266
Solomon, Lou 50
sophisticated state failure 6-7, 41, 73
South Africa 119; Black Economic Empowerment law 83; Chartered Director award 287; Code for Responsible Investing in South Africa (CRISA) 210; comply-and-explain approach 256; general duties of directors 21, 265, 280; immigrants 83; King Commissions 37, 131, 289; middle classes 83; national pension scheme 272; Public Investment Corporation Fund 272; stewardship-based approach 57; *Ubuntu* concept 184-5, 196, 198
South Sea Bubble 88
stakeholder capitalism 151, *see also* inclusive capitalism
stakeholders 154-5, 156, 173, 182-3; Blair government 261; ESG reporting 215; inclusive capitalism and 194, 283; NGOs 155; ownership 154, 195-6; power/control 93, 151; rights of 155; rise of 93, 213-15; Stewardship Code and 208, 209; UN Global Compact 213-14
Standard Life 182
Standing Commission on Corporate Governance 289-95; Boards of Directors' Forum 291-2; learning process 294-5; Legislators' Forum 293; Owners' Forum 292; Regulators' Forum 293

Starbucks 110
Steare, Roger: *Ethicability* 47; MoralDNA 39, 47
stewardship 182-3
Stewardship Code 149, 207-10, 253-4
Stockholm syndrome: professions 96, 99, 102; regulators 233, 260-1
Straw, Ed 270-1, 276
sub-prime mortgages 41, 96, 141-3
Sutherland, Euan 138
Swift, Jonathan 273

taxation: inclusive capitalism 109, 111; inclusive capitalism and 109, 111; offshore holdings 111; probity and 109-12; tax arbitrage 86, 111-12; tax avoidance 109, 264; tax limitation schemes 111-12; Vodafone 110-11
Taylor, Bernard 161
Techau, Jan 7, 8
technology 80; cyber-technology 180; information technology 65, 78, 79, 82, 92, 180
Ten Commandments of Moses 45
Tett, Gillian 48, 63, 66, 169
Thatcher, Margaret 9, 185; professionals and 19, 285, 286
Thurber, James 30
Tomorrow's Company 289
"too big to fail" 70, 77, 191
trades unions 193
Tragedy of the Commons 229-30
transparency 15, 31, 34, 36, 58, 70; Freedom of Information Act 105, 112; professionalism and 112-13; regulators 255, 263
Transparency International 94, 106
Treasury 110, 234, 236, 248; interventions 262; Select Committees 138, 193-4, 262, 282, 293
triple-bottom-line reporting 154, 214
Trollope, Anthony 80
Trompenaars, Fons 62
Trump, Donald 2, 8, 29, 37, 46, 54, 111, 119, 156, 194, 204, 213, 268
TSB 138
Tuckett, David 204
Twain, Mark 268
"two cultures" 147

Uber 110
Ubuntu concept 184-5, 196, 198
Ulster *see* Northern Ireland
UN Global Compact 61, 79, 106,
    154, 213-17; anti-corruption 216;
    environment 216; ESG reporting
    213-14; human rights 215;
    labour 215-16; principles 215-16;
    stakeholders 213-14
uncertainty: decision-making in 148-9;
    risk and 149
UNEP Finance Initiative 216
"unequals" 7, 18
Unilever 20
United Nations (UN): definition of
    "corruption" 36; Global Compact
    see UN Global Compact
United States: "American" values 46,
    54; chief executive officers (CEOs)
    129, 130; Commonsense Principles
    of Corporate Governance 200;
    compliance, risk and governance
    (CRG) 155-6; Declaration of
    Independence 171, 238; Delaware's
    Law of Plurality 151; directoral
    competence 137; extraterritoriality
    56, 57, 156, 256-7; Federal Deposit
    Insurance Corporation 243; Federal
    Housing Agency 242-3; Foreign
    Corrupt Practices Act 1977 37, 40,
    86, 108; foreign policy 56; freeing
    of capital markets 16; inclusive
    capitalism and 199; Institutional
    Shareholder Services 68; Joint
    Committee on Taxation 111;
    national culture 54-7; Nevada state
    law 151; Principles of Corporate
    Governance 200; ratings agencies
    96, 143; regulators 242-4; reporting
    system 155; rules-based system
    54-5; Sarbanes-Oxley Act 2004
    155, 257; shareholders 198; sub-
    prime mortgages 41, 96, 141-3
universal manhood suffrage 69
Universities Superannuation Scheme
    182

unlimited personal liability 119, 120,
    125, 128-9, 175, 176, 220

value sets 70, 106, 139, 185; of
    civil service 185; concept of 31;
    organizational 35; of other nations
    63; of society 17
values 12; "American" values 46, 54;
    basis of 29-30; as "belief in action"
    13-14, 43; business *see* accepted
    business values; communitarian
    values 46; corporate governance
    see corporate governance values;
    disjointed values 33; hard/
    soft sense 29-30; human *see*
    human values; international *see*
    international business values;
    lawful organizational values 31-2;
    meaning 13, 28; myth of "our
    business values" 30-1; of national
    leaders, defining 11-12; personal
    see personal values; societal values
    42; statements of 39; value clashes
    29; value of 28-66; values-in-
    practice 32; "Western" values 46,
    47, 152
viability statements 254
Vodafone 110-11
Volkswagen 183, 193, 242
voter disengagement 270

wage growth 81
Walker Report 41
Wall Street (film) 80, 171
Washington Mutual 242, 243
Webb, Merryn Somerset 169, 202
Weiner, Norbert 125
Welby, Justin, Archbishop of
    Canterbury 233
whistle-blowers 51, 109, 249
Wilde, Oscar 30
Willford, Christopher 245
Woolf Enquiry/Report 2008 61, 106
working classes 8; aspirant 73
Worshipful Company of Management
    Consultants 41, 103, 145-6